ARMS AND CONFLICT IN THE MIDDLE EAST

Contributions to
CONFLICT MANAGEMENT, PEACE ECONOMICS AND DEVELOPMENT VOLUME 13

SERIES EDITOR
MANAS CHATTERJI

BOOKS IN THE SERIES

Eurasia: A New Peace Agenda, edited by M. D. Intriligator

Cultural Differences between the Military and Parent Society in Democratic Countries, edited by G. Caforio

Managing Conflict in Economic Convergence of Regions in Greater Europe, edited by F. Carluer

Military Missions and their Implications Reconsidered: The Aftermath of September 11th, edited by G. Caforio and G. Kuemmel

Conflict and Peace in South Asia, edited by M. Chatterji and B. M. Jain

War, Peace, and Security, edited by Jacques Fontanel and Manas Chatterji

Armed Forces and Conflict Resolution, edited by G. Caforio, G. Kümmel and B. Purkayastha

Regional Development and Conflict Management: A Case for Brazil, by Raphael Bar-El

Crisis, Complexity and Conflict, by I. J. Azis

Putting Teeth in the Tiger: Improving the Effectiveness of Arms Embargoes, edited by Michael Brzoska and George A. Lopez

Peace Science: Theory and Cases, by P. Gangopadhyay and M. Chatterji

Advances in Military Sociology: Essays in Honor of Charles C. Moskos, 12A/B, edited by Giuseppe Caforio

Arms and Conflict in the Middle East, by Riad A. Attar

Contributions to
CONFLICT MANAGEMENT, PEACE ECONOMICS
AND DEVELOPMENT VOLUME 13

ARMS AND CONFLICT IN THE MIDDLE EAST

RIAD A. ATTAR
Murray State University, USA

Emerald

United Kingdom – North America – Japan
India – Malaysia – China

Emerald Group Publishing Limited
Howard House, Wagon Lane, Bingley BD16 1WA, UK

First edition 2009

Reprints and permission service
Contact: booksandseries@emeraldinsight.com

British Library Cataloguing in Publication Data
A catalogue record for this book is available from the British Library

ISBN: 978-1-84950-661-8
ISSN: 1572-8323 (Series)

CONTENTS

LIST OF FIGURES

LIST OF TABLES

FOREWORD

It was widely expected that when the Cold War was over, there will be peace dividends and the amounts of military spending will decrease. It was also believed that worldwide conflict will decline. However, these have not taken place. In place of international tension and conflict, we have intra-country/regional/ethnic conflicts and wars. Military spending in some geographical areas has increased. This is true for South Asia and the Middle East. This book addressed to the Middle East has two objectives. First, it makes a detailed analysis of the root causes of conflict in the Middle East, the amount of military spending in the region, and its opportunity cost for economic development.

In the second part, the author has adopted an innovative approach to reformulate the production function taking into account political variables not considered previously in the production function literature. It has given a fresh perspective of production function of arms spending in sociopolitical framework. This explains the distinction of economic abstraction and facts of economic life by inserting conflict variables in the production function. It also takes consideration of interstate and intrastate factors. The empirical findings have been supported by extensive data and using sophisticated econometric techniques and robust tests. If such a multidimensional production function can be perfected, it can be used to determine policy decisions to analyze the conflicts in the Middle East.

Manas Chatterji
Series Editor

CHAPTER 1

INTRODUCTION

This study assesses the effect of politics and conflicts on growth in sixty-nine developing societies. Political economists (e.g., Harrod, 1939; Domar, 1946; Solow, 1957, 1988; Denison, 1967, 1985; Feder, 1982; Ram, 1986; Mintz & Huang, 1990, 1991; Ward & Davis, 1992; Mueller & Atesoglu, 1993a, 1993b; Heo & DeRouen, 1998; Heo, 1998) have not empirically examined the results of political factors on economic development and growth (but see Heo & Mintz, 2002). In this study, I developed and applied an augmented production function (PF) model to sixty-nine developing countries from 1960 to 2002 and tested it with several political and conflict variables: political freedom, institutional freedom, regime type, stability, ideology, interstate conflicts, intrastate conflicts, and total conflicts. I utilized statistical methods: non-linear least squares (NLS) and cross-national time series (CNTS) analyses to investigate the impact of political and conflict variables on economic growth (EG) from 1960 to 2002. I used mathematical and formal modeling to investigate the Arab Israeli conflict and the political economy and arms in the Middle East (ME). And I used case studies to illustrate my theories.

1.1. THE PRODUCTION FUNCTION RESEARCH PROGRAM

The current study is an extension of the PF model research program that began after the Great Depression in the early 1930s. The purpose of the study is to introduce political dimensions to the PF defense-growth model and to assess the impact of political and conflict variables on EG. The study theorizes that excluding political factors from the PF defense-growth model hampers any realistic explanation of the problems of EG; that the influences of economic and military variables and their externalities effects vary across different political contexts; that political factors are at least as important as economic factors in determining the outcome of EG; that intrastate and interstate conflicts have differential effects on EG (both types of conflicts have negative effects on EG; however, intrastate conflicts have more damaging effects on growth than do interstate conflicts); and that the impact of conflicts on EG differs across regions.

By incorporating political and conflict variables such as political freedom, institutional freedom, regime type, regime stability, regime ideological base, and intrastate, interstate, and total conflicts, I augmented the PF to include the fundamental dimensions of political regimes. Consequently, the PF model should gain more explanatory power to predict EG and development of nations. I extended the applicability of the PF defense-growth model to the Third World, which has a level of economic and political development different from the First World. The main findings of the study offer important contributions to the study of EG in developing countries and provide guidelines to policy decision makers (PDMs) in evaluating their "guns versus butter" alternatives.

The study provides a preponderance of empirical evidence that the externality of military spending hinders EG, while the externality of non-military spending promotes EG in all political contexts. This finding is huge because it resolved a controversial issue that has been debated for more than three decades. Also, the results of the study show that the impact of the non-military sector on EG is positive and significant in the majority of countries, while the impact of the military sector on EG is positive and significant only in a minority of countries.

Despite the proliferation of studies on the impact of military spending on EG, it was inconclusive before the current research whether defense spending hinders or promotes EG. In fact, despite many research efforts, no strong conclusion about the relationship between military spending and EG can be drawn from the literature. The inconsistent results led Chan (1985, p. 405) to conclude that a review of the literature in this area is "as likely to bewilder as it is to enlighten" (see also Mintz & Stevenson, 1995, p. 283). Mintz and Stevenson (1995, p. 85) wrote, "The literature has failed to provide any meaningful consensus on the question of whether defense spending encourages or hinders economic growth. Indeed, any study that fails to address these issues is unlikely to contribute to such an answer." This study significantly contributes to settling such a question.

The current study is the first to add conflict variables to the PF defense-growth model and test them empirically across countries and regions. The CNTS analysis with external and internal conflicts (2,349 observations) shows unequivocally that both types of conflicts, intrastate and interstate, have negative effects on EG; however, the effects of intrastate conflicts have far more damaging effects on EG than do those of interstate conflicts. The impacts of intrastate and interstate conflicts in the ME are negative and significant under all political contexts, and the differential impact of the more damaging effects of intrastate conflicts on EG also hold under all political contexts. The CNTS analysis of five regions – the ME, Latin America, Asia, Africa, and the Caribbean region – shows that the impact of conflicts on EG differs across regions. The ME offers a preponderance of evidence that internal and external conflicts have a negative and significant impact on EG in all political contexts, more so than in other regions.

The current study has very important policy implications since it provides compelling empirical evidence and guidelines to PDMs on how to allocate the resources of their states and adopt policies that promote EG. The main guidelines that I believe are beneficial to PDMs are as follows. First, PDMs should reform their political system to contribute to EG. Improving levels of freedom, democracy, and openness of the political system are as important as economic factors to promote EG. Second, the reallocation of resources to the civilian sector is the *sine qua non* to improve the performance of the economy in developing countries. The leaders of Middle Eastern countries should pay closer attention to this point due to the enormous amount of resources that they spend on the military sector. Third, leaders of developing nations should pursue policies of national reconciliation between rich and poor and among ethnic and religious groups because domestic conflict has prodigious damaging effects on the performance of the national economy. In the ME in particular, economic development is more likely to improve if the leaders pursue policies that advance domestic reconciliation and international peace.

To illuminate the above-mentioned contributions of this study and show its importance in the evolution of the PF defense-growth model research program, I will first review the evolution of the neo-classic PF model; second, I will review the logic of the incorporation of defense spending factors into the neo-classic model of EG; and finally, I will review the logic of the incorporation of political and conflict variables into the PF defense-growth model.

1.2. THE EVOLUTION OF THE PRODUCTION FUNCTION

Solow (1988, p. xi) wrote, "Growth theory did not begin with my articles of (1956) and (1957), and it certainly did not end there. Maybe it began with

The Wealth of Nations; and probably even Adam Smith had predecessors." The Physiocratic school founded by François Quesnay (1694–1774) preceded Adam Smith in developing the fundamental ideas to achieve EG. The Physiocrats articulated the roles of economic activities that expand the country's revenue, such as industrialization, free trade, and investment. The Physiocrats believed that a country should concentrate on manufacturing only to the extent that the local availability of raw materials and of suitable labor enabled it to have cost advantage over its overseas competitors (Muller, 1978; Eltis, 1988). Thus, the complete lifting of all restrictions on local and foreign sales of agricultural products and sufficient private investments would only be forthcoming if the authorities improve the general economic climate. In accordance with the Physiocratic doctrine, the economic climate could be improved by desisting from mercantilist policies, terminating the state's policy of providing special privileges to certain manufacturers, abolishing excessive dues and tolls along transport routes, and overhauling the tax system so as to remove the disincentive effect of the existing system. As far as the private investment is concerned, Quesnay foresaw that the problem might arise through insufficient saving. Therefore, it was incumbent upon the proprietors (the major source of saving) to refrain as much as possible from unnecessary consumption (Muller, 1978; Eltis, 1988).

In all accounts, Adam Smith's *The Wealth of Nations* embodied a penetrating analysis of the processes whereby economic wealth is produced and distributed. The central thesis of *The Wealth of Nations* is that capital is best employed for the production and distribution of wealth under conditions of governmental non-interference, or "laissez passer-laissez faire" economy, and free trade. In Smith's view, the production and exchange of goods can be stimulated, and a consequent rise in the general standard of living attained, only through the efficient operations of private industrial and commercial entrepreneurs acting with a minimum of regulation and control by governments (Smith, 2000).

Although this view of "laissez passer-laissez faire" economy has undergone considerable modification by economists in the light of historical developments since Smith's time, many sections of *The Wealth of Nations*, notably those relating to the sources of income and the nature of capital, have continued to form the basis for theoretical study in the field of political economy. *The Wealth of Nations* has also served, perhaps more than any other single work in its field, as a guide to the formulation of governmental economic policies (Persky, 1989). It was Smith's attempt to define the institutional structure which will best harmonize the individual's pursuit of his selfish interests with the broader interests of society. The Smithian model is one of controlled freedom: freedom of behavior and choice exists only within the socially established norms of conduct. Self-love and self-interests go hand in hand with social control and socialization (Samuels, 1977, p. 196).

After the Great Depression, the main objectives of classical economists were to regain the stability of the market system and to redefine the steady-state conditions of EG within the parameters of industrially advanced societies. Struck by an unstable economic system after the Great Depression, Harrod (1939) and Domar (1946) attempted to integrate Keynesian analysis with elements of EG. They used the PF with little substitutability among the inputs to argue that the capitalist system is inherently unstable (Barro, 1999, p. 10). In pursuit of redefining economic stability, they each arrived by noticeably different routes at a classically simple answer: the national saving rate (s) has to be equal to the product of the capital-output ratio (v) and the rate of growth of the effective labor force (n); thus, they are compatible if and only if $s = vn$. Contrary to Harrod and Domar's expectations, their formula proved to be explosively unstable as a result of its simplicity and the rigidity of its assumptions (Deane, 1978, pp. 190–204; Solow, 1988, pp. x–xvi).

The advancement of the technological factor by Robert Solow (1957, 1988) opened up growth theory to a wider variety of real-world facts and a closer connection with general economic theory. Solow (1957, 1988) and Denison (1967, 1985) are credited for having developed the well-known neo-classical aggregate PF, which posits that EG is a function of changes in input of capital, effective labor force, and technology. An economy is growing at a "steady state," according to Solow (1988, p. 4), if "its output, employment, and capital stocks grow exponentially, and its capital to output ratio is constant." Thus, the growth of the output can be explained by the variations of capital and labor.

Later, it became a strong tradition to use the neo-classical PF approach in studying the defense-growth relationship (Heo, 1999, 2000; Sandler & Hartley, 1995; Heo & Mintz, 2002). Gershon Feder (1982) used this approach by dividing the aggregate economic output into export and non-export sectors. A number of studies have since followed Feder in exploring the relationship between exports and EG in which the GDP of a country is made as a function of the growth rates of different inputs such as labor, capital, and exports.

Following the logic of the neo-classical PF approach, Ram (1986) developed a two-sector growth (government and private sectors) model to examine the relationship between government spending and EG. Ram suggested that the public and private sectors differ with respect to productivity. The two-sector PF framework outlined by Ram (1986) was adopted from the reasoning developed by Feder (1982, pp. 61–67). In several articles, Mintz and Huang (1990, 1991) and Huang and Mintz (1990, 1991) developed a three-equation model employing a neo-classical PF model to test the impact of defense spending, including externalities on EG in the United States. Mintz and Huang (1990, 1991) and Ward and Davis (1992) have tested not only the economic effects of military and non-military public expenditures on growth but also the externality effects of these expenditures.

The defense-growth PF model prior to Mueller and Atesoglu (1993a, 1993b) did not include the impact of technological change on EG. Mueller and Atesoglu (1993a, 1993b) included technological progress in their model, utilizing the concept of the *Hicks neutral technological change*, which basically means that changes in technology do not change the share of income going to the factors of production and the factor ratios. In other words, this concept will allow us to measure the effects of technological progress separately without affecting the contribution that labor and capital make to the growth (Heo, 1999). Heo and Mintz (2002) noticed that the defense-growth PF model can be benefited by including technology progress. The authors concurred with Solow (1988, p. 35), who suggested that technological progress is necessary for steady growth to be possible, and with Denison (1985), who contended that the advancement in technology provides a way to produce at lower cost. Thus, Heo and Mintz (2002) concluded that technological progress is the cornerstone for the persistent long-term growth of output per unit of input.

Furthermore, Heo and DeRouen (1998) suggested that Mueller and Atesoglu (1993a, 1993b) implicitly assumed that technological progress in the non-military public sector and technological progress in the non-military private sector are identical. Thus, Heo and DeRouen (1998) argued that it is theoretically more reasonable to separate the private and non-military government sectors while keeping technological change effects in the model. They claimed that this division of the sectors allows the economic effects of defense spending on growth to be measured more accurately.

Despite the vast number of studies on the defense-growth relationship, the political variables were absent from the defense-growth PF model. Heo and Mintz (2002) extended the PF model of Ram (1986), Mintz and Huang (1990), and Ward and Davis (1992) to include a political factor (political party) and tested this model using empirical data on the United States from 1948 to 1996. The augmented Heo–Mintz (H–M) defense-growth-political

PF model introduced a new research program which paved the way to explore the impact of other political factors on the growth and development of nations. I argue that the H–M contribution was the most important contribution to the PF since Solow incorporated the technological factor into it.

1.3. THE POLITICAL ECONOMY OF DEFENSE

The political economy of defense (PED) is a relatively new field in international political economy (IPE). The PED approach attempts to fill the gap that existed in the literature by incorporating defense spending variables into the PF to narrow the gap between its theoretical construct and the realistic forces of production.

Therefore, the PED added explanatory power to the theories that attempted to explain the dynamics of development and growth. Nevertheless, there is no consensus among scholars about the impact of defense spending upon EG. Some scholars, such as Emile Benoit (1978, p. 276), argued that the defense programs of most countries help EG, while others, such as Nicole Ball (1983), suggested that they do not always promote EG. While many studies had been conducted, a dominant theoretical framework has not emerged. Therefore, in his review article, Chan (1987, p. 35) wrote, "Even though we understand the processes through which military spending can affect economic performance much better now than a decade ago, there remains much that we do not know or that we disagree about." Despite Chan's pessimistic assessment, Mintz and Stevenson (1995, p. 637) observed that "the question of how defense spending affects economic growth has been important to both academicians and the policy community." Indeed, the evolution of literature on the PED demonstrates its fundamental contribution to understanding and explaining numerous problems that face the EG of developing nations.

1.4. COMBINING POLITICS AND ECONOMICS

John Maynard Keynes was the most prominent political economist who seriously expounded a systemic and fundamental change of the free market economy and openly adopted an active governmental role in it. Keynes initiated a revolution in the free market economy by suggesting that national economy should function within political determinants. The Keynesian proposition of attaching national economy to political determinants was a retreat from the orthodox traditions of IPE. The net outcome of the Keynesian iconoclastic economic doctrine was the transformation to a new political economy with which to fortify a far-reaching program of sociopolitical reforms. Dillard (1946, p. 123) noted that in Keynes's later thinking, "he began to question aspects of the fundamental structure of capitalism, even to the point of foreseeing as a condition of its survival the disappearance of all rentier capitalism." In his *A Treatise on Money*, Keynes (1930) sought to explain why an economy operates so unevenly, with frequent cycles of booms and depressions. Like other treatments of the subject, his work failed to explain the problem of prolonged depression, a phenomenon that did not conform to the then-generally accepted notion that recessions were self-correcting. It was then felt that, during recessions, savings would accumulate, causing interest rates to fall and encouraging businesses to invest and the economy to expand.

Later, Keynes (1935) closely examined the problem of prolonged depression in his major work, *The General Theory of Employment, Interest, and Money*. In it, he provided a theoretical defense for programs that were already tried in Britain and by President Franklin D. Roosevelt in the United States. He proposed that there is no self-correcting mechanism in the free market system to lift an economy out of a depression. He argued that, since investment necessarily fluctuates, it cannot be depended on to maintain a high level of employment and a steady flow of income through the economy. Keynes proposed that government spending must compensate for insufficient business investment in times of recession and that the government must collect tax from citizens when the national economy is booming.

Shortly after Britain entered Second World War, Keynes (1940) published *How to Pay for the War: A Radical Plan for the Chancellor of the Exchequer*, in which he argued that a portion of every wage earner's pay should automatically be invested in government bonds. Keynes's idea was a pronouncement that the free motion of economic factors is not the ultimate determinate of EG; instead, the behavior of the political system and its relationship to the economic process is essential to the proper functionality of the economy. The Keynesian approach, which established the link between the political system and the economy, departed sharply from the orthodox IPE, which tended to insulate economic affairs from political contexts.

Numerous works exist on the effect of political variables on growth, variables such as the impact of party control of the polity on defense spending (Domke, 1992; Stoll, 1992; Mintz, 1988), the use of force and military actions (Ostrom & Job, 1986), the impact of domestic and international conditions on policy performance (Borrow, 1992), and the impact of politics on the timing of the use of force (DeRouen, 2000; Fordham, 1998). None of these studies has tested the effects of politics on growth in the context of the PF. More recently, Heo and Mintz (2002) tested the effect of the party control of the White House (Republican or Democrat) on EG. The authors found that Republican administrations affect growth negatively. However, they admit that further research is needed to cross-validate their findings. It is worth mentioning that Hibbs (1977) was the forerunner in reporting the systematic effects of party control of the executive on inflation and unemployment. Heo and Mintz (2002) conducted the first study that empirically introduced the political context to the PF and established a new paradigm from which to view the forces of production within a sociopolitical framework.

1.5. THE PRODUCTION FUNCTION AND DEVELOPING COUNTRIES

Sen (1999, pp. 3–11) noted that focusing on human freedoms contrasts with narrower views of development, such as identifying development with the growth of gross national product (GNP), or with the rise in personal incomes, or with industrialization, or with technological advance. Development requires the removal of major sources of unfreedoms: poverty as well as tyranny. Political and civil freedoms are constitutive elements of human freedom and are a necessary condition for scientific and technological creativity. According to Sen (1999, p. 37), "The relevance of the deprivation of basic political freedoms or civil rights, for an adequate understanding of development, does not have to be established through their indirect contribution to other features of development (such as the growth of GNP or the promotion of industrialization). These freedoms are part and parcel of enriching the process of development." Although freedom is an essential dimension for better understanding of the process of economic development, other characteristics of the political regime are equally important in understanding this process. The most relevant characteristics of the political regime are political freedom, institutional freedom, regime type, regime stability, and regime ideological base.

Although many scholars have tested the PF empirically and found overwhelming evidence that labor, investment, and technological progress have a positive impact on EG, I do not expect to obtain the same results when applying it within the framework of developing countries because the political contexts of Third World countries are different from those of the First World. The impact of political contexts of states on the performance of the economy is the core theoretical construct of this research. Another important factor is conflict.

1.6. THE IMPACT OF CONFLICTS ON ECONOMIC GROWTH

Van Raemdonck and Diehl (1989) identified and classified the major research investigations according to their theoretical perspectives on postwar EG and their spatial temporal domain (see also Chan, 1985) as follows:

Positive effects: The proponents of the positive impact of war on EG, led by Sombart (1913), Borton (1941), Schumpeter (1939), Foch (1918), and Herring (1941), claimed that war improves efficiency and protection of industry because it brings about technological progress. Other scholars, such as Dorn (1940) and Dulles (1942), emphasized enhancement of human capital, as in the managerial and organizational improvement in the field of decision-making processes. Gould (1972) suggested that, after the termination of war, redirecting resources to peacetime industries that were ignored during the war leads to EG.

Negative effects: This view was best expressed by Fraser (1926, p. 328): "Destroy the power of one country to produce, and you immediately destroy one side of the reciprocal demand, therefore, causing trade to cease." Waltz (1959, p. 1) noted, "Asking who won a given war, someone has said, is like asking who won the San Francisco earthquake. That in wars no victory but only varying degrees of defeat is a proposition that has gained increasing acceptance in the twentieth century." Most of the arguments for the negative economic effects of war are simply the opposites of the positive effects listed above. Rowthwell (1941) did not see the government control over the economy which is imposed during war as a transient effect but rather as a permanent effect because of the reluctance of institutions to give up power once it is acquired. Similarly, Ogawa (1926) attributes the negative effects of governments' mobilization of the credit markets and the distortion of the war effort as consumption and investment processes. Some scholars expect that states that participate in war, especially the losers, will experience immediate economic decline; Wheeler (1975) and Organski and

Kugler (1980) attributed this impact to the destruction of production facilities that usually results from war. Mendershausen (1943) and Thorp (1941) posited that economic stagnation will take place and human capital will be squandered in the battlefield rather than used properly in economic production. Other scholars argue that the negative effects of war may only be apparent indirectly, as war causes certain changes in the government's allocations of resources. Both Russett (1970) and Diehl and Goertz (1985) have found a "ratchet effect" in allocation to the military as the result of war. A ratchet effect is concerned with the growing pattern of chronic inflation characterized by much higher price increases at annual rates of 10–30 percent in some industrial nations and even 100 percent or more in a few developing countries. Chronic inflation tends to become permanent and ratchets upward to even higher levels as economic distortions and negative expectations accumulate.

A variety of overlapping perspectives emphasize the significant influence of war preparation and participation on the long-term capital formation of the system's most powerful states (Modelski, 1972; Tilly, 1975; Gilpin, 1987; Rasler & Thompson, 1985, 1988). Recent studies, such as Abadie and Gardeazabal (2003) and Ra and Singh (2005), affirm the negative effect of conflict on growth.

1.7. ORGANIZATION OF THE BOOK

This book consists of eight chapters. In Chapter 1, I introduce the problem and the contribution of my research, and I trace the evolutions of the PF model and theories of EG. I discuss the contribution of the PED in explaining problems of growth in developing countries. Moreover, I introduce conflict as a new variable in the PF.

In Chapter 2, I discuss the economic causes of conflicts in the ME and their impact on its economic development. I also discuss the nature of the Middle Eastern economy from the pre-Islamic era until the current time. The fact that the ME has been a zone of conflicts throughout its history is an indication of its relevance to great powers' strategic formulations. Ancient empires as well as contemporary major powers have competed for power and influence in the region to enhance their relative economic and military positions. The discovery of oil in the region has shifted the major focus of power to the ME and escalated struggle among them, thus hampering the normal development of the region due to the social dislocation that has been created. In this chapter, I use internal and external conflicts as control variables and test the impact of regime variables on EG for fifteen Middle Eastern countries (451 observations) using CNTS analysis.

In Chapter 3, I argue that conflicts between Arabs and Jews are constructed by radical national-religious elements. Political and cultural understanding of Middle Eastern politics will most likely overcome the root causes of conflicts in the region. I investigated the Camp David Accord (CDA) and the Wadi Araba Agreement (WAA) as examples of Pacta Sunt Servanda treaties and the Oslo Accords (OA) as examples of non Pacta Sunt Servanda agreements. I utilize the Nash Bargaining Approach to establish the conditions for successful or failing treaties. I also utilize Arrow's paradox to convey the idea that Palestinian Islamic radical choice is different from the Palestinian public choice.

In Chapter 4, I describe the key trends in defense spending and arms procurement in Middle Eastern sub-regions: Arab Mashreq, Arab Maghreb, and Gulf States. I explain the key characteristics of arms modernization and arms buildup and evaluate the future prospects of the region based on those trends. Furthermore, I explain the danger of transferring knowledge and technology of arms production to non-states actors in the ME. Finally, I discuss "guns versus butter" and the policy implications based on trends of defense spending as well as the impact of those trends on the severity of conflicts.

In Chapter 5, I survey the literature on IPE with a focus on several dimensions: classical PF, the PF defense-growth model, and the defense-growth-political and conflict model. I extensively evaluate the existing models to explain the evolutionary relationship, the conceptual framework, and the background of my alternative model.

In Chapter 6, I augment the H–M model by incorporating into it eight political and conflict variables: political freedom, institutional freedom, regime type, regime stability, regime ideological base, intrastate conflicts, interstate conflicts, and total conflicts. Therefore, I extend the applicability of the H–M model to capture most of the fundamental characteristics of political regimes. Moreover, I extend the applicability of the augmented model to the Third World, which has a different level of economic and political development than the First World.

In Chapter 7, I show the sources of my data, explain the process involved in preparing my data for actual analysis, and explore their relative advantages to other datasets. I utilize time series data on sixty-nine developing countries in Asia, the ME, Africa, Latin America, and the Caribbean region from 1960 to 2002. The data of this research consists of four types: economic, military, political, and conflict data. The study involves NLS analysis, CNTS analysis, and an in-depth case study of the ME. The data in the ME chapters extends to current events. In Chapter 8 (Conclusion), I summarize the main findings of this book and the ideas that make this research unique in explaining problems of growth and development in the Third World as well as describe the policy implications of my research.

CHAPTER 2

THE POLITICAL ECONOMY OF THE MIDDLE EAST

2.1. INTRODUCTION

The fact that the ME has been an area of conflicts throughout its history is an indication of its utmost relevance to the strategy formulations of major powers. The ME can be called "the land bridge of civilization" because it links Africa with Eurasia, and it has been the trade route of peoples from Asia, Africa, and Europe. Ancient empires, as well as contemporary major powers, have competed for power and influence in the region to enhance their relative economic and military positions. The discovery of oil in the region escalated the struggle among major powers, created societal dislocations, and increased internal and external conflicts. The ME has been the major artery of contact for over 3000 years (Weatherby, 2001, pp. 1–4). One hundred years ago, scholar-adventurer John L. Stoddard recognized this fact when he described a small portion of the region, Palestine. According to Stoddard, "Palestine has an area only a little larger than the state of Massachusetts, while Russia occupies one seventh of the habitable globe: yet in the scales of intellectuals and moral value the little province of Judea outweighs beyond comparison the empire of Czar" (Weatherby, 2001, pp. 1–4).

In this chapter, first, I argue that throughout Middle Eastern history, nations of the region have continued, with minor variations, the same "conquestal" economic trends of the pre-Islamic era (Jahilliah). The main feature of the conquestal economy is the absence of a base of production accompanied by a heavy role of state power exercised through the military. In the past, Middle Eastern states maintained their survival by extracting resources from invaded countries. Today, their survival depends on foreign aid and oil resources. Although the appearance of modern Middle Eastern states has changed, the essence of the mode of production has remained the same: there has been a parasitic mode of production and over-dependence on peripheries' resources,[1] which has been a main factor in the implosion of consecutive Islamic empires. Secondly, the last Islamic Caliphate (the Ottoman Empire) depleted resources, damaged the environment, and left a backward administrative system in the Arab world such that any potential for economic and political development were eliminated. In other words, when the Arabs entered an era of renaissance, they could not find tangible or intangible resources to allow them to pursue the process of modernization. And finally, interstate and intrastate peace must be a strategic choice because it is a necessary condition for economic development in the region. The key to understanding the chronic problems of economic and political backwardness in the ME is to investigate the impact of conflicts on the economic and political life of the region; conflicts propagate in all layers of the political and economic systems in the region and hold them back from achieving any significant progress. Thus, I have placed particular emphasis in this chapter on understanding the dynamics of conflict in the region.

2.2. EVOLUTION OF THE MIDDLE EAST'S POLITICAL ECONOMY

In the works *Man Makes Himself* and *What Happened in History*, Gordon Childe (1936, 1940) developed his theories about the rise and fall of ancient civilizations in the ME. Childe argued that these civilizations were shaped by conflicts between progressive groups, which endorsed flexible social structures and embraced technological change, and conservative groups, which favored a rigid social hierarchy and opposed any developments that might undermine the power of the elite. Childe suggested that the increasing dominance of conservative forces ultimately undermined the civilizations of the ancient ME.

One wonders whether Childe had ever read *The Muqadamah* of Ibn Khaldoun, who considered the conflict between *badu* (nomads) and *hadar* (urbanites) to be a major category in his sociological analysis. Ibn Khaldoun[2] (1322–1406) analyzed the conflict between the nomads and urbanites in his *Muqadamah,* explaining the evolution of societies in the ME and North Africa (Ibn Khaldoun, 1967, pp. 91–123; Ayubi, 1999, pp. 38–86). Ibn Khaldoun theorized that the nomads despise agriculture and crafts and are disinclined to engage in them (the Arabic word for a "craft" or profession is derived from the same root of "humiliation," imtihan), but they are at the same time tempered by the riches of the settled people's lands and inclined to take them over and control their producers. A cyclical pattern then often is set in motion: nomadic fighters relying on their strength and group solidarity (*asabia*) take power, but over time, those nomads are softened by the luxury of settled urban life, leading to its weakening and decay. As a result, another wave of nomads whose group solidarity still is strong attacks and takes power, and the cycle continues (Ayubi, 1999, pp. 49–50). Ali Al-Wardi (1981) [as cited by Ayubi, 1999, p. 50] held that conflict between *badawa* (nomadism) and *hadara* (civilization) characterizes the entire social history of the Arab world.

The most prominent Moroccan thinker, Abid Al-Jabiri (1982, pp. 404–431), found Ibn Khaldoun's theory interestingly indicative of a certain mode of production that he called a "conquestal mode of production" or a "military mode of production." Al-Jabiri (1982) indicated that the term "production" obviously has a different meaning than its general economic usage, for this is basically a consumerist or circulationist, not a producing, type of economy. In such a political economy, the "booty" (al-ghanima) takes pride of place: it is a source of income reflected in distribution (which is based on donation), and it promotes a certain "rentier mentality" that is averse to production and to a work ethic.

According to Nazih Ayubi (1999, p. 41), the idea of the existence of a distinct "orient mode of production" is not entirely new. Adam Smith classified China with ancient Egypt and "Indostan," making the point that governments in these societies paid much attention to the canal system. The idea of an "Oriental society" was put forward some years later by James Mill and also by John Stuart Mill. Furthermore, Karl Marx, who was familiar with such writers, developed a theory about "an Asiatic mode of production." According to Ayubi (1999, p. 42), "Oriental society as Marx understood was nevertheless something more complex than a system of canals. It had to do, on the one hand, with centralized – i.e., despotic – regulation of the basic economic functions and, on the other, with a self sufficient village economy" Ayubi (1999, pp. 49–51) suggests that the "Asiatic mode of production" – inasmuch as it applies to the ME – cannot be understood without taking into account another mode of production that was never very far away from any Middle Eastern society: the nomadic, kin-ordered mode of production. A nomadic community has not only to be sensitively tuned to nature and its changes but also critically alert to the movement of other nomadic communities that are trying to use the same limited resources. Thus, the vital role of social organization is absolute internal solidarity and external antagonism.

The tribal society of Arabia about a century before Islam was by no means a simple one of autonomous and egalitarian tribes. It knew poverty, wealth, injustice, and tribal warfare. It also chiefly witnessed authority based on some degree of ownership and elements of control over the means of production. Markets existed for the interchange of both goods and ideas (through poetry in particular), and in Hijaz, especially around Mecca, a commercial semi-aristocracy (mainly Quraishi) was involved in local and distance trade and was capable of possessing herds, large areas of pasture land, slaves, and a long trade route extending to Iraq, the Gulf, Yemen, Ethiopia, and Syria (Ayubi, 1999, pp. 54–56; Cleveland, 2000, pp. 4–8). This level of economic development in Arabia was accompanied by a high level of injustice, deep social antagonism, and ultimately a deep threat to internal social cohesion.

Islam then came in the seventh century as a unifying force, forging most of Arabia into a more integrated society subject to one law, the new Islamic *shari'a.* However, the unifying process was not comprehensive and fixed, as evidenced by the ridda[3] (apostasy) wars that followed the death of Prophet Muhammad. The ridda wars (632–634) cost the newly established Islamic state an enormous amount of resources and weakened internal social cohesion. Thus, through conquest, the Islamic state achieved a higher level of social integration and vast economic resources vital to the life of the newly established state.

The origin of the Islamic state, as Waddah Sharara (1981, pp. 125–142) pointed out, can be traced to a process of the traditional conquest (ghazw) practice and more specifically to the traditional rules of "distribution" following war. Ayubi (1999, p. 57) noted,

> Distribution of the spoils of war was at first equitable among Arabs regardless of differences; it then became increasingly based on a system of degradation. Abu Baker, the first caliph, related the distribution directly to internal consideration of Arabian society by adopting the (nomadic) principle of equal share of the booty. With Umar, the second caliph, however, gradation in compensation was introduced according to Islamic 'seniority' (how long in Islam and whether the crucial battle of Bader[4] had been attended or not).

Furthermore, according to Ayubi (1999), Umar made the grant to the fighters annual after accumulating the money and not occasional with each conquest collection. Umar was assassinated in 644 and was succeeded by Uthman, who faced opposition from the military from the beginning of his reign. In 656, a group of soldiers broke into Uthman's home and murdered him. They then prevailed upon Ali to accept the caliphate, which was contested by the Umyyad clan. Two major civil wars erupted between Ali's partisans (*shaia*) and the Umyyads: the "great strife" (al-fitna al-kubra[5]) lasted from 656 to 661, and a battle occurred in 657 at Siffin.[6] Ali was assassinated by the Kharijites in 661, marking the end of the first phase of the Islamic community (Cleveland, 2000, pp. 13–16).

2.3. THE UMAYYADS AND THE ABBASIDS

After Ali's death, Múawiya became the fifth Caliph and the first Umayyad ruler. Like their predecessors, the umayyads took advantage of the disunity and overconfidence of their Christian, Zoroastrian, and Hindu rivals to create the largest empire in the world. As they expanded to become the largest empire in the world, they proved incapable of controlling the territories they acquired. Over time, the Arab traditions gave way to the more sophisticated administrative practices of the Greek and Persian converts. As a result, non-Arabs ran the empire for the Arabs and performed the same administrative jobs that they had done for their former Byzantine and Persian masters. When the Umayyads banned them from the top positions of authority, they were dissatisfied. In addition, the policy of Arab *exclusivism* adopted by the Umayyads (discrimination against non-Arab converts to Islam) created widespread discontent. The Persians, the Shia, and the discontented Arab tribes revolted and succeeded in overthrowing the Umayyads in AD 750. The new rulers called themselves Abbasids after Abbas, the uncle of Prophet Muhammad (Weatherby, 2001, pp. 121–124; Roskin & Coyle, 2008, pp. 30–32; Cleveland, 2000, pp. 15–18).

The office of the Caliphate remained with the Abbasids from AD 750 to AD 1258. Under the Abbasids, the "heroic" age of the conquest gave way to the development of administrative institutions, commercial enterprise, and a legal system. The Abbasids abandoned the Arab exclusiveness that had generated so much discontent under the Umayyads. In its place, they adopted a universalistic policy accepting the equality of all Muslims, regardless of their racial origins. The universalism of the Abbasids was symbolized by the transfer of their capital from Damascus (a predominantly Arab city) to Baghdad. The new location of the Islamic center brought about more contact with the Iranian imperial traditions and more dependence on Sasanian practices. The Abbasids' administration was developed based on the Sasanian model and depended largely on Iranian bureaucracy. In 945, an Iranian military dynasty, the Buyids, took over temporal power in Baghdad, reducing the Caliph to a titular position. The weakness of the Abbasids caused an Islamic political, economic, and cultural decline that ultimately led to the collapse of the Abbasid Empire in 1258 (Cleveland, 2000, pp. 17–20; Weatherby, 2001, pp. 122–27; Roskin & Coyle, 2008, pp. 30–33).

2.4. THE OTTOMANS

During the last centuries of Abbasid rule, areas at the periphery of the empire started to separate from the core. In Anatolia, Turkish tribes migrating from central Asia established a string of small states that separated the Muslim lands from Byzantium. When the Abbasid Empire collapsed, these small states plunged into a struggle to control much of the old Abbasid territories. In the Anatolian Peninsula, Osman Ertuğrul managed to defeat his rivals to establish the Ottoman Empire. As a centralized, imperial state, the Ottomans drew on the administrative traditions of the Byzantines, the Iranians, and the Arabs in operating their civil services. According to Cleveland (2000, p. 51),

> External factors, most prominent among them the penetration of European merchant capital into the empire, caused a wrenching dislocation of the Ottoman economy. Beginning in the late sixteenth century, Ottoman raw materials, normally channeled into internal consumption and industry, were increasingly exchanged for European manufactured products. This trade benefited Ottoman merchants but led to the decline in state revenues and shortage of raw materials for domestic consumption. Without these revenues, the institutions that supported the Ottoman system, especially the armed forces, were undermined.

According to Cleveland (2000, pp. 51–52), the once-prevalent idea that the Ottoman Empire entered into a period of precipitous decline following the reign of Süleman al-Kanuni ("the law giver," better known in the West as "the Magnificent") is no longer accepted. Indeed, some historians now question whether the term "decline" is an accurate description of the reason that the Ottoman Empire lost its dominant position. Cleveland (2000, p. 51) argued, "It is preferable to view the Ottoman experience from the seventeenth to twentieth centuries as a period of transformation during which the Ottomans struggled to find a new imperial synthesis in a changing international environment." The penetration of the European-manufactured goods into the empire and the eventual domination of Ottoman commerce by Europeans and their protégés were facilitated by a series of commercial treaties, known as "the capitulations," that the Ottoman sultans signed with the Christian states of Europe. The first capitulation with France in 1536 allowed French merchants to trade freely in Ottoman ports, to be exempted from taxes, to import export goods at low tariff rates, and to permit French merchants to be under the jurisdiction of the French consul in Istanbul. This first treaty was the model for subsequent agreements signed with other European states. External factors combined with a gamut of domestic problems rendered the Ottoman Empire less effective than at the time of al-Kanuni.

The defeat of the Ottomans at the battle of Lepanto, their failure in 1683 to take Vienna for the second time, and the 1699 Treaty of Karlowitz were clear indications of the decline of the Ottoman Empire's capabilities. Why could the Ottomans not respond to these defeats by modernizing their society and beating the Europeans at their own game? Roskin and Coyle (2008, pp. 278–280) argued that in 1908, the Young Turk movement officers (including Mustafa Kemal, later known as Atatürk [father of the Turks]) attempted to reform and modernize the Empire. They only partially were successful because key elements of the Empire did not wish to become like Europe. The Ottoman Empire was old, complex, carefully balanced, and based on an Islamic legitimacy in which the temporal ruler, the Sultan, was also the spiritual ruler, the Caliph (successor of the Prophet). Instead, the Ottoman Empire embarked on a path to attempt partial modernization, copying Europe in some areas but preserving the overall traditional system. This was not possible, as partial modernization leaves the job undone. In short, you cannot become a little bit modern; you have to go all the way, which the Ottomans refused to do.

Roskin and Coyle (2008, p. 281) drew a comparison between the Ottoman and Japanese modernization experiences. They argued that the Japanese did not fear Western ways because they were so secure in their Japaneseness (nihonjinron). In one generation, Japan went from traditional to modern, copying the West in everything from industry and education to medical care and naval warfare. Why could the Japanese do it and the Turks not? Roskin and Coyle (2008, p. 281) indicated that the answer in part is cultural: "Japan had long imported foreign culture – for example, Buddhism and Confucianism from China – but always bent and shaped it to suit Japanese needs. Japanese religion is vague and flexible, and there is no barrier to modernization." They claimed that many Arabs concur that the underlying problem is an Arab cultural antipathy to modernization that urgently needs to be overcome. For example, several Arabs coauthored a series of UN studies, the *Arab Human Development Reports*, which found corruption, declining economies, lagging science and technologies, widespread illiteracy, suppression of women, poor governance, and no political freedoms, elections, or media. The reports urged the Arab world to reform their political regimes.

The Ottoman transformation experience was not limited to Turkey; rather, it was the model that most Middle Eastern countries followed to varying degrees. The fact remains that partial modernization failed to form the grounds for any significant political and economic development in the ME. The indecisive attitude toward modernization in the ME caused fluctuations in economic and political development to the extent that the process of modernization in the ME since the early 1980 has yielded economic and political decline. Some major countries in the ME such as Egypt and Iran took some successful steps toward political and economic development in the 1940s and 1970s, respectively, but they have been reversed in both government and society since the late 1970s.

Al-Jabiri (1982, pp. 404–431) proposed that Ibn Khaldoun's observation, which I mentioned earlier in this chapter, can be generalized to most phases of the history of Middle Eastern states: monies are collected to be distributed among fighters and the officials for consumption but not for investment. The "conquestal" economy, as Al-Jabiri (1982, pp. 404–431) suggested, is based on wealth accruing to the state through a statist method to be spent by the statesmen. The main feature of the conquestal economy is the absence of a base of production accompanied by a heavy role for state power exercised through the military. Although the role of the state in the modern ME has changed, the essence of the mode of production remains the same. If conquest is replaced with external aid or oil revenues, it leads to an unproductive economy in which the state eliminates social economic activities and proposes itself as the sole "entrepreneur."

Ayubi (1999, p. 3) suggested, "The Arab state is not a natural growth of its own socio-economic history or its own cultural and intellectual tradition. It is a 'fierce' state that has frequently to resort to raw coercion in order to preserve itself." Consequently, the divergence between the people and the state in the ME became a fact of life, and it increased as more privileges were offered to the military and other coercive state apparatuses. Thus, it is difficult to understand the problems of development in the ME without taking into account and providing clear direction regarding the dynamics of internal and external conflicts and their influences on the economic and sociopolitical development of the region.

2.5. CONTEMPORARY MIDDLE EASTERN POLITICAL ECONOMY

According to Attar (2009), "the Middle East, a region that spans southwestern Asia and northeastern Africa, was coined in 1902 by naval officer Alfred Thayer Mahan and popularized in the United Kingdom. Determining which states the Middle East includes is both subjective and objective. It is subjective in the sense that those member states would be included or excluded from the region following the rise of an international hegemon, a reaction to the regional imbalance of power, or a shift in public opinion in one or more Middle Eastern countries. For example, until the 1950s, few included Pakistan and Afghanistan as part of the Middle East; however, following the rise of the United States after the Second World War as the international hegemon and the adoption of the Baghdad Pact in 1955 in order to counter the threat to the regional balance of power, Pakistan has been included as part of the Middle East."

Similarly, the Soviet invasion of Afghanistan in December 1979 and the resurgence of terrorism in Afghanistan and Pakistan, particularly after September 11, 2001, helped incorporate both countries into the ME region to recruit Arab Muslim fighters against the Soviets during the Afghani war of liberation and attract the Pakistani military establishment and intelligence agencies to cooperate against extremist organizations in Pakistan and Afghanistan. On the contrary, according to Attar (2009), "Turkey has been considered a Middle Eastern country for the past century, but many Turks today, including the Islamic government, insist that they are Europeans and ought to be admitted to the European Union."

The objective element of including or excluding a country from the region refers to how similar or different that country is from the regional core (the Arab countries). Thus, Arab culture, language, politics, physical features, and economic structures may represent determining criteria to include or exclude a country from the region. For example, Iran is very much similar to the regional core in all dimensions. On the contrary, Israel is physically in the ME but differs from the regional core economically, politically, and socially. In fact, Israel looks more like a European country than a Middle Eastern one (Attar, 2009; Anderson, Seibert, & Wagner, 2009, pp. 246–320; MacMillan, 2002, pp. 381–455; Fromkin, 1989; Hudson, 1977, pp. 56–81; Microsoft Encarta, 2007; Owen, 1992, pp. 239–250; Weatherby, 2002, pp. 1–4; Weatherby et al., 2009, pp. 240–290).

In this study, Middle Eastern countries are divided into the categories of Arab ME and non-Arab ME. The Arab ME includes Algeria, Bahrain, Comoros, Djibouti, Egypt, Eritrea, Iraq, Jordan, Kuwait, Libya, Mauritania, Morocco, Oman, the Palestinian National Authority (PNA), Qatar, Saudi Arabia, Somalia, the Sudan, Tunisia, the United Arab Emirates, and Yemen. The non-Arab ME includes Afghanistan, Israel, Iran, Pakistan, and Turkey.

In Section 2.6, I apply David Easton's structural approach to understand the problem of growth and development in the region. Easton's systemic approach suggests that any system includes inputs and outputs. The inputs, consisting of supports and demands, are processed through a converting mechanism (government) to produce outputs: policies and decisions. As displayed in Fig. 2.1, I used economic, military, non-military, conflict, and political variables as the inputs of the system to produce the output when processed though the "converting mechanism" of the PF. It is worth noting that I am not trying to affirm or disaffirm Easton's model; rather, I am employing it as a paradigm to clarify the problems of growth and development in the ME.

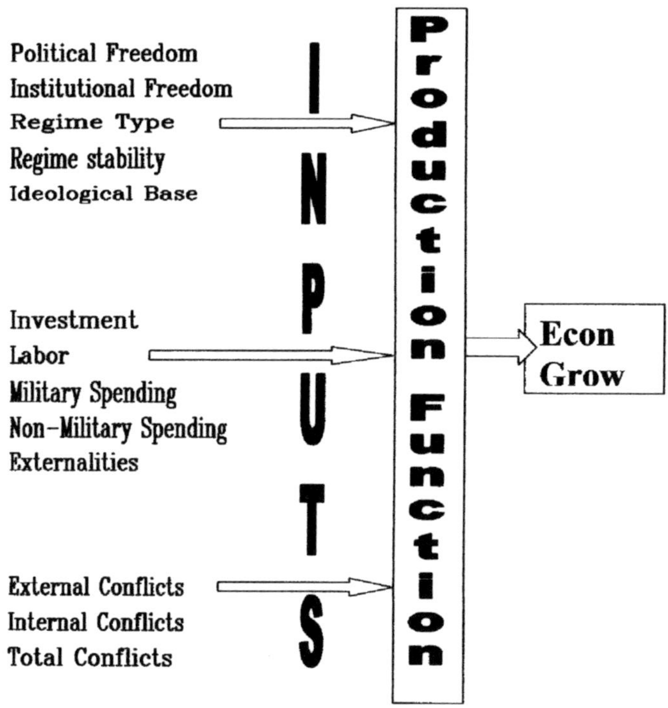

Fig. 2.1. The Production Function Defense-Growth Model Based on Easton (1965, p. 32).

2.6. STRUCTURAL APPROACH TO POLITICAL SYSTEM

I believe that the structure of the political system approach[7] as developed by Easton is the most appropriate level of analysis with which to examine the problems of political and economic development in the ME; thus, I would like to elaborate on some of Eaton's concepts. In this respect, it is essential to distinguish between a political regime and a political system: "specifically, to what might we refer when speaking of the regime of a political system? A political system is more comprehensive than a political regime such that within a political system, we have political authorities, a political community, and a political regime. A regime refers to the goals or values of a political system, the norms or rules of the game, and the structure of authority" (Easton, 1965, p. 26, 1990, p. 12).

Easton (1967, p. 12, 1990, pp. 190–212) theorized that each of these elements of political regime has its own structure, which typically draws our attention to the relationships among political authorities and, in turn, their relationship as political authorities, to other members of the political system. In Easton's (1990, p. 12) words, "it points to the distribution of that kind of power we call authority and the informal political power relationships associated with such authority." Easton (1990, p. 13) reminded us to bear in mind that the structure of the political regime is narrower than that of the political system as a whole or of the regime itself:

> The structure of the political system, for example, would include the structure of nonauthoritative power in a system (elite-mass relationships or class-based power, for example); the patterns of nonauthoritative relationships among interest groups and political parties; various roles such as those of opinion leaders, political bosses, and voters; electoral and other political cleavages; and all those other groups and roles that wield political power (except the kind we call political authority), which is characteristic of the influence exercised through regime.

The regime, as a set of constraints on political interaction in all systems, may be broken down into three components: values (goals and principles), norms, and structure of authority. The values serve as broad limits with regard to what can be taken for granted in the guidance of day-to-day policy without violating the deep feelings of an important segment of the community. The norms specify the kind of procedures that are expected and acceptable in the processing and implementation of demands as well as support and conversion processes. The structure of authority designates the formal and informal patterns in which power is distributed and organized with regard to the authoritative making and implementing of decisions – the roles and their relationships through which authority is distributed and exercised. The goals, norms, and structure of authority both limit and validate political actions and in this way provide what tends to become a context for political interactions. This context changes more slowly than other kinds of political relationships (Easton, 1967, pp. 259–266, 1990, pp. 12–13).

Easton (1965, p. 138) noted, "If we select political systems for special study, we do so because we believe that they have characteristically important consequences for society, namely, authoritative decisions. These consequences I shall call the outputs. If we judged that political systems did not have important outputs for society, we would probably not be interested in them."

The author went on to say that "Unless a system is approaching a state of entropy – and we can assume that this is not true for most political systems – it must have continuing inputs to keep it going. Without inputs the system can do no work; without outputs we cannot identify the work done by the system. The typical demands that will find their way into the political process will concern the matters in conflict that are labeled important by the culture" (Easton, 1965, p. 138).

Easton (1965, p. 138) suggested, "We cannot hope to understand the nature of the demands presenting themselves for political settlement unless we are ready to explore systematically and intensively their connection to the culture." Support is fed into the political system in relation to three objects:

1. *The political community*: No political system can continue to operate unless its members are willing to support the existence of a group that seeks to settle differences or promote decisions through peaceful action in common.
2. *The regime*: Support for the regime helps to keep the system running. This kind of support is related to all those arrangements that regulate the way in which demands put into the system are settled and the way in which decisions are put into effect.
3. *Converting mechanism*: If a political system is going to be able to handle the conflicting demands put into it, the political community must support the government. Supporting the government is essential because it is the mechanism that converts inputs to outputs, making and interpreting the rules and representing social interests (Easton, 1967, pp. 25–33, 155–170, 171–172). The government also provides feedback to various agencies to

enhance proficiency. Feedback helps the system to persist in the face of stress due to information and other influences that return to its actors and decision makers and assist them in rectifying past mistakes (Easton, 1965, p. 25).

2.7. ECONOMIC GROWTH BASED ON EASTON'S MODEL

Considering Easton's (1965, p. 112) model as an analytical framework to describe economic growth (EG) in the ME reveals a system of EG as shown in Fig. 2.1. The system of EG consists of inputs, a converting mechanism, and outputs.

The system of EG as shown in Fig.2.1 receives three different types of inputs:

- *Political input*: Political freedom, institutional freedom, regime type, regime stability, and ideological base.
- *Conflict input*: External conflicts, internal conflicts, and total conflicts.
- *Economic input*: Investment, labor, military spending, non-military spending, and the externality effects of capital, labor, and defense spending.

The PF represents the converting mechanism through which the inputs are transformed to outputs. The PF transforms the impacts of political, economic, and military variables; the externality effects (labor, capital, and defense spending); and the impact of conflict variables to output (EG). The output increases if there is a positive impact from the input variables; on the contrary, it decreases if the impacts of the input variables on EG are negative. Utilizing Easton's (1965, pp. 111–117) terminologies, the positive impact on EG provides "support" to the system of EG; conversely, the negative impact on EG imposes "demand" on it. Therefore, when demands outweigh supports, the system becomes dysfunctional, or at best inefficient.

2.8. APPLYING EASTON'S FRAMEWORK TO THE MIDDLE EAST

I tested fifteen countries in the ME – Jordan, Morocco, Saudi Arabia, Algeria, Bahrain, Egypt, Kuwait, Mauritania, Tunisia, United Arab Emirates, Sudan, Pakistan, Turkey, and Iran – using CNTS. The model consists of the standard PF in addition to external and internal conflict as control variables plus one political variable in each test.[8] Time series data[9] from 1960 to 2002 for the countries listed above (451 observations) were used in the CNTS analysis. The results[10] are summarized in Table 2.1 and explained below.

Political input variables: Political freedom has an insignificant negative impact on EG; institutional freedom has an insignificant positive impact on EG; regime type has an insignificant negative impact on economic on EG; regime stability has an insignificant positive impact on EG; and ideological base has a significant negative impact on EG.

Conflict input variables: The external conflicts variable has a negative and significant impact on EG under all political contexts. Likewise, the internal conflict variable has a negative and significant impact on EG under all political contexts. However, the internal conflict variable shows a more

Table 2.1. Cross-National Time Series Analysis Results of Fifteen Middle Eastern Countries with External and Internal Conflict as Control Variables.

Parameter	Pol Free	Inst Free	Type	Stability	Ideology
Labor estimate *t*-stat	1.422	1.437	1.422	1.424	1.422
	4.61**	24.58**	24.62**	24.57**	24.64**
Investment	−1.924	−0.748	−0.797	−0.748	−0.857
	−1.335	−1.093	−1.168	−1.096	−1.254
Military sector	−0.002	0.003	0.004	0.225	0.004
	−0.050	0.064	0.086	0.047	0.093
Military externalities	0.14E−3	0.14E−3	0.14E−3	0.13E−3	0.14E−3
	20.38**	20.14**	20.27**	20.19**	20.28**
Non-military sector	0.394	0.675	1.471	0.655	1.081
	0.097	0.166	0.361	0.162	0.268
Non-military externalities	−0.899	−0.757	−0.816	−0.743	−0.785
	−0.927	−0.783	−0.845	−0.776	−0.815
External conflict	−0.44E−5	−0.41E−5	−0.433E−5	−0.40E−5	−0.45E−5
	−2.251*	−2.083*	−2.219*	−2.058*	−2.289*
Internal conflict	−0.382	−0.396	−0.373	−0.391	−0.358
	−2.625**	−2.341*	−2.206*	−2.293*	−2.111*
Political variables	−0.163	0.410	−0.319	0.038	−0.383
	−1.474	0.022	−1.440	0.0204	−1.839*
	$N = 451$	$N = 451$	$N = 451$	$N = 451$	$N = 451$
	$R^2 = 0.72$	$R^2 = 0.72$	$R^2 = 0.72$	$R^2 = 0.72$	$R^2 = 0.72$
	DW = 1.16	DW = 1.15	DW = 1.16	DW = 1.14	DW = 1.16

*, significant at 0.05 level; **, significant at 0.01 level.

significant negative impact on EG than the external conflict variable under all political contexts.

The PF input variables: An increase in labor growth has a positive and significant impact on EG under all political contexts; investment shows an insignificant negative impact on EG under all political contexts; the combined effects of technological progress and productivity of the military sector show an insignificant negative impact on EG under the context of political freedom and an insignificant positive impact under institutional freedom, regime type, stability, and ideological base; the externality effects of defense spending have an unequivocal positive and significant impact on EG under all political contexts; the combined effects of technological progress and productivity of non-military spending have a insignificant positive impact on EG under all political contexts; the externality effects of non-military government spending show an insignificant negative impact on EG under all political contexts.

The results in Table 2.1 indicate that the system of EG in the ME receives significant "supports" from labor and the externality effects of military spending. On the contrary, internal and external conflicts impose demands on the system of EG. The effect of internal conflicts on EG in tribal societies, particularly the ME, is much greater than in civilized juridical societies. In the ME, where societies are based on *assabia* (strong tribal solidarity), domestic conflicts have a more disruptive and profound impact on socioeconomic activities than in other regions. The strong tribal lineage in the ME further explains how internal conflicts severely hamper the region's EG.

Internal conflicts create societal dislocation and provide an opportunity to certain organizations to grow in strength and influence. Examples are Harakat al-Moukawama al-Isalmia (HAMAS) and the Islamic Jihad Movement (IJM) in the Gaza Strip and the Party of God (Hezbollah) in Lebanon. Those organizations are supported financially and militarily by external powers (mainly by Iran and Syria) and may shift societal priorities to meet the agenda and objectives of their financiers; consequently, the social agenda and programs are paralyzed. In fact, those organizations end up as oligarchic entities that coerce members and leaders of their societies to implement and accept the agenda of others. In states where such organizations operate, it becomes unfeasible to attain a national developmental plan because those organizations disrupt the developmental process upon the request of their financiers. Because such organizations possess military and economic capabilities that are equal to or beyond the power of their respective states, the problem is exacerbated. Due to internal conflicts, in many countries in the ME, such as Egypt, Lebanon, Iraq, Somalia, the Sudan, and Algeria, political economic development becomes directionless, and the developmental efforts do not add up to make constructive socioeconomic development happen.

Internal conflicts in the ME have become the most destructive factor affecting economic development. The propagation of the culture of death by some Islamic organizations and the proliferation of suicide bombers in several Arab and Islamic countries have disrupted all types of economic activity. The insecurity caused by the culture of death discourages investments and shuts down vital sectors of the national economy, such as tourism.

In general, interstate regional armed conflicts in the developing world have similar characteristics, which are described below.

- The conflicts are dyadic, occurring between two states without direct interference from other states. Examples today include conflicts between India and Pakistan, Iran and Iraq, and Libya and Chad.
- The military operations are conducted on the peripheries of the participating states, not in their centers. Both states avoid the population centers; therefore, economic activities continue without disruption during conflicts. An example is the Iran–Iraq War.
- Usually, one or both countries receive military and economic assistance from one or more major powers. For example, during the Pakistani–Indian conflict over Bangladesh, the former received assistance from the United States of America, while the latter received assistance from the former Soviet Union. The military and economic assistance contributed positively to the general state of the economies in both countries.
- Countries engage in intermittent military operations. Although interstate conflicts continue, military activities are not continuous. There are some intermittent bursts, but they do not last long. Examples are Eritrea versus Ethiopia, Libya versus Chad, and Pakistan versus India over Kashmir.
- Interstate conflicts may induce the rally-round-the flag effect; the domestic front might grow stronger than it is during ordinary times, and the motivation for productivity might be enhanced.

It would be useful for PDMs to see Wimberley's (2003) satire, *The Mouse that Roared*, and follow the logic of the fictional Duchy of Grand Fenwick as a source of economic utility during interstate conflicts.

On the contrary, internal or intrastate conflicts have far more damaging effects on EG than interstate conflicts, whether weapons are involved, such as between the Kurdish and the Iranians or the Iraqis and the Turks, or passive domestic clashes like the one between the Iraqi Shia and Sunni sects during Saddam Hussein's regime. There are two levels of armed conflicts:

- They can be destructive when military operations are conducted in cities and towns of a country, which harms the infrastructure, the flow of business, and kills or injures innocent individuals.
- They can be passive. During times of non-military operations (truce, ceasefire, or agreements between the central government and the "rebels"), the dissatisfied populace continues passive resistance against central government development programs, or at least they do not participate fully to achieve the government's objectives.

2.9. THE INDIRECT EFFECT OF CONFLICTS

Based on the literature on defense spending and economic performance, Mintz and Huang (1991, pp. 738–757) hypothesized that increased levels of military expenditures dampen investment, which reduces growth, thereby reducing the ability of government to allocate more funds to welfare programs (Chan, 1985, 1987; Denoon, 1986; Lindgren, 1984; Rasler & Thompson, 1988; Smith, 1980; Smith & Georgiou, 1983).

Specifically, Mintz and Huang (1991) hypothesized that military spending and investment compete for the nonconsumption portion of the total productive capacity of the economy. Increased levels of military spending crowd out investment (Rasler & Thompson, 1988), which in turn may have a dampening effect on growth "by impeding the renewal and expansion of existing capital stock as well as the rate at which technical progress and innovation are spread through the economy" (Mosley, 1985, p. 65, as cited by Mintz and Huang, 1990; Mintz & Huang, 1991). Thus, the economy of the ME must be restructured such that support must come from investment instead of military expenditures' externalities.

2.10. SHADOW ECONOMIES AND SUB-ECONOMIES

Shadow economies and sub-economies are economic activities that bypass the converting mechanism (the PF in this chapter as shown in Fig. 2.1 or government in the original model of Easton, 1965, p. 32) such that those economic activities create inaccurate planning due to PDMs' incomplete knowledge of inputs and outputs of the economic system.

Schneider's (2005, pp. 114–115) "The Size of Shadow Economies in 145 Countries from 1999 to 2003" clarified the meaning of shadow economy. Schneider suggested that a shadow economy includes unreported income from the production of legal goods and services from either monetary or barter transactions and thus includes all economic activities that would generally be taxable were they reported to state authorities. The ME includes a very high number of shadow economies compared to any other region in the world. The average size of shadow economies in 145 nations was 33.6 percent of the gross domestic product (GDP) in 1999/2000. Five Middle Eastern countries top the regional average: Tunisia (38.4 percent), Pakistan (36.8 percent), Morocco (36.4 percent), Egypt (35.1 percent), and Algeria (38.4 percent). The regional average of shadow economies in 2001/2002 among 145 nations was 34.5 percent of GDP. Three countries in the Middle East and North Africa (MENA) topped the regional average: Tunisia (39.1 percent), Pakistan (37.9 percent), and Morocco (37.1 percent) (Schneider, 2005, pp. 118–127).

The Islamic investment companies illustrate the meaning of sub-economies, especially in Egypt and Pakistan. Zubaida (1992, p. 9) observed, "These companies only functioned freely because they recruit influential high-ranking officials, both retired and in post, to their board of directors and consultancies at high fees." According to Zubaida (1992, p. 9), "[T]hese companies were involved in all kinds of irregularities and doubtful practices." Zubaida alluded to the infamous investment companies (sharikat tawzif al-amwal) that came to prominence in Egypt from 1985 to 1988. They were "investment companies" in the sense that they invited deposits from the public on which they paid very high rates of return but in a form which did not go against the Islamic interdiction on interest dealing. According to Zubaida (1990, p. 154), "The volume of investment attracted by these companies was enormous. Estimates vary between 4.5 and eight billion Egyptian pounds by 1988, deposited by an estimated half a million customers. This represented a movement of capital out of the banks and saving investments, which caused considerable dislocation in the financial markets."

Thus, without a qualitative change to the inputs regarding the political system, we will not be able to accurately evaluate EG in developing countries. Middle Eastern governments must combat economic irregularities such as sub-economies and shadow economies because those types of financial dealings preclude a realistic evaluation of EG and make it impossible for PDMs to develop a realistic economic plan due to insufficient information about economic transactions.

NOTES

1. The Umayyads and Abbasids depend on the Persians, Byzantines, and Greeks resources; the Ottomans depend on the Arab and Balkan resources; and most Arab countries depend on oil and foreign aid.

2. Born in Tunisia, he went into seclusion near modern Frenda, Algeria, taking four years to compose his monumental *Muqaddamah*, the introductory volume to his *Kitab al-Ibar* (*Universal History*). In the *Muquadamah*, Ibn Khaldun outlined a philosophy of history and theory of society that are unprecedented in ancient and medieval writing and that are reflected closely in modern sociology. He argued that social change and the rise and fall of societies follow laws that can be discovered empirically.

3. Shortly after the news of Prophet Muhammad's death, many Arab tribes renounced their allegiance to Islam in favor of new, local leaders. This was less a religious choice than a political and economic one, since the tribes used this as an excuse to govern themselves and stop paying the zakāt, or alms tax. Though most Arab tribes did not challenge the prophecy of Muhammad, others apostatized and returned to their pre-Islamic religion and traditions, classified by Muslims as idolatry. The tribes claimed that they had submitted to Prophet Muhammad and that with the Prophet's death, they were again free. Abu Baker insisted that they had not just submitted to a leader but joined the Muslim religious community, of which he was the new head, and Abu Baker declared war on the rebels. The severest struggle was the war with Ibn Habib al-Hanefi, known as Musailimah Al-Khadab (Musailimah the Liar), who claimed to be a prophet and Muhammad's true successor. The undefeatable Muslim general Khalid bin Walid finally defeated al-Hanefi at the Battle of Akraba (Cleveland, 2000, p. 13; Microsoft Encarta Reference Library 2004; http://en.wikipedia.org/wiki/Abu_Bakr#The_Ridda_Wars).

4. In March 624, Prophet Muhammad and about 300 of his men battled a Meccan force three times their size at the oasis of Badr. It was a great victory for the Muslims, and later generations of Muslims considered it a mark of nobility to have fought at Badr.

5. Ali went north to Al Başrah-Iraq with his loyal troops, where in December 656, he defeated an army of Aisha's (the wife of Prophet Muhammad) supporters in what is considered the first round of the first Islamic civil war. This war, which lasted from 656 to 661, later became known as the first fitnah because it tested the unity of the Islamic community. It was also known as the Battle of the Camel.

6. Ali moved from Medina to Al Kufah-Iraq, where he had more support. There he was challenged by Muawiyah, the Umayyad governor of Syria. Muawiyah refused to recognize Ali as caliph and engaged Ali's forces in a battle at Siffin, in northern Syria, in 657.

7. I am more inclined to utilize the system level of analysis as developed by David Easton (1965) because a system analysis of political life enables the investigator to look at the whole picture and understand the interactions among the units of the system and the reasons that some systems are ineffective.

8. For a complete explanation and formulation of the cross-sectional model, see Chapter 6 and Eqs. (6.10)–(6.14).

9. A description of the data that have been used in this analysis can be found in Chapter 6.

10. For more details about the CNTS results, see Appendix C.

CHAPTER 3

ARAB ISRAELI CONFLICT

In this chapter, I investigate the root causes of the Arab–Jewish conflict from the pre-Islamic era to the present and explain the impact of historical residuals on the Middle East peace processes for the past 30 years. I developed a set of theoretical conditions for stable and enduring treaties, and those are not. I analyzed the CDA and the WAA in light of the Nash bargaining solution (NBS) using complete information and explained why both agreements met the conditions of an efficient NBS. On the contrary, I argue that the Oslo Accords (OA) were negotiated using incomplete information and under an Israeli uncertainty of the Palestine Liberation Organization (PLO) intentions and ability to enforce the deals. Therefore, the OA were not efficient NBS. I explain the factors that preclude the Palestinians and the Israelis from reaching stable and enduring agreements and provide suggestions to both the Palestinians and the Israelis that would enable them to make peace negotiations and bargaining more successful.

3.1. INTRODUCTION

For more than nine decades, the Jewish–Palestinian conflict has dominated all aspects of life in the Arab world. The Arabs have disregarded and neglected their political, economic, and social development since 1916 because of their obsession with defeating the Jews or driving them into the sea. When the Arab armies collectively failed to destroy the newly established Jewish state in 1948, the dynamics of the conflict changed. On the one hand, Arab rationalists such as King Abdullah ibn al-Husyan (King Abdullah-I) (d 1951) of the Hashemite Kingdom of Jordan (HKJ) suggested accepting the United Nations Partition Plan as proposed by the UN General Assembly on November 29, 1947. On the other hand, most Arab countries followed the lead of Egyptian President Gamal Abdul Nassir, who advocated the destruction of Israel. The latter view was also adopted by the PLO during Ahmad Shukeiri's reign (1964–1967) and later by Yasir Arafat (1969–2004) and most Palestinian armed factions.

However, the Arab defeat in the 1967 Six-Day War discredited the Nassirite radical approach and strengthened the realists' view led by Tunisian President Habib Bourguiba who advocated a lasting peace between Arabs and Jews. Bourguibia's apocalyptic vision was revived by King Hassan-II (d 1999) of the Kingdom of Morocco and carried out during the visit of Egyptian President Anwar Sadat to Jerusalem on November 19, 1977. Sadat's visit paved the way for peace between Israel and the Arab world, shaped new political alignments in the region, and normalized future visits of Arab leaders to Israel.

The Madrid conference convened on October 30, 1991, and involved Israel and the PNA as well as some Arab countries including Egypt, Syria, Lebanon, and Jordan recognized the need for peace in the region and redeemed the reputations of Abdullah-I, Bourguiba, Hassan-II, and Sadat. The Arab–Israeli negotiations in Madrid led to the successful WAA between Jordan and Israel and to a series of agreements and marathon negotiations between the PLO and Israel. The focus of the following section is on determining the conditions that make some agreements pacta sunt servanda while other agreements that utilize the NBS framework are not.

3.2. BARGAINING

Most rules of international law find their sources in the explicit agreements made by states. Such international agreements are commonly called treaties, although they are also termed conventions, pacts, protocols, or accords. Treaties create legal rights and duties, and it is the obligatory aspect that makes them part of international law. Agreements among states are *pacta sunt servanda* Latin for a fundamental principle that means that treaties must be observed and respected (Janis, 2003, p. 9). It is a fact that treaties are not reached quickly. Rather, they are preceded by a process of negotiations and bargaining, which might lead to agreements between nations or not. It is reasonable to think that the process of negotiations and bargaining and their outcomes affect the endurance and success of agreements and the *pacta sunt servanda* of the signatories. Morrow (1994, p. 112) notes that, "the critical question in cooperative games is how the players divide the surplus above the minimum they can achieve on their own." Bargaining as a cooperative political process focuses on what deals the players will strike to divide the surplus among them.

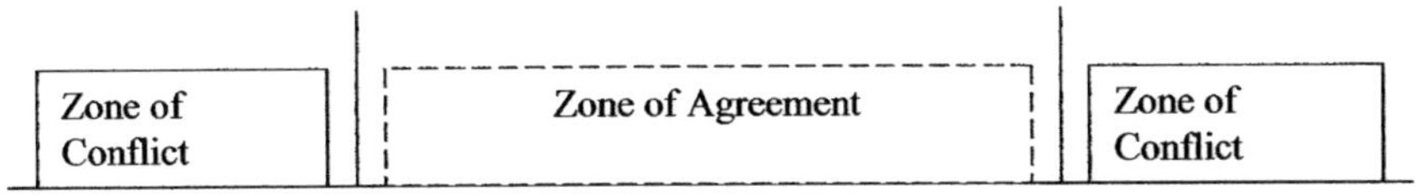

Fig. 3.1. Zone of Agreement and Conflicts in Bargaining.

I want to discuss the NBSs that Israel negotiated with Egypt, Jordan, and the PNA, respectively. Before I proceed, it is important to clarify and determine the meaning of the reservation levels of the negotiators in those cases. For convenience, I assume the range of possible deals can be modeled by a set of points on a line as in Fig. 3.1. If the two sides reach an agreement using complete information, meaning that the possible set of deals is known to both of them, the agreement will be an efficient solution that endures and is respected. In this case the reservation level is very small or does not exist, so there are no conflicts that hinder the agreement such as those that occurred in the CDA and the WAA. On the contrary, if the set of deals is unknown to both sides, the efficient solution may not be implemented. This may happen for two reasons. First, the actual set of deals is bigger than the expected one so no one has thought of the efficient solution. Second, the actual set of deals is smaller than the expected one. Here, the signed deal may not be enforceable, so the conflict level is very large. Concerning the OA, I would argue that the actual set of deals was indeed smaller than the expected one. Israel expected the PLO to be able to control groups like HAMAS and al-Jihad al-Islami. In fact, this was crucial to their deal. Afterwards, they found out that this was not the case. Hence, they signed a deal that was not enforceable. Each side has a reservation level, or reservation point, that expresses its value for a no agreement. In between the reservation levels of the two sides is a zone of agreement. This zone provides information about all the bargains that both parties prefer to the conflict zone. In coming to the negotiation table, the two sides have concluded that they have more to gain from bargaining than from the status quo, which is a continual source of tension and overt military conflict. We transfer the problem form set of points on a line to a two-dimensional space representing all the possible bargains as shown in Fig. 3.2, where the gains to be made by the Israelis increase as we move eastward along the horizontal dimension and the gains to be made by the PNA, Egypt, and Jordan increase as we move northward along the vertical dimension. That is, any bargain in this space will provide utility, an improvement over the status quo, to Israel the PNA, Egypt, and Jordan (Morrow, 1994, pp. 112–115; Osborne, 2004, pp. 465–477; Russett, Starr, & Kinsella, 2006, pp. 126–127).

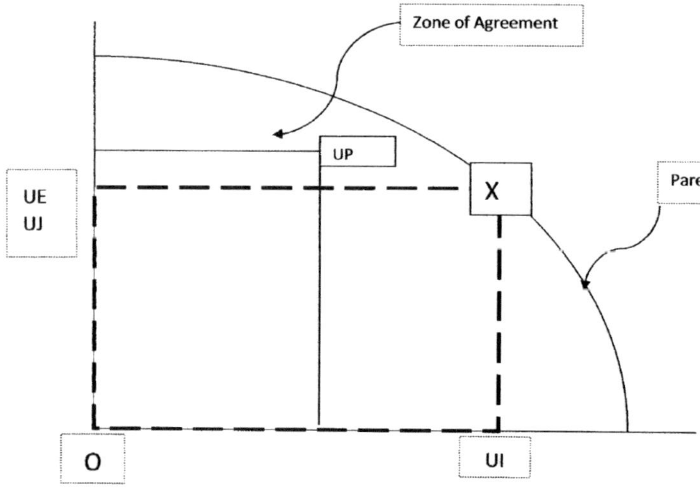

Fig. 3.2. Nash Bargaining Solution of Israel versus Egypt, Jordan, and the PNA.

This bargaining space is bounded by a frontier, shown as a curve, which represents the limits of all possible bargains that could be made by both the PNA and the Israelis. A particular bargain, X – to formally recognize Egyptian, Jordanian, or Palestinian authority on land, for example – will be an improvement for Israel, equal UI, and an improvement for Egypt, Jordan, or PNA equal UE, UJ, or UP. A bargain anywhere inside the large zone of agreement but not on the frontier can be improved upon. The frontier is often called the Pareto optimal frontier, after the Italian economist Vilfredo Pareto, whose concepts of economic efficiency are employed widely in the social sciences today. A Pareto optimal outcome is one in which neither side can do better without making the other side worse-off. One can see that any point on the frontier meets that condition; these outcomes are thus socially optimal (Morrow, 1994, pp. 112–115; Osborne, 2004, pp. 465–477; Russett et al., 2006, pp. 126–127).

The challenge for negotiators is first to define the bargaining space and identify the zone of agreement and then to strike a bargain at or near the Pareto frontier. That is not easy or possible when there is incomplete information as occurred during the bargaining process between the Israelis and the Palestinians. Imagine that Israel and Egypt, in the process of negotiations, are zeroing in on a bargain at point X, but Israel is having second thoughts and wants to increase the portion of land recognized as sovereign Israeli territory. While any point on the frontier southeast of X is still Pareto optimal, Egypt could be expected to reject that move. The two sides, perhaps with the help of third-party mediators, need to try to find a bargain that is both socially optimal and perceived as fair. One solution is to find a bargain that maximizes the products of the two sides' utilities (i.e., a point on the frontier tangent to the largest rectangle that could be drawn inside the zone of agreement, which in this case is point X as shown in Fig. 3.2). A solution at point X is an efficient NBS, which is possible when complete information is available. As the bargainers move closer to one axis or the other – as they disproportionately favor one side or the other – this conception of fairness will not be met.

3.3. THE MODEL

There are two players, $i = 1, 2$, who must divide a single resource denoted by X as displayed in Fig. 3.2. It is useful to think of these resources as security, land, holy sites, people, water, and independence. In this model, i_1 denotes Israel which bargains with the PNA, Egypt, and Jordan denoted by i_{2P}, i_{2E}, and i_{2j} respectively; u_1 denotes the payoff of Israel; and u_{2p}, u_{2E}, and u_{2J} denote the payoffs of the PNA, Egypt, and Jordan, respectively. We denote by $x_i \geq 0$ the initial amount of the resources held by a player. We assume that there is a single unit of resources; thus, $x_1+x_{2p} = 1$; $x_1+x_{2E} = 1$, and $x_1+x_{2J} = 1$ represent the resources bargains made between Israel and the PNA, Israel and Egypt, and Israel and Jordan, respectively. In addition, each side has a reservation level denoted by c_1, c_{2E}, c_{2J}, and c_{2P} refers to the reservation levels of Israel, Egypt, Jordan, and the PNA, respectively.

Let f_1, f_{2E}, f_{2J}, and f_{2P} be the utility function of Israel, Egypt, Jordan, and the PNA, respectively.

The utility function of each country is the difference between the utility of making a deal and the reservation level. Thus,

The Utility function of Israel: $f_1 = [(u_1(x) - u_1(c_1)]$
The Utility function of Egypt: $f_{2E} = [(u_{2E}(x) - u_{2E}(c_{2E})]$
The Utility function of Jordan: $f_{2J} = [(u_{2J}(x) - u_{2J}(c_{2J})]$
The Utility function of the PNA: $f_{2P} = [(u_{2J}(x) - u_{2P}(c_{2P})]$

I argue that the CDA and the WAA are efficient NBSs because they were signed under conditions of certainty with complete information and sets of enforceable deals available. The reservation levels of Egypt and Jordan were very low; therefore, the CDA NBS is the maximization of the joint utility functions of Israel and Egypt:

$$\text{CDA: Max } f_1\, f_{2E} = \text{Max}\{[(u_1(x) - u_1(c_1)]^*[(u_{2E}(x) - u_{2E}(c_{2E})]\} = 0$$

Similarly, the WAA NBS between Israel and Jordan is expressed:

$$\text{WAA: Max } f_1\, f_{2J} = \text{Max}\{[(u_1(x) - u_1(c_1)]^*[(u_{2J}(x) - u_{2J}(c_{2J})]\} = 0$$

On the contrary, the OA between Israel and the PNA were not NBS because they were negotiated and signed without complete information, and when the bargainers were experiencing mistrust, doubts about the enforceability of deals, and high reservation level; therefore:

$$\text{OA: Max } f_1\, f_{2J} = \text{Max}\{[(u_1(x) - u_1(c_1)]^*[(u_{2P}(x) - u_{2P}(c_{2P})]\} \neq 0$$

(see Hirshleifer, Boldrin, & Levine, 2009, pp. 197–199; Morrow, 1994, pp. 112–115; Osborne, 2004, pp. 465–477; Russett et al., 2006, pp. 126–127).

3.4. RESERVATION LEVELS

There are some important issues that must be addressed before peace can occur between Arabs (Egypt and Jordan in this case), Palestinians, and Israelis. These issues involve land, water, refugees, Palestinian prisoners in Israeli jails, Jerusalem, and Palestinian independence. Negotiations that ignore these issues will pose a high level of reservations on both sides and make treaties unstable. These issues are more relevant to the PNA than Egypt and Jordan. I begin by articulating these issues concerning the Palestinian, and I explain them later in this chapter within the context of CDA and WAA.

3.4.1. Land

Land is at the center of one of the oldest, most contentious disputes between the Jews and Palestinians. During most of the period of the Ottoman rule, land title was not important. Country people lived on land following tradition, and there was common land for grazing. In 1858, the Ottoman authorities enacted a land code that required registration of agricultural land. This was a new idea for peasants who were using land that had no official owners. Fearful that registration meant taxation or the drafting of their sons for military service, many Palestinians either failed to register or had merchants in the cities or towns register the land in their names. With a stroke of a pen, these peasants moved from having the status of independent farmers to being tenants of absentee landlords. Later, some of the absentee "owners" sold their land to Jewish groups. Following European custom, the Jewish immigrants holding legal titles proceed to occupy the land after expelling the Palestinian residents. To the European, this action was a reasonable step for a landowner to take. To the evicted Palestinians, their expulsion at the hands of the new arrivals was land theft (Weatherby, 2002, p. 158). From the Palestinian point of view, Palestine is their homeland inherited from their ancestors, and the Jews are occupiers who displaced them from their homes. The Palestinians believe that they were in Falestine (Palestine) before the Jews immigrated and seized their land by force. However, the Palestinian definition of "land" has changed over time. For example, until the 1980s, the PLO defined land as the whole of Palestine, that is, the West Bank, Gaza, and land beyond the green line (at that time Israel was not recognized by the PLO). This claim was modified after the PLO engaged in negotiations with Israel, and now it is defined as control of the West Bank and the Gaza strip (Roskin & Coyle, 2008, pp. 107–124; Weatherby, 2002, p. 158).

Opposing the Palestinian viewpoint, the Jews suggest that Palestine has never existed as an autonomous entity. Philistines, according to the Jews, were migrant people from the Aegean Sea and the Greek Islands who settled on the southern coast of the land of Canaan. There they established five independent city-states (including Gaza) on a narrow strip of land known as Philistia. The Greeks and Romans called it "Palastina." In the First Century CE, the Romans crushed the independent kingdom of "Judea." After the failed rebellion of Bar Kokhba in the Second Century CE, the Roman Emperor Hadrian determined to wipe out the identity of "Israel-Judea." Therefore, he took the name Palastina and imposed it on all the Land of Israel. After the Roman conquest of Judea, "Palastina" became a province of the pagan Roman Empire, then of the Christian Byzantine Empire, and then, very briefly, of the Zoroastrian Persian Empire. In 638 CE, Umar ibn al-Khatab, the second Muslim Caliph, took Palastina away from the Byzantine Empire and made it part of an Arab-Muslim empire. The Arabs, who had no name of their own for this region, adopted the Greco-Roman name Palastina, which they pronounced "Falastin." During the First World War, the British took Palestine from the Ottoman Turks. At the end of the war, the Ottoman Empire collapsed, and as one of its subject provinces, "Palestine" was assigned to the British, who were to govern it temporarily under a mandate from the League of Nations. Therefore, the Jews believe that they were the original inhabitants not immigrant occupiers of this land (Palestine Facts, 2009). These divergent views on land make this reservation level very important to both sides.

On the contrary, the issue of land was more specific in the case of Egyptian–Israeli negotiations. Egypt wanted to get back the land that it had lost after the Six-Day War, the Sinai Peninsula. Similarly, HKJ resolved the issue of land a long time before the direct Jordanian–Israeli negotiations. King Hussein bin Talal resolved this issue in two stages. First, during the Arab Summit on September 6–9, 1982 in Fez, Morocco, he accepted that the PLO was the sole legitimate representative of the Palestinian people. Second, the king announced the severance of all administrative and legal ties between the HKJ and the West Bank. In both stages, King Hussein was responsive and accommodating to the PLO's wishes and demands. Therefore, the land reservation level was very well understood by the Egyptians and was not an obstacle to the HKJ; this implies that Egypt and Jordan were bargaining under a condition of complete information and a very well known set of deals. The red line to Jordanians has been the Kingdom's territorial integrity. Jordanians are deeply concerned about any settlements between the Palestinian and Israelis because they worry about establishing a Palestinian homeland in Jordan.

3.4.2. Water

In the Middle East, water is the region's major deficit. Nowhere in the region is this issue more contentious than in Jordan because the kingdom was overloaded with waves of refugees following the regional conflicts and received no significant help from Arab countries or from the world community. With the expansion of urban areas, population, and modernization, the need for water became a primary issue for Jordan. Therefore, the reservation level for Jordan concerning water is higher than it is for Egypt and the PNA (Roskin & Coyle, 2008, pp. 107–124; Weatherby, 2002, p. 159).

3.4.3. The Right to Return

Palestinian refugees in Arab countries or in the world represent one of the critical problems in any Israeli–Palestinian negotiations. The fact that surrounding Arab states have resisted moves to assimilate the Palestinians refugees left the Palestinians in destitute refugee camps for over 60 years. The Palestinian side considers the right to return as one of the critical issues in any negotiation. On the contrary, the Israeli side considers the right to return tantamount to committing suicide (Roskin & Coyle, 2008, p. 117). The right to return is not an issue for the Egyptians. On the contrary, it is an important issue to Jordanians because many Palestinians live in Jordan as refugees, and the Jordanian government wants to settle this problem in any future negotiations (Roskin & Coyle, 2008, pp. 107–124; Weatherby, 2002, p. 160).

3.4.4. Palestinian Prisoners in Israeli Jails

The Palestinians want to see a speedy release of people whom they consider to be freedom fighters. However, Israel considers these individuals to be saboteurs (*Mukharebeen*) who ought to be in jail. This issue is not significant to either Egyptians or Jordanians. Several Jordanians held in Israeli jails were released following Jordanian governmental efforts to free them.

3.4.5. Jerusalem

The future status of Jerusalem is the most serious issue dividing the Arabs, the Palestinians, and the Jews. Although the Palestinians are Arabs, for the purposes of this study, they are considered as a separate entity. Leaders from all groups have made inflammatory demands from which it is difficult if not impossible to retreat. The religious symbols of Judaism, Christianity, and Islam have been manipulated by various leaders to serve their own ends. The following statements illustrate the difficulty of resolving the question of who controls Jerusalem. According to Israeli Prime Minister Ehude Barak, "No Israeli prime minister could agree to let the Palestinians have sovereignty over the Temple Mount, which is the holy site for the Jewish people for generations" (Mideast Mirror, 2000). The Israeli side made it very clear to the whole world that it considers Jerusalem to be the eternal capital of Israel. This position is the cornerstone of any Israeli negotiations with the Arabs. On the contrary, the Palestinians believe and have also iterated in many places that Jerusalem is the capital of their future state. Nevertheless, the PLO suggested partitioning the city between Israel and the future Palestinian state.

Egypt and Jordan look at the issue from an Islamic vantage point, so they oppose any Israeli incursion into Muslim holy sites and warn from any provocative Jewish activities against those sites. Egyptian President Husni Mubarak made the following comment, which was published in the Mideast Mirror (2000), regarding the sensitive issue of Jerusalem and the consequences of any provocative activities: "No one is entitled to say that Jerusalem, or al-Aksa Mosque, is under Israeli sovereignty. We presented ideas to the Palestinian side and asked that they discuss them from all angles. It is up to the Palestinians to make the decision compatible with their interests and which is simultaneously acceptable to the Arab and Islamic world." In the same interview, President Mubarak suggested, "Giving up Jerusalem would invite endless violence."

The aforementioned statements are further complicated because of the proximity of the holy sites of Muslims, Christians, and Jews. They all occupy an area about the size of an American university campus. However, the issue of Jerusalem did not prevent Egyptians and Jordanians from making successful and enduring peace agreements with Israel because both Jordan and Egypt accepted the PLO and later the PNA as the sole representative of the Palestinian people. On the contrary, the Jerusalem issue is a demarcation line in any Israeli–Palestinian negotiations, especially with the growing strength of Islamic fundamentalists in Gaza and the West Bank such as HAMAS and al-Jihad al-Islami organizations (Roskin & Coyle, 2008, pp. 107–124; Weatherby, 2002, p. 160–161).

3.4.6. Palestinian Independence

The Palestinians want to establish their state, but they are not clear about what its border should be. For example, after Arafat signed a treaty with the Israelis, he went to South Africa and gave an enthusiastic speech to the Muslim community, declaring that he signed the peace treaty as a step toward the complete liberation of Palestine, using rhetoric that reminded people of Arafat's speeches during the 1970s. This reservation point is very tricky and poses a real problem in any negotiations because there are people within the inner circles of Palestinians who do not believe in Israel's right to exist. Peace talks have been corrupted with tactical intentions not strategic beliefs about coexisting with Israel. This reservation point creates distrust, doubts, and hesitation in implementing the deals, and it clouds the enforceability of a signed agreement. Thus, we believe that the OA were not an efficient NBS. Uncertainties have always been very high during

Israeli–Palestinian negotiations and after the signing of any deals. On the contrary, independence is not an issue to Egyptians and Jordanians in any peace talks. Egypt achieved its complete territorial sovereignty with the return of the Sinai Peninsula, and Jordan is focused on the kingdom's territorial integrity and all aspects of sovereignty related to the kingdom (Weatherby, 2002, p. 161).

3.5. WHO TO BELIEVE?

U.S. President Bill Clinton aptly remarked that in the Arab-Israeli conflict, "No side has a monopoly on pain, or virtue." But does anyone have a monopoly on truth? One need not be a regional expert to perceive that the way the story of the Arab–Israeli conflict is told depends on the perspective of the storyteller. This creates a quandary for the would-be objective political scientist: to whose story do we listen? How do we judge the truth of one story and not another? Edward. H. Carr (1961) remarked with tongue in cheek, "I hope that I am sufficiently up-to-date to recognize that anything written in the 1890s must be nonsense. But I am not yet advanced enough to be committed to the view that anything written in the 1950s necessarily makes sense" (as cited by Isacoff, 2005, p. 71).

Taking Carr's point to heart, how can we substantiate what we think we know about the past? The literature on the philosophy of history speaks at length about the debates among relativists, objectivists, and positivists during the past century and a half. The matter is typically portrayed as a pendulum that was set in motion in the 1830s with the establishment of Rankean positivism, which emphasized "feeling for and a joy in the particular in and by itself," or what many have since referred to as the past "as it really was." Since Ranke's time, positivists and relativists have each sought to prevail on the question of whether history should be either objectively or subjectively grounded (Isacoff, 2005, pp. 71–73).

That said, I agree with Jonathan Isacoff (2005) that we need a pragmatic approach to history in the tradition of John Dewey and Richard Rorty. If we did so, historical truth would not be predicated on a perceived correspondence to ontological reality. Nor is it purely relative. Rather, understandings of history and historical knowledge are produced to solve problematic situations in human experience. Historical accounts are a function of their ability to account for and reconcile anomalous facts and their ability to further practical political needs.

It has been said that those who do not learn from history are doomed to repeat it. And nowhere has the past been so heavily invoked in a discussion of the present and the future than in negotiations between the Arabs and the Jews. The past of both Arabs and Jews was so brutal that one think their histories are conspiring against their present and future. Histories of any nation are constructive. In other words, historical events have nationalistic and religiously biased interpretations. In this sense, no history can claim objectivity. As a result, national and religious histories form barriers to peace and reconciliation among nations. This is true of the relationship between Jews and Arabs and Jews and Muslims. Therefore, one fundamental step forward to peace and understanding between Arabs and Jews is that both groups not only review their national religious histories but also revise and dismantle historical coverage of incidents and ideas that have been constructed over centuries to serve national and religious biases.

Let us follow the advice of David S. Milton (2009, p. 1): and "take the past by the hand and coax it from the shadows, parade it before us, look at it clearly, without sentimentality or hypocrisy." How have Palestinians and Jews reached this desperate place? The near past is rich enough, but we must go beyond that and plunge to the heart of hate. Mystical, tribal, religious, fanatical ferocity is rooted deep in the psyches of each. To comprehend the fury that exists between Arabs and Jews, we must go to the roots. We must examine, simply, without dogma or deception, in the most precise ways, the relationship between Jews, Muslims, and Christians – and we must go way back to do this – or we will understand nothing. There's a crystal clarity that links three of the world's major religions, a relationship that transcends borders and armies and occupation and the knot of political problems that seem so intractable today. Yes, they are intractable, but for reasons far different, deeper, yet clearer, purer than what we believe them to be. Jews and Arabs have a more common past than any other religious or ethnic groups in the region.

In the Arabian Peninsula, there were thriving Jewish communities, none more so than at Yathrib (al-Medina), which was an important center of trade and agriculture. As they were in Arab communities, the people were organized into tribes. They had Arabic names, wrote in Arabic. Some of the most glorious literature from that era was composed by Jews. They were successful farmers who had introduced the date palm and irrigation into the desert. They were smiths, working in gold and silver, fashioning swords, and knives (Milton, 2009, p. 2). To the north of al-Medina was the settlement of Khaibar, another Jewish oasis, also plump with wealth, the richest Jewish settlement on the peninsula. Prophet Muhammad had great support among the people of al-Medina. In 622, Prophet Mohammed and Abu Bakr emigrated to al-Medina to escape the persecution of the Arab tribes of Quraish. Many prominent Jews in al-Medina believed in the message of Prophet Mohammed and converted to Islam. Thus, the common past extends from the pre-Islamic era, to the Islamic era, to their common and harmonious coexistence in Spain where they later faced a common and miserable fate at the hands of Ferdinand and Isabella in 1492. Furthermore, the Ottoman Islamic caliphate welcomed the Jews to live under the *millet* system among their Muslims countrymen, and when they did so, there were no significant problems.

In the remainder of this chapter, I examine several treaties between the Arabs and Israel in light of NBS. I investigate CDA and WAA as two treaties that were signed under conditions of complete information and a well known set of deals. In addition, I examine the OAs as an example of accords that were signed under a condition of incomplete information, distrust, and uncertainties that rendered them inefficient accords that were not enforceable. It is imperative to discuss the two United Nations Security Council Resolutions 242 and 338 before investigating the above treaties because they form the bedrock on which those agreements are built (Wikisource, 2009).

3.6. UNITED NATIONS SECURITY COUNCIL RESOLUTIONS 242 AND 338

In the UNSC 242 Resolution signed on November 22, 1967, the UN Security Council expressed its concern about the grave situation in the Middle East and emphasized the inadmissibility of the acquisition of territory by war and the need to work for a just and lasting peace in which every state in the area would live in security. The resolution further emphasized that all member states in their acceptance of the Charter of the United Nations have undertaken a commitment to act in accordance with Article 2 of the Charter, which affirms as a requirement the establishment of a just and lasting peace in the Middle East, which should include the application of the following principles: Withdrawal of Israeli armed forces from territories occupied in the recent conflict, that is, the Six-Day War in June 1967; termination of all claims or states of belligerency and respect for and acknowledgment of the sovereignty, territorial integrity and political independence of every state in the area and their right to live in peace within secure and recognized boundaries free from threats or acts of force.

Moreover, the resolution affirmed the necessity of guaranteeing the freedom to navigate through international waterways in the area; achieving settlement of the refugee problem; and guaranteeing the territorial inviolability and political independence of every state in the area (UNSC Resolutions 2009).

On the contrary, UNSC Resolution 338, signed on October 22, 1973, was written during a late stage of the October War (called the Yom Kippur War by the Israelis) after international efforts to stop the fighting were intensified (see UNSC, 1973). American Secretary of State Henry Kissinger flew to Moscow on October 20, and, together with the Soviet government, the United States proposed a ceasefire resolution in the UN Security Council. The Council met on October 21 at the urgent request of both the Unites States and the Soviet Union, and by a vote of 14 to 0 adopted Resolution 338. The Security Council called upon all parties to terminate all military activity immediately, no later than 12 hours after the adoption of the decision. Second, it called upon all parties concerned to implement SC Resolution 242 in all its parts and immediately and concurrently with the ceasefire, to start negotiations under appropriate auspices aimed at establishing a just and durable peace in the Middle East (UNSC Resolutions 2009; Wikisource, 2009). We must read the CDA, the Wadi Arab Agreement, and the OA within the contexts of Resolutions 242 and 338 to understand the reasons behind the success or failure of these treaties (*Ibid.*).

3.7. THE CAMP DAVID ACCORDS

Muhammad Anwar al-Sadat, president of the Arab Republic of Egypt, and Menachem Begin, prime minister of Israel, met with Jimmy Carter, president of the United States of America, at Camp David from September 5 to September 17, 1978, and agreed that the search for peace in the Middle East must be guided by, first, the United Nations Security Council Resolutions 242 and 338 in all their parts. Second, they agreed that after four wars during 30 years, despite intensive human efforts, the Middle East, which is the cradle of civilization and the birthplace of three great religions, does not enjoy the blessings of peace. As stated in the preamble of CDA (kataeb.org).

"The people of the Middle East yearn for peace so that the vast human and natural resources of the region can be turned to the pursuits of peace and so that this area can become a model for coexistence and cooperation among nations. Their purpose is to achieve peace and good neighborly relations. They recognize that for peace to endure, it must involve all those who have been most deeply affected by the conflict. They therefore agree that this framework, as appropriate, is intended by them to constitute a basis for peace not only between Egypt and Israel, but also between Israel and each of its other neighbors which is prepared to negotiate peace with Israel on this basis." With that objective in mind, they agreed to proceed in the following way: Egypt and Israel undertake not to resort to the threat or the use of force to settle disputes. Any disputes shall be settled by peaceful means in accordance with the provisions of Article 33 of the UN Charter.

To achieve peace between them, the parties agree to negotiate in good faith with a goal of concluding within three months from the signing of the Framework a peace treaty between them while inviting the other parties to the conflict to proceed simultaneously to negotiate and conclude similar peace treaties with a view to achieving a comprehensive peace in the area. The Framework for the Conclusion of a Peace Treaty between Egypt and Israel will govern the peace negotiations between them. The parties will agree on the modalities and the timetable for the implementation of their obligations under the treaty (Jimmy Carter Library and Museum, March 30, 2009).

3.8. WADI ARAB AGREEMENT

Bearing in mind the Washington Declaration signed by them on July 25, 1994, the government of the State of Israel and the government of the HKJ, aiming at the achievement of a just, lasting and comprehensive peace in the Middle East based on Security Council Resolutions 242 and 338 in all their aspects, reaffirmed their faith in the purposes and principles of the Charter of the United Nations and recognized their right and obligation to live in peace with each other as well as with all states, within secure and recognized boundaries. Both sides ensured lasting security for both their states and in particular to avoid threats and the use of force between them. They recognized and agreed to respect each other's sovereignty, territorial integrity, and political independence; they recognized and agreed to respect each other's right to live in peace within secure and recognized boundaries and to refrain from the threat or use of force against each other and to settle all disputes between them by peaceful means (Jewish Virtual Library, March 20, 2009).

The following are sections from articles in the agreement that deal with the matters raised in this Chapter. Those articles can be found in Jewish Virtual Library: http://www.jewishvirtuallibrary.org/jsource/Peace/isrjor.html).

3.8.1. Article 4 on Security Matters

Both Parties, acknowledging that mutual understanding and cooperation in security-related matters will form a significant part of their relations and will further enhance the security of the region, take upon themselves to base their security relations on mutual trust, advancement of joint interests and cooperation, and to aim toward a regional framework of partnership in peace. The Parties undertake, in accordance with the provisions of this Article, the following:

To refrain from the threat or use of force or weapons, conventional, nonconventional or of any other kind, against each other, or of other actions or activities that adversely affect the security of the other Party;
To refrain from organizing, instigating, inciting, assisting, or participating in acts or threats of belligerency, hostility, subversion, or violence against the other Party;
To take necessary and effective measures to ensure that acts or threats of belligerency, hostility, subversion, or violence against the other Party do not originate from, and are not committed within, through or over their territory (hereinafter the term "territory" includes the airspace and territorial waters).

Consistent with the era of peace and with the efforts to build regional security and to avoid and prevent aggression and violence, the Parties further agree to refrain from joining or in any way assisting, promoting or cooperating with any coalition, organization or alliance with a military or security character with a third party, the objectives or activities of which include launching aggression or other acts of military hostility against the other Party, in contravention of the provisions of the present Treaty (see Jewish Virtual Library).

The Parties undertake: to take necessary and effective measures to prevent acts of terrorism, subversion or violence from being carried out from their territory or through it and to take necessary and effective measures to combat such activities and all their perpetrators. The Parties undertake to work as a matter of priority, and as soon as possible in the context of the Multilateral Working Group on Arms Control and Regional Security, and jointly, toward the following: the creation in the Middle East of a region free from hostile alliances and coalitions; the creation of a Middle East free from weapons of mass destruction, both conventional and nonconventional, in the context of a comprehensive, lasting, and stable peace, characterized by the renunciation of the use of force, reconciliation, and goodwill (*Ibid.*).

3.8.2. Article 6 on Water

With the view to achieving a comprehensive and lasting settlement of all the water problems between them, the Parties agree mutually to recognize the rightful allocations of both of them in Jordan River and Yarmouk River waters and Araba/Arava ground water. The Parties, recognizing the necessity to find a practical, just and agreed solution to their water problems and with the view that the subject of water can form the basis for the advancement of cooperation between them, jointly undertake to ensure that the management and development of their water resources do not, in any way, harm the water resources of the other Party. The Parties recognize that their water resources are not sufficient to meet their needs. More water should be supplied for their use through various methods, including projects of regional and international cooperation (see Jewish Virtual Library, 1994).

3.8.3. Article 7 on Economic Relations

Viewing economic development and prosperity as pillars of peace, security, and harmonious relations between states, peoples and individual human beings, the Parties, taking note of understandings reached between them, affirm their mutual desire to promote economic cooperation between them, as well as within the framework of wider regional economic cooperation (*Ibid.*).

3.8.4. Article 8 on Refugees and Displaced Persons

Recognizing the massive human problems caused to both Parties by the conflict in the Middle East, as well as the contribution made by them toward the alleviation of human suffering, the Parties will seek to further alleviate those problems arising on a bilateral level. Recognizing that the above human problems caused by the conflict in the Middle East cannot be fully resolved on the bilateral level, the Parties will seek to resolve them in appropriate forums, in accordance with international law (*Ibid.*).

3.8.5. Article 9 on Historical and Religious Sites

Each party will provide freedom of access to places of religious and historical significance. In this regard, in accordance with the Washington

Declaration, Israel respects the present special role of the HKJ in Muslim Holy shrines in Jerusalem. When negotiations on the permanent status will take place, Israel will give high priority to the Jordanian historic role in these shrines. The Parties will act together to promote interfaith relations among the three monotheistic religions, with the aim of working toward religious understanding, moral commitment, freedom of religious worship, and tolerance and peace (*Ibid.*).

3.8.6. Article 23 on Aqaba and Eilat

The Parties agree to enter into negotiations, as soon as possible, and not later than one month from the exchange of the instruments of ratification of this Treaty, on arrangements that would enable the joint development of the towns of Aqaba and Eilat with regard to such matters, inter alia, as joint tourism development, joint customs, free trade zone, cooperation in aviation, prevention of pollution, maritime matters, police, customs, and health cooperation. The Parties will conclude all relevant agreements within 9 months from the exchange of instruments of ratification of the Treaty (*Ibid.*).

3.9. CAMP DAVID ACCORDS AS PACTA SUNT SERVANDA

Reading through items that Egypt and Israel agreed upon might lead one to think that Egypt gained far more than Israel from the CDAs. I strongly argue that this was not the case and I will clarify my reasons stating the main items or gains of both sides from the CDA. The main items Egypt gained are as follows: (1) the full exercise of Egyptian sovereignty up to the internationally recognized borders; (2) the withdrawal of Israeli armed forces from the Sinai; (3) the use of airfields left by the Israelis near al-Arish, Rafah, Ras en-Naqb, and Sharm el-Sheikh for civilian purposes only, including possible commercial use by all nations; (4) the right of free passage by ships of Israel through the Gulf of Suez Canal on the basis of the Constantinople convention of 1888 applying to all nations; (5) the Strait of Tiran and Gulf of Aqaba are international waterways to be open to all nations for unimpeded and nonsuspendable freedom of navigation and overflight; (6) and Egypt and Israel should establish among themselves a relationship normal to states at peace with each other. To that end they should undertake to abide by all the provisions of the UN Charter: full recognition, abolishing economic boycotts; guaranteeing that under their jurisdictions the citizens of the other parties shall enjoy the protection of the due process of law (see Jimmy Carter library.org).

It is clear that the Egyptians obtained all that they needed from the CDAs, and from the beginning to the end, Egypt knew the set of deals it desired: return of its occupied land; national security; American and international financial, economic, and technical assistances; and international political support, especially forgiving to Egyptians their violation of human rights. On the contrary, as stated earlier, it appears that the Israeli gains were fewer than those of the Egyptians. Had this been the case, the agreement would have violated the joint efficiency condition of bargaining, which means that negotiators did not reach a Pareto-optimal solution; but this was not the case. The fact that the CDAs have endured for more than three decades now attests that the agreement was jointly efficient par-excellence. Thus, we can infer that Israel signed the CDA with the complete knowledge of the set of deals involved and was confident in its enforceability. Israel, in fact, obtained gains that from its perspective seemed greater than those of the Egyptians. To understand this, let us look at the most important issues that Israeli negotiators wanted to discuss and achieve at Camp David that would provide them equal gains and satisfy the condition of joint efficiency: security and Jerusalem.

Gil Merom (1999, pp. 411–412) articulated this dimension in Israeli minds and demonstrated the deep-rooted security concerns in the Jewish political culture. According to Merom, "David Ben Gurion, the founding father of modern Israel, in a speech delivered to Israeli youths in 1960, masterfully meshed the theme of moral exceptionalism with the idea of inherent national security exceptionalism." He said, "You ... know that we were always a small people, always surrounded by big nations with whom we engaged in a struggle, political as well as spiritual; that we created things that they did not accept; that we were exceptional.... Our survival-secret during these thousands of years ... has one source: Our supreme quality, our intellectual and moral advantage, which singles us out even today, as it did throughout the generations."

Essentially, the strategic foundations of exceptionalism contain three elements: the perception of the basic imbalance of power between the Arab world and Israel, the perception of Arab declared hostile intentions, and the perception of Arab aggressive behavior. The basic imbalance of power element refers to Israel's inherent quantitative inferiority in the face of the demographic, budgetary, and military resources that the whole Arab world possesses, and to Israel's geostrategic vulnerability, that is, lack of a measure

Zone of Conflict	Zone of Agreement	Zone of Conflict

Fig. 3.3. Camp David Accord and Wadi Araba Agreement Zones of Conflict and Agreement of Nash Bargaining Solution.

of strategic depth. The intention element refers to voices in the Arab world that define the destruction of the Jewish state as the Arab strategic objective and occasionally discuss the extermination of the Jewish citizens of Israel. The behavior elements refer to the de jure state of war, occasional wars, continuous terror, and repeated efforts to deny Israel international recognition and legitimacy (Merom, 1999, pp. 413–416).

In 1988, for example, forty years after the establishment of Israel, Prime Minister Yitzhak Shamir explained in reference to the idea that "the Arabs want to throw the Jews to the sea" that: "If we carefully examine our reality, it has not changed. The Arabs are the same Arabs; the sea is the same sea. The objective is the same objective – the extermination of the Israeli state... ." The second important consequence of the image of national security exceptionalism is the conviction that Israel must devise strategic solutions that will match the level of the challenges Israel faces. Indeed, Ben Gurion had already concluded that: "We [Israelis] will not solve [our security problems] by means of simple answers, drawn from our past or adopted from other people. Whatever [solution] was adequate in the past, and for others, will not be adequate for us, since our security problem is one of a kind... . We will not withstand" (Merom, 1999, p. 414).

The earlier statements of Israeli leaders demonstrate the crucial importance of Israeli security. Israel bargained and signed the CDA with complete knowledge of the set of deals that they were looking for, and with high certainty that Egypt, the greatest Arab state, could provide security to it; Israel's gains from the CDA matched Egypt's gains. As shown in Fig. 3.3, the zone of agreement between Egypt and Israel was very large compared to the zone of conflict. Both countries knew that they had a great stake in peace, and they had complete knowledge about their gains and confidence in the enforceability of the deals.

3.10. WADI ARABA AGREEMENT AS PACTA SUNT SERVANDA

Jordan and Israel had very good knowledge and assessment of the set of deals set forth in WAA. Israel knew that Jordan, especially the late King

Hussein, had a history of honoring agreements. King Hussein was an internationally respected ruler who always pursued stability and peace in the region. Given the reputation and the stature of King Hussein, Israel had no doubt about the enforceability of the deals. Both sides knew that the gains achieved by signing WAA exceeded the status quo, especially since the reservation levels were relatively low.

Both realized that security, water, and regional stability were mutually fundamental concerns, and both would benefit from cooperation much more than from conflicts. Jordan has the longest borders with the West Bank, so Israel wanted to be sure that these borders were protected and safe. On the contrary, Jordan wanted to be sure that any settlement between Israel and the Palestinians would not involve Jordan, which had particular concerns about the idea of an alternative Palestinian homeland in Jordan. WAA was an efficient solution because Jordanian and Israeli leaders during and after King Hussein have clear ideas about each other, and they were certain that both sides respected what the signed. In hindsight, WAA stood up to the turbulent events in the Middle East because both sides signed it with complete information, knowledge, and confidence in its enforceability.

3.11. OSLO ACCORDS

On September 13, 1993, representatives of the state of Israel and the PLO signed the Declaration of Principles on Interim Self-Government Arrangements, a document also known as the OA. The agreement was signed at a Washington, D.C., ceremony hosted by U.S. President Bill Clinton, and Palestinian leader Yasser Arafat and Israeli Prime Minister Yitzhak Rabin ended decades as sworn enemies with an uneasy handshake. This agreement was the fruit of secret negotiations between Israel and the Palestinians, represented by the PLO, following the Madrid Conference in 1991. The OA contain a set of mutually agreed-upon general principles regarding a five-year interim period of Palestinian self-rule. So-called permanent status issues are deferred to later negotiations, to begin no later than the third year of the interim period. The permanent status negotiations were intended to lead to an agreement that would be implemented to take effect at the end of the interim period (Palestine Facts, 2009). The details of OA can be found on MEMRI (http://www.memri.org/docs/oslo1.html).

3.11.1. Framework

The framework of the Middle East peace process initiated at Madrid in October 1991 reaffirmed the determination of both sides to put an end to decades of confrontation and to live in peaceful coexistence, mutual dignity, and security, while recognizing their mutual legitimate and political rights and their desire to achieve a just, lasting, and comprehensive peace settlement and historic reconciliation through the agreed-upon political process.

3.11.2. Recognizing

Both parties recognized that the peace process and the new era that it has created, as well as the new relationship established between the two parties as described earlier, are irreversible, and the determination of the two parties to maintain, sustain, and continue the peace process. They understood that the aim of the Israeli–Palestinian negotiations within the current Middle East peace process was, among other things, to establish a Palestinian Interim Self-Government Authority for a transitional period not exceeding five years from the date of signing the Agreement on the Gaza Strip and the Jericho Area on May 4, 1994, leading to a permanent settlement based on Security Council Resolutions 242 and 338.

Recognizing these principles, both parties reaffirmed their understanding that the interim self-government arrangements contained in this agreement are an integral part of the whole peace process, that the negotiations on the permanent status, that would start no later than May 4, 1996, were meant to lead to the implementation of Security Council Resolutions 242 and 338, and that the Interim Agreement would settle all the issues of the interim period and that no such issues would be deferred to the agenda of the permanent status negotiations. According to Palestinian Facts (2009), both parties agreed to the following.

3.11.3. Land

The two sides view the West Bank and the Gaza Strip as a single territorial unit, the integrity and status of which will be preserved during the interim period. The two sides agree that West Bank and Gaza Strip territory, except for issues that will be negotiated in the permanent status negotiations, will come under the jurisdiction of the Palestinian Council in a phased manner, to be completed within 18 months from the date of the inauguration of the Council, as specified below.

3.11.4. Arrangements for Security and Public Order

To guarantee public order and internal security for the Palestinians of the West Bank and the Gaza Strip, the Council shall establish a strong police force. The Palestinian police force established under the Gaza-Jericho Agreement will be fully integrated into the Palestinian Police and will be subject to the provisions of this Agreement. Except for the Palestinian Police and the Israeli military forces, no other armed forces shall be established or operate in the West Bank and the Gaza Strip.

3.11.5. Confidence Building Measures

With a view to fostering a positive and supportive public atmosphere to accompany the implementation of this Agreement, to establish a solid basis of mutual trust and good faith, and to facilitate the anticipated cooperation and new relations between the two peoples, both Parties agree to carry out confidence building measures as detailed herewith:

Israel will release or turn over to the Palestinian side Palestinian detainees and prisoners, residents of the West Bank and the Gaza Strip. The first stage of release of these prisoners and detainees will take place on the signing of this Agreement and the second stage will take place prior to the date of the elections. There will be a third stage of release of detainees and prisoners.

3.11.6. Palestinian National Charter

The Executive Committee of the PLO and the Palestinian Central Council will reaffirm the letter of January 22, 1998, from PLO Chairman Yasir Arafat to President Bill Clinton concerning the nullification of the Palestinian National Charter provisions that are inconsistent with the letters exchanged between the PLO and the Government of Israel on September 9/10, 1993. PLO Chairman Arafat, the Speaker of the Palestine National Council, and the Speaker of the Palestinian Council will invite the members of the PNC, as well as the members of the Central Council, and the Palestinian Heads of Ministries to a meeting to be addressed by President Clinton to reaffirm their support for the peace process and the aforementioned decisions of the Executive Committee and the Central Council.

3.12. OSLO ACCORDS AND THE CRISIS OF IMPLEMENTATION

Reading a list of the items that PLO and Israel agreed upon demonstrates that the PLO obtained most of its demands, and Chairman Arafat struck a great deal with Israeli PM Rabin. The most important gain Israel was looking for in Oslo was a solution to the security issue, but Israel was seriously doubtful that the PLO could deliver or enforce it. The OA states clearly, "Except for the Palestinian Police and the Israeli military forces, no other armed forces shall be established or operate in the West Bank and the Gaza Strip. Except for the arms, ammunition and equipment of the Palestinian Police, and those of the Israeli military forces, no organization, group or individual in the West Bank and the Gaza Strip shall manufacture, sell, acquire, possess, import or otherwise introduce into the West Bank or the Gaza Strip any firearms, ammunition, weapons, explosives, gunpowder or any related equipment." Obviously, this item explicitly requires the Palestinian side to end the armed presence of the HAMAS organization and other Palestinian armed groups, including Arafat's armed factions.

The PLO and its formal entity the PNA failed at each and every stage to implement the security items that they agreed upon with Israel. The PNA did not possess enough power to eliminate or contain HAMAS and other smaller armed factions such as al-Jihad al-Islami and the Popular Front for the Liberation of Palestine (PFLP). The inability of the PNA to control armed groups extended to Arafat's faction, the Palestine National Liberation Movement (FATEH) and one of its military arms the al-Aqsa Martyrs Brigades (AMB), which carried out several bloody attacks against Israel. It was obvious that the AMB was under the control of Marwan al-Barghouthi, a member of the Fateh Revolutionary Council and a member of the Palestine National Council (parliament), not under the control of Arafat. As a result, the OA were not *pacta sunt servanda* from the Palestinian side, and consequently, the Israelis did not feel obligated to implement its items because the security issue was not delivered by the PNA.

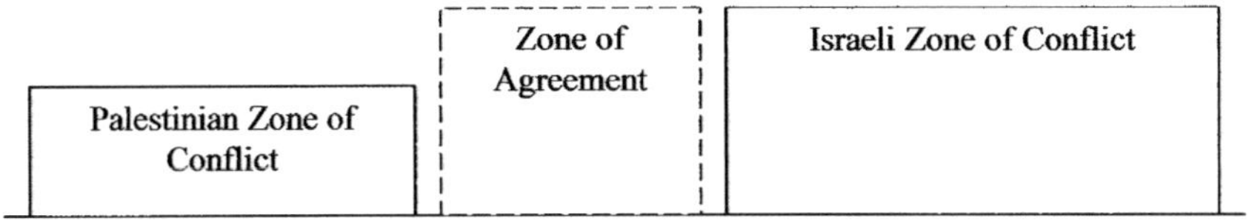

Fig. 3.4. The Oslo Accords Zones of Conflict and Agreement between Israel and the PNA.

Realizing Arafat's inability to enforce the agreement that had been signed, the Israeli side preferred not to continue the preservation of the OA. Thus, the OA were unstable treaty because there was uncertainty and doubt from the beginning to the end about the enforceability of the deals. Furthermore, the reservation levels (zone of conflict) were very high, as shown in Fig. 3.4, especially, on the question of Jerusalem. The OA were not efficient NBS because the actual set of deals was smaller than expected. Therefore, the signed deals were not enforceable, and the OAs were not *pacta sunt servanda.*

3.13. LACK OF PROGRESS IN THE MIDDLE EAST PEACE PROCESS

The Middle East Peace Process that centered on finding a workable and substantial solution to establish a Palestinian state next to Israel has defied a solution for decades now. The problem finding a solution to this complex conflict has been compounded by set of strategic, military, political and religious overtones. The parties involved are mired in global and regional rivalries. Thus, the Israeli–Palestinian conflict, unlike Israel's conflicts with Egypt and Jordan, is not a simple bi-lateral issue between Israel and the PNA because it involves several layers of influence on the Palestinian side, which hampers the possibility of reaching a stable and workable agreement with Israel. Even when agreements are concluded, as in the OA, the possibility of *pacta sunt servanda* is very low because those involved in the process lack trust, genuine information, and sincerity. All those uncertainties were enveloped in regional intervention, external agendas, vague religious slogans, internal Palestinian schisms, and a lack of popular accountability. All those factors make the OA inefficient and unenforceable.

3.14. NESTED INFLUENCE ON PALESTINIAN DECISION MAKERS

Historically, the Palestinian movements were not a reflection of domestic interactions or an embodiment of the Palestinian people's concerns. Rather, they reflect external interests and agendas. Chairman Arafat attempted to keep the Palestinian national decision independent of foreign influences, especially Arab influence, but the growing strength of HAMAS precluded him from exercising effective Palestinian sovereignty. Therefore, the PNA leadership was influenced by a nested domestic and regional agenda. For example, HAMAS disrupted each phase during the implementation of the OA by launching rockets and suicide bombing attacks on Israel that gave the latter justification to halt the implementation of the OA. In addition, other organizations such as al-Jihad al-Islami and the al-Aksa Martyr Brigades used the same tactics. HAMAS and al-Jihad al-Islami did not show concerns for the Palestinian agendas because they were more concerned about the Iranian or the Syrian agendas.

Throughout the peace process between the PNA and Israel, Iran and Syria wanted to make Arafat understand that he had no power to move toward an independent stable and peaceful settlement with Israel, that he needed their approval, and unfortunately, this was the case. We have noticed since the return of the PLO leadership to Ramallah that the relationship between HAMAS and the PNA at certain stages looked like episodes in a cartoon. Finally, Arafat lost his credibility as an able enforcer with the Americans and the Israelis. Later, Israel, with the consensus of the United States, decided not to rely on him since he failed to deliver what he promised them in the OA.

Even when some rational leaders in HAMAS attempted to deal with the peace process, the divergence between HAMAS's internal leadership (in Gaza) and its external leadership (in Damascus or Tehran) obstructed those attempts by firing missiles or suicide attacks. The divergence within HAMAS's leadership made it impossible to rely on their decisions or words. On the one hand, Khalid Mashaal represents HAMAS's external leadership in Damascus; on the other hand, Mahmoud al-Zahar represents HAMAS in Gaza, and each leader is subjected to different influences and has a different agenda. This duality of leadership in the principal Palestinian organizations creates an obstacle to an agreement, even among themselves, and it is, therefore, almost impossible for them to negotiate a deal with Israel. Moreover, if a treaty is negotiated and signed, they render it impossible to implement.

That fragmented picture was apparent in the so-called Cairo reconciliation talks that took place mainly between FATEH and HAMAS, although most factions were included in several meetings. Months of negotiation among those factions failed to reach any common ground, and they squandered resources on lodging and food in Cairo, among other things. They seem to show no concern for the future of their children and the misery of their people, except when they search for a needy child to recruit for "a holy suicide bombing" mission. Palestinian organizations, religious as well as secular, portrayed themselves as merchants of death. Billions of dollars have been wasted over the years, not on their people but on their personal luxury. For example, Ali Hassan Salameh, the late PLO chief of intelligence spent an unknown amount of money on his marriage with Miss Universe Georgina Risk; and many sources affirmed that Arafat's widow seized about $1.3 billion after his death since there was no accountability. Why, then, do the Palestinian people blame the whole world but not their leaders for their misery?

3.15. THE IRON LAW OF OLIGARCHY AND THE PALESTINIAN LEADERSHIP

It looks as if the Palestinian leaders are the last individuals concerned about finding a solution to their problems. It is as if they are proved Abba Ebban's statement, "The Palestinians never miss an opportunity to miss an opportunity." It looks as if some Palestinian leaders have turned their cause into public entrepreneurship. The evolution of Palestinian movements affirms Robert Michels's (1962) *Iron law of oligarchy*: "it is an organization which gives birth to the domination of the elected over the electors, of the mandataries over the mandators [sic], of the delegates over the delegators [sic]. Who says organization says oligarchy." (p. 15). The leadership of the PLO evolved to become one of the corrupt oligarchic groups in the Middle East, and the HAMAS movement is heading in the same direction. The PLO and HAMAS turned their Palestinian cause into a profitable trade that earned them money from Arab, Muslim, and European countries. However, the wealth that they acquired in the name of Palestine was not spent on the welfare of their people or to find a reasonable solution to their problems.

The public entrepreneurship role was transferred to HAMAS, and its leaders turned their organization into a political agency to implement the Iranian agenda in the region. This time the transition of domination from PLO to HAMAS was fatal because it left the Palestinian people totally dependent on the "welfare system" of the new masters who possess the power of the purse and who have the power to distribute food, clothes, jobs, and security to those who agree with them. As Michels (1962, p. 219) correctly pointed out, "how fatal is the transition from an authority derived from 'the favor of the people' to a right based upon the 'grace of God'... A right of sovereignty born of the plebiscite soon becomes a permanent and inviolable dominion."

What kind of logic is the HAMAS movement following? Why has it aborted all of Arafat's attempts to implement the deals of the OA which gave Arafat more than 90 percent of his demands? They are trying now to attain lesser deals than what Arafat achieved. Does HAMAS have alternatives to make the lives of the Palestinian people better?

HAMAS reduced the Palestinian demands to opening the check point at Rafah so that the Palestinians can buy something to eat from Egypt; that is, if they have money to buy anything! Who decides the fate of the Palestinian people? Is it HAMAS leaders in Damascus who await orders from Iran to strap explosives on hapless Palestinian kids without the knowledge of their parents? Did HAMAS realize that it destroyed the Palestinian cause and spirit with these random and indiscriminate attacks? Did HAMAS realize the danger of linking the group to an Iranian-led universal Islamic scheme? Why should the Palestinian people bear the brunt of those adventures? Why don't they reconcile with PNA and become part of the peace process to find a reasonable solution for their people? Palestinian democracy should not be, as Arafat once described it, "democracy among guns." Instead, it should be a democracy of the Palestinian people's competing interests. Otherwise, we have reason to believe that the Palestinian people became the hostages of HAMAS and other armed groups.

The important point is that we should not assume that violence is preferred by the Palestinians just because their leaders chose that course of action. It is important to know which groups were vocal in making their preferences known, but we also need to know which groups were able to seize the agenda of political debate. In the Palestinian case, HAMAS seized the political debate because Iran provides it with abundant arms and money to dictate their choices regarding the Palestinians. Thus, the path of HAMAS is not necessarily the path of the Palestinian people.

3.16. PALESTINIAN DEMOCRACY

HAMAS brags that it won democratic and free elections; thus, it has the right to decide the fate of the Palestinian people. The problem with this argument is that we cannot assume that the Palestinians chose HAMAS freely when its members hold guns in every corner of Gaza, nor can we make the assumption that its choices reflect the public's opinion. If Arafat was correct, and Palestinian democracy is a "democracy among guns," therefore, equating HAMAS's winning the election with Palestinians having a free choice is inaccurate. Kenneth Arrow explained this delusion in what came to be known as "Arrow's impossibility theorem" or, more commonly, Arrow's paradox. A simple example can illustrate the above case, and demonstrates that different groups in society backed by external forces can exercise their influences and shift the domestic political debate such as the groups that monopolize guns, finances, and food to make decisions on behalf of the entire society.

Following Arrow's logic (Russett et al., 2006, pp. 138–139) and focusing it on Gaza after the PLO signed the OA in 1994, the debate among different groups in Gaza was about the appropriate response to the OA. Suppose there were three possible courses of action: armed conflict, implementing Oslo deals, and doing nothing. Suppose also there were only three groups in Gaza: HAMAS, FATEH, and independents with strongly held preferences, each roughly equal in size. Further suppose that they had the following preferences and "〉" is read as preferred to:

HAMAS	armed conflict〉continuing implementation〉nothing
FATEH	continuing implementation〉nothing〉armed conflict
INDEPENDENT	nothing〉armed conflict〉continue implementation

How could these groups' preferences be aggregated into a social choice? If society was asked to vote between armed conflict and implementation of the OA, society would prefer armed conflict (both HAMAS and independents preferred armed conflict to the implementation of OAs). If the choice was between implementation of the accords and doing nothing, the social choice would be implementation (HAMAS and FATEH preferred the implementation of the OA to doing nothing). Finally, if the social choice was between armed conflict and doing nothing, the choice would be to do nothing (the preference of FATEH and independents). Aggregating these paired contests presents a paradox:

SOCIETY armed conflict〉continue implementation〉nothing〉armed conflict

How could society prefer armed conflict to implementation and prefer implementation to doing nothing, but at the same time prefer doing nothing to armed conflict? There is an inconsistency or "cycling" in society's preference ordering. We say that its preferences are intransitive, which means they violate rationality. The important point here is that we should not assume that armed conflict is preferred by the Palestinians just because that was the chosen course of action. It is important to know which groups were vocal in making their preferences known, but we also need to know which groups were able to seize the agenda of political debate and learn why they were able to do so. In the case of Gaza, it was the external will that had been imposed on the Palestinians, not their own free will. The Palestinian political debate was, as is usually the case, seized and hijacked by regional powers exploiting the pain and suffering of innocent Palestinians. In the Palestinian case, HAMAS and its allies seized the political debate because Iran provides them with abundant arms and money to dictate its choices on the Palestinian people and turned them into hostages in Gaza (Arrow, 1963, p. 2; Russett et al., 2006, p. 138–139).

CHAPTER 4

ARMS IN THE MIDDLE EAST

In this chapter, I explain the key trends in defense spending and arms procurement in the ME, and test whether those trends were subject to Louis F. Richardson's action-reaction model. I assessed the "guns-versus-butter" trade-off and the future prospects for peace in the region in light of these trends. I explained the danger of transferring weapons knowledge and technology to non-state actors in the ME. I conclude the chapter with policy implications and recommendations for achieving permanent peace in the region.

4.1. INTRODUCTION

It is generally believed that Middle Eastern countries are homogenous. Although this belief holds some truth, Middle Eastern countries have more differences than similarities. They differ in language, race, psychology, perception of threats, historical and colonial backgrounds, and political and economic developments. Realizing these differences, I expect that these countries have varying perceptions and interpretations of external threats and different methods of dealing with those threats. It is theoretically implausible to contemplate a general trend in defense spending across Middle Eastern countries; however, it is theoretically sound to view several broad trends within the region.

According to Attar (2009), "Middle Eastern countries are divided into Arab Middle, and non-Arab ME. The Arab ME includes Algeria, Bahrain, Comoros, Djibouti, Egypt, Eritrea, Iraq, Jordan, Kuwait, Libya, Mauritania, Morocco, Oman, Palestinian National Authority (PNA), Qatar, Saudi Arabia, Somalia, the Sudan, Tunisia, the United Arab Emirates, and Yemen. The non-Arab ME includes Afghanistan, Israel, Iran, Pakistan, and Turkey. North Africa constitutes Algeria, Libya, Morocco, Mauritania, and Tunisia. The Arab countries of Egypt, Jordan, and Syria have constituted the "front lines" against the state of Israel since its establishment in 1948. In this chapter, I investigate four sub-regional trends in defense spending and procurements in the ME: North Africa, the front-line states, the Gulf states, and the Indian subcontinent region with a focus on Pakistan and India."

I investigate the trend in defense spending based on Richardson's action-reaction model by considering rival pairs in each sub-region: Algeria–Morocco in North Africa; Egypt–Israel, Jordan–Israel, and Syria–Israel in the front-line states; United Arab Emirates–Iran in the Arab–Persian Gulf; and Pakistan–India in the Indian subcontinent. My investigation includes empirical testing for countries with available data such as Algeria, Morocco, Egypt, Iran, Jordan, Syria, Israel, and UAE, as well as qualitative explanations for countries that do not have data in SIPRI Yearbooks such as Afghanistan, Lebanon, Mauritania, and Somalia. It is important to know that my objective is not to prove or disprove Richardson's model; rather, I utilized it as a paradigm to investigate defense spending trends in those sub-regions.

4.2. RICHARDSON'S MODEL AND RELEVANT STUDIES

The arms race model proposed by British meteorologist Lewis Frye Richardson (1960) has become one of the most widely studied mathematical models in international relations. Until recently, however, arms race models and arms races have been studied as phenomena in themselves (see Simowitz, 1976) and have not been directly related to other theories in international relations. In this chapter, I relate this study to the general theory of peace economics and development.

Richardson (1960) postulated the law of interaction as follows. He supposed the rate of growth of the armament budget of each nation to be stimulated in proportion to the already existing size of its rival's armament budget and inhibited in proportion to the nation's own armament budget. To compare the theory's predictions with observations, it is necessary to select a pair of rival blocks whose armament budgets are known over some period of time (Clausewitz, 1968, pp. 42–46). Richardson's (1960) original model is shown in Eqs. (4.1) and (4.2) below

$$dx/dt = ly - \alpha x + g \ldots \tag{4.1}$$

$$dy/dt = kx - \beta y + h \ldots \tag{4.2}$$

The coefficients l and k measure each nation's reaction to its opponent's armaments, which Richardson (1960) referred to as "threat." Coefficients

α and β measure each nation's reaction to its own armament, which Richardson (1960) called "fatigue and expense"; and coefficients g and h are reactions to general "grievances" that are not dependent on the amount of arms (see Schrodt, 1978).

Richardson's (1960) model is about general trends shared by all nations: how they interpret defense as threats and aggression; how expenditures on armaments become a heavy burden on the national budget; and how grievances become impediments to permanent peace. There are several motives that lead nations in times of peace to increase military spending, though there are no immediate threats: dissatisfaction because of historical grievances, fear because of misperceptions of other nations, and rivalry because of national arrogance. All these factors could be eliminated or at least reduced through sincere negotiations to relieve some pressure on national budgets.

As Eqs. (4.1) and (4.2) show, if g, h, x, and y all are made zero simultaneously, the values of x and y remain zero, which are ideal conditions for permanent peace through disarmament and satisfaction. Eqs. (4.1) and (4.2) further imply that mutual disarmament without satisfaction is not permanent peace. For example, if x and y instantaneously vanish, it does not imply the absence of grievances: $dx/dt = g$ and $dy/dt = h$. The fact that g and h did not vanish indicates the presence of potential conflicts despite disarmament. As a result, disarmament is necessary but not sufficient for permanent peace. Thus, disarmaments must occur with a general regional scheme to attain genuine peace based on eradicating grievances and dissatisfaction on all sides. Permanent peace takes genuine, frank, and sincere negotiations between disputants to be achieved. National grievances endanger the enforceability of permanent and just peace in the region.

In "Arms Imports as an Action-Reaction Process: An Empirical Test for Six Pairs of Developing Nations," Alex Mintz (1986) attempted to determine whether arms imports into Third World nations follows an action-reaction behavior pattern. Using Richardson's (1960) formulation, six major races were analyzed: three in the ME and three in East Asia. The major findings revealed that while Middle Eastern nations clearly react to the armament behavior of their rivals, this has not proved to be the case in the East Asian region. Mintz (1986) suggested that in the developing world, the most conventional channel for acquiring military stockpiles is through arms imports, and the arms race models should therefore be applied not only to total arms expenditures figures but also to arms import data.

Prior scholarly analysis of Israeli military spending has focused on national security questions. Alex Mintz and Michael Ward (1989), in

"The Political Economy of Military Spending in Israel," present a mathematical model incorporating security threats as well as electoral cycles and corporate profits. The results support the idea that in Israel, the military budget at the margin provides a favorable election climate for incumbents. Mintz and Ward (1989) analyzed the political-economic context and security context in Israel. In the former, investment in the defense sector accounts for as much as 50% of all industrial investment in Israel; two major parties are struggling to achieve power highly competitively; and the pervasive influence of military spending makes it difficult for elected politicians to vote against increases in the budget. Mintz and Ward (1989) concluded that even in highly security-conscious societies such as Israel, the government uses the defense budget at the margins to respond to political and economic pressures.

An alternative, "Explanations of Competitive Arms Processes," offered by W. Ladd Hollist (1977, pp. 313–340), the author reported on part of a research endeavor dealing with the multivariate empirical analysis and computer simulation of competitive arms processes in four settings – the United States/Soviet Union, Israel/Egypt, Iran/Iraq, and India/Pakistan pairs of nations. This particular chapter presented a comparative empirical analysis of eight rival explanations (models) of changes in arms in the four pairs of nations listed earlier. He found that arms processes often tended to be context-specific. He also found that certain internal factors (technology, cost constraints, and fatigue) in some cases tended to be relatively more significant in explaining changes in arms than did the basic action-reaction factor originally postulated by Lewis F. Richardson (1960). To test the models, Hollist (1977) examined the hypothesized relationships via multiple regressions utilizing the ordinary least squares method (OLS).

4.3. EMPIRICAL ESTIMATION OF ACTION-REACTION MODEL OF THE MIDDLE EAST

I begin by analyzing six "action-reaction" pairs of Middle Eastern countries based on Richardson's (1960) equations (Eqs. (4.1) and (4.2) in this chapter), and using military expenditure data[1] from the *SIPRI Yearbook: World Armament and Disarmament* (1969, 1974, 1976, 1980, 1983, 1984, 1990, 1991, 1992, 1996, 1997, 2001, 2002, 2007, 2008), published annually by the Stockholm International Peace Research Institute. I will explain the results of each pair and justify the compliance or noncompliance of these results with Richardson's (1960) model. I follow the empirical analysis

Table 4.1. Richardson's Action-Reaction Model Applied to Middle East (Eqs. (4.1 and 4.2)).

Rival Dyads	*N*	Reaction Parameters	Fatigue Parameters	Grievances Parameters	*R*-Squared
Algeria	41	$l = 0.076$	$\alpha = 0.0014$*	$g = 0.143$*	0.86
Morocco		$\kappa = -8E\text{-}06$*	$\beta = 0.0014$*	$h = 0.05$	0.60
UAE	21	−0.53	0.46	20.24	0.47
Iran		−7.9E-17	1.00	−1.5E-12	1.00
Egypt	24	−0.05	−0.04	0.056	0.09
Israel		0.36	0.50*	−0.32	0.22
Jordan	25	−0.014*	0.002*	0.03	0.95
Israel		−0.142	0.0092	−1.55	0.004
Syria	18	−0.008	4E-10*	0.04	0.99
Israel		−0.24	8E-4*	0.92	0.72
Pakistan	43	0.165*	5E-4*	6E-3*	0.95
India		4E-5*	0.198*	6E-4*	0.98

(*) significant at 0.05 level.

with a qualitative discussion of Middle Eastern countries that were not involved in the empirical estimation. Following Hollist (1977), I utilized OLS regression analysis to estimate the model. The results are shown in Table 4.1. It is apparent that this model does not adequately account for the arms expenditure behavior as specified by Richardson (1960). Nevertheless, the results provide us with a starting point to understand and explain defense trends of the countries under investigation.

4.4. NORTH AFRICA

North Africa in this analysis includes Algeria, Morocco, Tunisia, and Mauritania. North African countries differ from the front-line states (Egypt, Jordan, and Syria) in that their military expenditures are not in reaction to Israeli military expenditures; rather, they are in reaction to each other.

4.4.1. Algeria–Morocco Dyad

As shown in Table 4.1, the Algeria–Morocco dyad has 41 observations (from 1962 to 2005). The reaction's parameters for Algeria and Morocco are insignificant (0.076 and -8E-6, respectively). Algeria holds a similar positive sign in Richardson's model (Eq. (4.1)), whereas Morocco holds a different sign from Eq. (4.2); the fatigue's parameters are significant (+0.00014 and+0.00014), and the grievance parameters are significant (+0.143) and insignificant (+0.05); and the values of R-squared are 0.86 and 0.60, very high for Algeria and acceptable for Morocco.

Algeria, officially known as the Democratic and Popular Republic of Algeria, is the second largest country in the African continent after the Sudan. The military blocked radical Islamists from taking power after winning the election of 1991. As a result, the military has been engaged in bloody fighting with Islamist armed groups ever since. The size of the National Liberation Army (NLA) was 137,000 as of 2004. This was distributed among the army, navy, and air force, with 110,000, 7,500, and 10,000 personnel, respectively. The army has 1,000 main battle tanks (320 T-54/55, 330 T-62, and 350 T-72). The navy deploys 2 submarines, 3 frigates, and 25 patrol boats. The air force has 175 combat aircraft (Su-24, MIG-23, MIG 25, MIG-29, and MIG-21). The NLA does not possess any nuclear weapons. It is equipped mainly with weapons from the former Soviet Union (Attar, 2009; *CIA World Factbook,* 2009; Cordesman, 2002, pp. 107–128; Microsoft Encarta, 2007; *World Desk Reference*).

The size of the Moroccan armed forces was 196,300 in 2002. The number was distributed among the army, navy, and air force, with 175,000, 7,800, and 13,500 personnel, respectively. The Moroccan army has 744 main battle tanks (224 M-48A5, 420 M-60, and 100 T-72.) The navy deploys 2 frigates and 27 patrol boats. The Moroccan air force has 95 combat aircraft including 39 F-5 s, 29 Mirage F-1 s, 4 0V10 s, and 23 Alpha jets (see *World Desk Reference*). As Table 4.2 shows, the pattern of Moroccan military expenditures is very similar to the Algerian pattern since it is mostly a reaction to external pressure from Algeria. However, the Moroccan political system is more stable as reflected by the endurance of its political regime measured based on Polity-IV dataset.

As shown in Table 4.2, Algerian military expenditures reflect reactive behavior to Moroccan military expenditures because of general grievances that have plagued the relationship between the two countries since the revolutionary regime of Houari Boumedienne came to power in 1965. Under Boumedienne, the army became the dominant force. Boumedienne formed a 26-member Council of the Revolution as supreme authority; his members were army commanders and his close civilian associates. Factionalism and personal rule were strictly prohibited. Although Boumedienne remained first among equals – he was simultaneously president,

Table 4.2. Algerian and Moroccan Military Expenditures (Constant Values) in Million $US, 1962 to 2006.

Year	Algerian Military Expenditures	Moroccan Military Expenditures	Year	Algerian Military Expenditures	Moroccan Military Expenditures
1962	537.78	215.14	1984	1028.05	796.37
1963	734.44	229.03	1985	953.30	606.47
1964	749.29	300.81	1986	1004.27	641.29
1965	716.99	270.11	1987	991.42	690.64
1966	723.47	235.95	1988	804.42	770.25
1967	652.43	247.31	1989	611.23	813.07
1968	611.80	267.18	1990	580.12	836.86
1969	588.10	313.10	1991	275.40	848.58
1970	566.17	336.79	1992	341.13	84.55
1971	543.21	315.33	1993	392.09	121.09
1972	562.81	339.93	1994	317.63	786.47
1973	645.77	415.05	1995	226.37	925.53
1974	822.95	599.00	1996	224.38	898.18
1975	997.80	663.41	1997	256.04	850.14
1976	1292.83	1026.60	1998	266.04	745.03
1977	1142.43	1350.46	1999	247.73	730.19
1978	1297.51	1521.58	2000	254.32	780.82
1979	1294.95	1464.77	2001	NA	758.79
1980	1492.37	1568.78	2002	268.01	744.36
1981	1168.38	1787.97	2003	275.05	96.04
1982	797.47	1387.59	2004	337.30	99.57
1983	1116.80	1241.94	2005	346.38	91.66
			2006	357.36	92.00

prime minister, and minister of defense – the principle of collegial leadership was maintained. In 1976, a national charter and subsequent new constitution reaffirmed Algeria as a socialist state solely under the National Liberation Front (FLN) leadership. The de facto side of the national charter was the linkage of military power to socialism; thus, Algeria was best described as an "army with a country, rather than a country with an army" (Attar, 2009; *CIA World Factbook*; Microsoft Encarta, 2007).

During the years of Algerian revolutionary fervor, Morocco was on high alert because the monarchical regime of King Hassan II worried about the Algerian influence on Moroccan political leftist movements such as the Socialist Union of Popular Forces (USFP), the Moroccan Communist party, and other leftist factions. However, the biggest threat to Moroccan national security was the flagrant support of Algeria for the West Sahara people to secede from Morocco. Algeria has lent its full-fledged support to the Popular Front for the Liberation of Saguia el Hamra and Rio De Oro (Polisario Front). The Algeria-backed Polisario Front proclaimed the Sahrawi Arab Democratic Republic on February 27, 1976, and waged a guerrilla war against Morocco and Mauritania. Thus, the behavior of Morocco military expenditures fundamentally changed in 1976. The border clashes between Algeria and Morocco proved that the Moroccan armed forces were more effective and modern than the Algerian armed forces.

As Table 4.2 shows, Moroccan military expenditures rose gradually and normally from 215.14 $US million in 1962 to 663.41 $US in 1975; that is, the difference was only 448.27 $US million over 13 years. However, the increase in Moroccan military expenditures over only a one-year period (from 1975 to 1976) was 363.19 $US million. The Moroccan grievances against Algeria continued to motivate their military expenditure behavior until 1982, when military expenditures began to drop from 1787.97 $US million in 1981 to 1387.59 $US million in 1982. This sudden decline of Moroccan military spending was caused by the Moroccan perception of Boumedienne's successor Chadli Benjedid (born 1929), who was elected president of the Algerian Republic in 1979. Representing a so-called middle-of-the-road faction, Benjedid steered Algerians on a moderate path in foreign and domestic matters until he was deposed by a military junta in 1991.

In spite of his moderate tendencies, Benjedid attempted to acquire political legitimacy by strengthening his military forces in response to the poor Algerian air and land forces during the 1976 clashes with Morocco. Bendjedid's government resorted to a military buildup that reached 1492.37 $US million in 1980. In the following years, it was obvious that the Benjedid government's spending consistently was decreasing military spending, which reached 275.40 $US million in 1991; this decline might be one of the reasons that led the junta to depose him in 1991. After 1991, Algeria plunged into a bloody civil war that changed the whole dynamic of Algerian priorities from acting/reacting to Morocco to reacting to its own internal conflicts. The primary Algerian grievances became unemployment, national debt, inflation, poverty, and civil strife. In reference to Table 4.1, the changing dynamic of Algerian grievances from external to internal grievances would be a plausible explanation for the inadequate sign of the fatigue parameters for both Algeria and Morocco.

Algeria maintained low military expenditures after 1991. As shown in Table 4.2, there was no significant increase or decrease in its military expenditures until 2006. The increase in Algerian defense spending from 1991 to 2006 was only 81.96 $US million. It is obvious as shown in Table 4.2 that Morocco reacted to Algerian military spending changes by decreasing its military expenditures from 1387.59 $US million in 1982 to 836.86 $US million in 1990. Morocco maintained low military expenditures until 2002 744.36 $US million and significantly decreased its spending in the following four years from 2003 to 2006 with 96.04, 99.57, 91.66, and 92 $US million, respectively. The West Sahara conflict remains the main grievance causing the tense relationship between the two countries.

Similar to most socialist countries, Algeria was significantly affected by the fall of the Soviet Union in 1991. The Soviets under Mikhail Gorbachev and later the Russians under Boris Yeltsin, Vladimir Putin, and Dimitri Medvedev no longer accommodated the arms demands of their former clients such as Algeria and Syria without cash in advance for purchasing Russian weapons and technology. This new reality placed Algeria in a disadvantageous position with respect to Morocco, which unlike Algeria has provided its armed forces with access to alternative sources of sophisticated weapons systems from the United States and western European countries, particularly France. Unlike Algeria, Morocco has not suffered from conflicts in Morocco proper.

4.4.2. Tunisia–Libya Dyad

Similar to most countries in the ME, the modern histories of Tunisia and Libya are not difficult to understand because they are linked to one or two political figures that dominate all aspects of the state: political, economic, military, and other minor states' activities. Habib Bourguiba (1903–2000), first president of Tunisia (1957–1987) and the maker of its independence, dominated all aspects of Tunisia until he was ousted by his newly appointed prime minister, Zine al-Abidine Ben Ali. Bourguiba was one of the most sophisticated and visionary leaders in the ME because he could read the path of conflicts in the ME several decades ahead of others. For example, he suggested solutions to the Arab–Israeli conflict in 1968, which subjected him to attacks from most Arab regimes; ironically, the Arab regimes that attacked him at that time adopted his schemes decades later. Bourguiba pursued a policy of political non-alignment but maintained close relations with France and the United States.

Bourguiba's legitimacy as the hero of independence allowed him to rule his country without any significant internal conflicts. This is one major reason that Tunisia has kept a relatively small army. The main focus of Bourguiba was not on the military but on economic development and social programs such as education and women's rights. The size of the Tunisian armed forces was 35,000 as of 2002. The army, navy, and air force have 27,000, 4,500, and 3,500 personnel, respectively. The army has 84 main battle tanks (54 M-60A3 and 30 M-60 A1). The navy deploys 19 patrol boats, and the air force possesses 29 combat aircraft (12 F-5E/F, 12 L-59, and 5 MB-326 K/L) (Attar, 2009; *World Desk Reference*).

Table 4.3 shows that the pattern of Tunisian military spending changed as Tunisia's relations with Libya were tainted after Tunisia annulled a brief agreement to form a union with Libya in 1974. Alerted by Qadhafi's erratic behavior, Bourguiba placed more focus on strengthening his armed forces. Tunisian military expenditures steadily increased beginning in 1976 with 19.9 $US million more than its expenditures in 1973. The Tunisian–Libyan relationship deteriorated in 1980 when Libyan-trained rebels attempted to

Table 4.3. Tunisian, Mauritanian, and Libyan Military Expenditures from 1960 to 2006 in Constant $US Million.

Year	Tunisian Military Expenditures	Mauritanian Military Expenditures	Year	Tunisian Military Expenditures	Mauritanian Military Expenditures	Libyan Military Expenditures
1961	8.6	1	1984	296	NA	
1962	6.6	1	1985	357	NA	
1963	7.1	2	1986	249	NA	
1964	8.6	1	1987	226	NA	
1965	7.4	2	1988	261	NA	
1966	8.8	2	1989	269	29	
1967	8.4	2	1990	287	28	
1968	10.5	3	1991	315	26	
1969	10.5	3	1992	319	24	
1970	10.5	3	1993	347	17	
1971	10.5	NA	1994	301	16	
1972	13.8	NA	1995	324	14	
1973	16.1	5	1996	387	13	
1974	20.3	5	1997	396	11	173.96
1975	30.3	17	1998	417	9	212.15
1976	36	24	1999	424	8	158.91
1977	52.2	32	2000	442	7	157.95
1978	61.8	37	2001	459	6	170.74
1979	65.4	31	2002			259.94
1980	78.6	32	2003			297.41
1981	113	NA	2004			292.86
1982	284	20	2005			272.93
1983	364	NA				

seize the town of Gafsa. Moreover, in 1984, Libya allegedly aided in the sabotage of the pipeline between Algeria and Tunisia. In 1985, Qadhafi put pressure on Tunisia by expelling some 25,000–30,000 Tunisians working in Libya. He also provided funding to labor and radical Islamist groups that opposed Bourguiba (see Cordesman, 2002, p. 246). All of these events led Bourguiba to place more emphasis on defense in reaction to Libyan behavior. As shown in Table 4.3, the amount of spending in 2001 reached as high as 459 $US million.

The eruption of violence between Islamic groups and Algerian authorities in the early 1999 created deep concerns in Tunisia as well as in other North African countries. As shown in Table 4.3, Tunisian military expenditures have increased significantly since 1991 to address the surge of Islamic groups and to avoid a repeat of an internal conflict similar to the Algerian civil war. As of 2001, Tunisian military expenditures reached 459 $US million, an increase of 172 $US million from 1990 (see Attar, 2009; Cordesman, 2000, p. 248).

The Great Socialist People's Libyan Arab Jamahiriya is the official name of Libya, which has been ruled by Colonel Muammar Qadhafi since 1969. In 1973, Qadhafi engaged in military operations in northern Chad's Aozou Strip but was forced to abandon his last military stronghold in Chad at Faya Largeau in 1987. Qadhafi's adventure in Chad cost him heavily in terms of casualties and equipment. His blunt rhetoric made many Middle Eastern countries, including Tunisia, Egypt, and Saudi Arabia, aware of his adventurous schemes (see Attar, 2009; *CIA World Factbook/Leaders*; Cordesman, 2000, p. 183; Gadhafi, 1977; Microsoft Encarta, 2007).

As displayed in Table 4.3 Libyan military expenditures from 1997 to 2005 do not show any abnormal changes. However, most totalitarian countries such as Libya, Iraq, and Syria do not declare their defense spending because they consider that to be a part of their national security. It also suggests that the UN sanctions imposed on Libya in 1992 have been effective.

Fearing a fate similar to that of Saddam Hussein, Qadhafi voluntarily abandoned his nuclear program less than a year after the invasion of Iraq. On January 27, 2004, the United States airlifted out of Libya components of the nuclear weapons program that the country agreed to give up. The White House hailed Libya for its cooperation and said that its good faith in dismantling weapons would be reciprocated. The announcement was made several hours after the U.S. transport plane had landed in the central state of Tennessee carrying some 25 metric tons of Libyan weapons program components including centrifuge parts, uranium, and sensitive documentation. The airlift was the most dramatic move since Qadhafi concluded an agreement on December 19, 2003 with the United States and Britain to give up weapons of mass destruction programs in a bid to end two decades of international isolation and U.S. sanctions (Global Security, 2008).

4.5. FRONT-LINE STATES AND ISRAEL

Before Egypt and Jordan signed peace treaties with Israel, they formed, along with Syria, what used to be called the "front-line states." The name derived from the fact that those countries are located on the front lines of the occupied territories, the West Bank and Gaza Strip (see Abu-Qarn & Abu-Bader, 2008). After the Camp David Accords in 1979 between the most important Arab state (Egypt) and Israel and the Peace Treaty of Wadi Araba in 1994 between Jordan and Israel, only Syria remains a front-line state. Nevertheless, Syria has no inhibition from peace negotiations with Israel because they have engaged in several rounds of indirect negotiations, though in the same hotel, with Israel coordinated by Turkey over the past couple of years. It was expected that action-reaction evidence between Egypt, Jordan, and Israel would not be found because the grievances of Egypt and Jordan no longer are caused by Israel but by other sources in the ME. These sources of threats are a mix of states and non-state actors such as Iran, al-Qaeda, HAMAS, Hezbollah, and other fringe groups.

King Abdullah II of the Hashemite Kingdom of Jordan revealed his concerns and grievances regarding the growing influence of Iran in the region. Late in 2004 in an Interview with Time (2004, www.time.com/time/world/article/0,8599,1533384,00.html)

> The region is going through throes where there are other regional powers that are vying for supremacy in this area. Usually when that happens the net result is conflict and violence. [The Palestinian issue] is the core issue, one that should be dealt with very easily because there is something looming over the horizon that is a lot worse. (see Mackeod, 2006)

The alliance between Iran and the Alawites (a Shia sect) of Syria has frightened Sunni rulers in the region. King Abdullah II described this alliance as the "Shia crescent." The Arabs feel that U.S. intervention in Iraq has given Iran a unique opportunity to exercise a dominant regional role and to threaten their stability.

It is generally believed that Iran can muster an alliance that is powerful enough to dominate the ME, or at least to destabilize it. The current imbalance of power in the region is dictated by the Dawa Party rule in Iraq, the Alawite minority rule in Syria, the powerful Hezbollah and HAMAS in Lebanon and Gaza, and the rise of Shia political movements in Yemen, Saudi Arabia, and Bahrain. It is no wonder, then, that even key players feel that they are surrounded by Iran. Therefore, the grievances of the Egypt and Jordan are no longer about Israel but about the rising threats from states and non-state actors in the region. Similarly, Iran and its proxies in the region have become the main threats to Israel.

4.5.1. Egypt–Israel Dyad

As shown in Table 4.1, the reaction parameters of both Egypt and Israel are insignificant (−0.05 and +0.36); the fatigue parameters are insignificant (+0.04) for Egypt and significant (0.5) for Israel; the grievances parameters are insignificant (+0.065 and −0.32); and the values of R-squared are 0.09 and 0.22. It is obvious that the results do not reflect Richardson's (1960) model; however, Table 4.4 displays the Israeli reaction to Egypt's defense spending after the October (Yom Kippur) War in 1973 due to the poor performance of the Israeli army at the beginning of the war. Moreover, the Israeli reaction to Egyptian defense spending was obvious after Israel and Egypt signed the Camp David Accords in 1977. As shown in Table 4.4, there was significant decrease in Israeli defense spending in 1980, 1982, 1983, and 1984: 82.36 $US million, 185.03 $US million, 351.03 $US million, and 893.80 $US million, respectively, compared to 357,632.33 $US million in 1979. However, Egypt had a consistent decrease in defense spending after the October (Yom Kippur) War in 1973. As shown in Table 4.4, Egyptian defense spending in 1974 was (15,154.15 $US million) and steadily declined to only 436.83 $US million in 1998. However, Israel's defense spending increased significantly and consistently from 893.80 $US million in 1983 to 73,846.67 $US million in 1998. As Table 4.4 shows, the Israeli increase in defense spending was not in reaction to Egypt, Jordan, or Syria; rather, it might have been in reaction to Iran and Hezbollah. Another possibility might be an Israeli perception of general threats during that period or a means of domestic political manipulation as most democratic countries engage in order to manipulate voters during elections, as suggested by Alex Mintz (1989).

The armed forces of Egypt are among the largest in the region, consisting of an army, navy, and air force. The army is the largest military establishment in Egypt; it is estimated to number around 320,000 personnel.

Table 4.4. Egyptian, Jordanian, Syrian, and Israeli Military Expenditures from 1974 to 1998 in Constant $US Million Values.

Year	Egypt Military Expenditures	Jordan Military Expenditures	Israel Military Expenditures	Syria Military Expenditures
1974	15154.15	401.91	6948.20	
1975	14730.15	401.04	94794.96	
1976	12804.00	626.93	133967.61	
1977	13398.55	516.99	174783.08	
1978	7518.49	1090.71	194151.13	
1979	3990.40	639.46	357632.33	
1980	2824.94	592.81	82.36	5730.84
1981	2873.02	584.82	185.03	5289.08
1982	3241.90	570.65	351.03	4388.65
1983	3636.29	577.50	893.80	4433.68
1984	3763.60	528.21	4486.56	4084.32
1985	3011.43	555.80	11488.29	4254.78
1986	2875.27	694.57	13079.08	3146.30
1987	2642.13	748.41	13173.50	2315.91
1988	2343.76	647.61	13607.06	494.08
1989	1467.63	330.31	16444.02	917.58
1990	780.43	247.24	19697.72	278.98
1991	471.43	235.95	34753.50	229.67
1992	469.22	229.75	38609.02	173.58
1993	483.53	260.54	40520.07	157.01
1994	483.63	276.35	49519.10	141.20
1995	448.13	437.17	53582.24	104.10
1996	442.21	288.60	62911.14	95.51
1997	445.71	298.90	68914.14	95.23
1998	436.83	319.90	73846.67	635.29

The navy has a total of 20,000 personnel and 375,000 reservists. The paramilitary forces number around 330,000, including the Central Security Forces, the National Guard, the Border Guard Forces, and the Coast Guard (Attar, 2007, pp. 225–240). Egypt has not engaged in conflicts with any country after it had participated with the coalition forces in the liberation of Kuwait in 1991. As Fig. 4.1 shows, Egyptian defense spending from 1998 to 2006 remained low in spite of dramatic events that have had deep repercussions for the region such as the September 11, 2001 terrorist attack on the United States and the invasions of Afghanistan and Iraq. Egypt's trend of defense spending indicates that it is engaged in peaceful relationships with its neighbors, and that the focus of its leadership is on its domestic affairs.

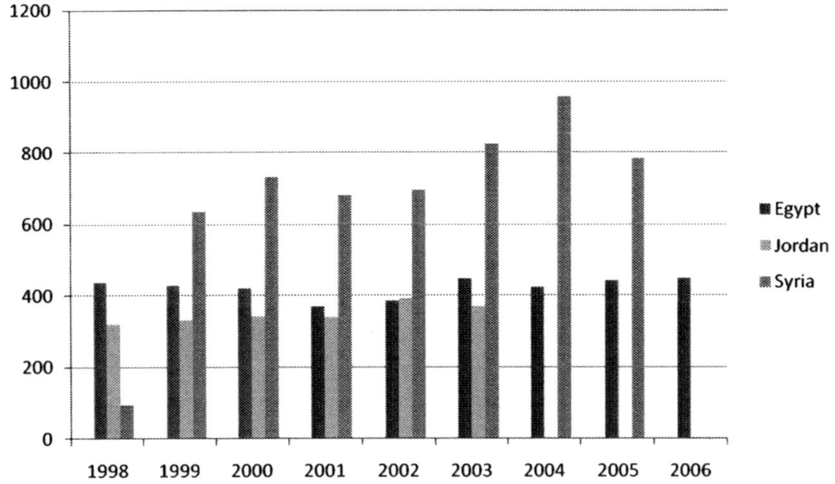

Fig. 4.1. Egyptian, Jordanian, and Syrian Military Expenditures from 1998 to 2006 in $US Million (Constant Values).

The trend of defense spending in Egypt reflects its foreign policy as advocated by Sadat after the Camp David Accords in 1979. In his speech to the Israeli Knesset on November 20, 1977, Sadat pronounced,

> I introduce to the entire world the image of the new man in this area so that he might set an example to the man of our age, the man of peace everywhere. Ring the bells for your sons. Tell them that those wars were the last of wars and the end of sorrows. Tell them that we are entering upon a new beginning, a new life, a life of love, prosperity, freedom and peace.

This peaceful path of foreign policy also was adopted by Egyptian President Husni Mubarak as Egyptian official foreign policy not only toward Israel but also toward all other countries. This line of foreign policy was in stark contrast to the foreign policy of President Gamal Abdul Nassir (1954–1970) who engaged the Egyptian army in several conflicts such as the Yemeni civil war between 1962 and 1967.

4.6. ISRAELI DEFENSE ARMY

The size of Israel's armed forces as of 2002 was 167,600. This was distributed among the army, navy, and air force with 125,000, 7,600, and

35,000 personnel, respectively. The Israeli army has 3,950 main battle tanks (Centurion, M-60A1/3, Magach 7, and Merkava). The navy deploys 3 submarines and 53 patrol boats. The Israeli air force has 688 combat aircraft (50 F-4 E-2000, 62 F-15, and 203 F-16). It is widely believed that Israel has nuclear capabilities with up to 100 warheads, deliverable via Jericho 1 and Jericho 2 missiles (Attar, 2009; Feldman & Shapir, 2001, pp. 63–71, 163–185; Peled, 1992; *World Desk Reference*).

Israel buys a lot of American weapons (mainly major systems, like jet fighters). It has developed a lot of unique and combat-proven weapons and military technology. A lot of these weapons used American weapons as a starting point and then were improved on. However, Israel became one of the largest exporters of weapons. According to Strategy Page (2007), "Israel has displaced Britain as the fourth largest exporter of weapons on the world market. Israel exported over $4 billion worth of weapons this year." The United States is the biggest buyer of Israeli military gear, accounting for nearly 20 percent of Israeli exports. Such sales have been increasing year-by-year. The latest buy includes items such as Lightning targeting pods, high-tech helmets for fighter pilots (Israel supplied most of the technology for the new U.S. JHMCS helmets), and numerous other bits of military components and technology. Recently, Russia purchased Israeli unmanned aircraft because the Russians experienced their effectiveness during the Russian-Georgian conflict in South Ossetia on August 8, 2008.

One of the most insightful views on Israeli military spending comes from Alex Mintz (1989), who suggested that those domestic political-economic considerations are so dominant in the calculus of decision makers that they influence military expenditures, at least at the margins. He hypothesized that declining corporate profit leads to increased military spending; whereas security considerations play a key role in influencing military spending, electoral competition and concerns for the economic well-being of major corporations also influence spending. Mintz (1989) argues that the military in Israel is the government's single most important fiscal mechanism for stimulating the economy and influencing elections, and that the government simply is not able to overlook its political and economic significance. If a society like Israel, which faces continuing and periodically intensified threats to its security, also utilizes the defense budget as an instrument of macroeconomic and electoral policy, such practices would appear to be widespread.

4.7. JORDANIAN SURVIVAL POLICY

Since the founding of the Emirate of Transjordan in April 11, 1921, Emir (later King) Abdullah-I realized the need for a capable security force to establish and ensure the integrity of the state in defense, law, taxation, and other matters. Accordingly, he set up the fabled Arab Legion as one of cornerstone of the fledgling state. The heroism and comparative effectiveness displayed by Jordan's army during its defense of Palestine are widely acknowledged. After the successful defense of East Jerusalem by the Arab Legion, King Abdullah-I traveled regularly to al-Aqsa mosques to participate in Friday prayers. On Friday July 20, 1951, the King was assassinated in an al-Aqsa mosque by a Palestinian assassin. The killer also fired a shot at the young Prince (later King) Hussein bin Talal, but the bullet ricocheted off a medal on his chest (see King Hussein, 1962, pp. 10–12).

At the core of Jordan's founding fathers' policy has been survival of state, monarch, and society. Nevertheless, no Jordanian statesmen took the survival concept more seriously than King Hussein, who witnessed first-hand the annihilation of his family (the Hashemites) in Iraq in July 1958. However, the high tide of Arab radical nationalism, which was responsible for the Hashemite massacre in Iraq, continued with the support of the United Arab Republic[2] (a union between Egypt and Syria 1958–1961) until late 1960. During those years of turbulence, Jordan's survival was at the brink to the extent that the Eisenhower administration recognized that "the indefinite continuance of Jordan's present political status has been rendered unrealistic by recent developments" (Dann, 1999, pp. 93, 101–102, 110–111). Nevertheless, with deft leadership, King Hussein was able to haul Jordan out of that turbulent time. Amidst all these events, the loyalty of the Arab Legion (the official name of Jordan's army) was the safeguard against external threats.

In 2004, the Jordanian armed forces totaled 100,500 personnel. The number is distributed between the army, the navy, and the air force with 85,000, 500, and 15,000 personnel, respectively. The Jordanian armed forces are loyal to the monarch. It has a reputation for thorough training and professionalism. The forces are dependent on Western support for credit for purchasing advanced arms and equipment (Attar, 2009; Feldman & Shapir, 2001, pp. 185–195; *World Desk Reference*).

The pattern of Jordanian military expenditures, as shown in Tables 4.1 and 4.4 and Fig. 4.1, does not follow an action-reaction trend with respect to

Israel. Jordanian military expenditures reflect normal defense spending for a state concerned mainly with its survival and the safety of its society. However, the effects of peace between Jordan and Israel on military spending have been obvious since the beginning of the negotiation process in Madrid in 1991 that led to the Wadi Arab Treaty in 1994. As Table 4.4 shows, Jordanian military expenditures declined from 647.61 $US million in 1988 to 229.75 $US million, 260.54 $US million, and 276.35 $US million in 1992, 1993, and 1994, respectively. Jordan does not possess any nuclear or biological weapons. Its main sources of weapons are the United States and Britain, in addition to other western countries.

4.8. SYRIA FROM FATHER TO SON

The most enduring regime in Syrian politics has been the Assad regime (1971-current). Hafez Assad belonged to the Alawite, a version of Shia Islam. The majority of Syrians are Sunni Muslims (74%), whereas other Muslims (including Alawite and Druze) comprise 16% (see *CIA World Factbook*). This means that it takes a lot of political skills for an individual like Hafez Assad to survive in volatile Syrian politics. Survival was the name of the game for Assad and the Alawites within a contending Sunni majority. Thus, the survival of Assad and the Alawites has rested on mercilessly controlling and suppressing contending groups. With this in mind, Assad devised a political system in which the army would provide protection against external threats, as well as serve as a coercive machine designed to maintain control of the discontented Syrian Sunni majority. On many occasions, the Syrian army was used against the Syrian people with unimaginable ruthlessness: a clear example was the Hama massacre on February 2, 1982. Assad also oversaw the establishment of an effective police and spying apparatus in every layer of society: family, schools, universities, factories, parties, and all societal aggregations. Syria, with its army, police, and massive intelligence agencies (Mukhabarat), became a model of totalitarianism in the ME.

In the early 1980s, President Assad achieved two important goals that consolidated his regime more than at any other time during his reign: (1) his "victory" on the domestic front in the early 1980s eradicated any internal opposition or threats to his regime and (2) the defeat and expulsion of the PLO in Lebanon by Israel removed the main rival in his vital space. However, Assad never felt secure or comfortable with the Israeli occupation in Lebanon; thus, he wanted to find a way to overcome that threat.

According to Daniel Pipes's (1994), "Understanding Assad" in *The Middle East Quarterly*:

> Syrian forces have engaged in impressive military buildups several times before, but the post-1991 effort has been unprecedented in terms of size, quality, and reach; for the first time, Syrian armaments challenge not just the Israel Defense Forces but Israel's civilian population. Israeli analysts concluded by late 1991 that the Syrian military arm had attained a stronger position vis-à-vis Israel than ever before.

In 1980, Syria signed a 20-year treaty of friendship and cooperation with the USSR. The Syrian army was not only merely supplied but also trained by the Soviets, inheriting their centralized, top-down, take-no-initiative style of warfare. Nonetheless, President Hafez Assad insisted that he would develop a "strategic parity" with Israel, but after the Israeli stripped bare the myth of Syrian defenses in 1982, Assad abandoned his goal of achieving "strategic parity" with Israel and instead aimed for "strategic deterrence." President Assad died on June 10, 2000, but before he died, he introduced a new era in Syrian politics: "republican hereditary" or "Ba'athi monarchy." His son Bashar became the ruler of Syria after his father and continued the same policies with the same old guard and the same allies.

As of 2002, the Syrian armed forces were comprised of an army, navy, and air force with 215,000, 4,000, and 40,000 personnel, respectively. The army has 4,500 battle tanks (T-55/MV, T-62M/K, and T-72/72 M); the navy possesses 2 frigates and 18 patrol boats; and the air force deploys 548 combat aircraft such as Su-22/24 and MIG-21/23/25/29 jetfighters (CSIS, Israel and Syria Conventional Military Balance; Feldman & Shapir, 2001, pp. 289–300; *World Desk Reference*). In early September 2008, the Syrian government sought to purchase from Russia MIG-29-SMT fighters, Pantsir SIE air-defense systems, Iskander tactical missile systems, Yak-130 aircraft, and two Amur-1650 submarines.

Before the Gorbachev era (1985–1991), the Soviet Union used to sell weapons systems to some countries in the ME under favorable conditions, Syria in particular because it had a treaty of friendship and cooperation with the USSR. The growing economic problems and the policy shift towards the end of the Cold War during Gorbachev's rule led Moscow to lose interest in its former clients. Consequently, the Soviet Union required cash when selling their weapons systems (Attar, 2009; Feldman & Shapir, 2001, p. 17). The declining trend in Syrian defense spending as shown in Table 4.4 reflects the change in the Syrian–Soviet relationship during Gorbachev's rule, and later with the Russian Federation. Syrian defense spending decreased from 5,731.84 $US million in 1980 to 229.67 $US million in 1991.

The decline in Syrian military spending continued until 1997, with spending dropping as low as 95.23 $US million. As shown in Fig. 4.1, Syrian defense spending picked up after 2002 and reached as high as 873 $US million in 2006.

4.9. PAKISTAN AND INDIA

India and Pakistan have a long and complicated history with each other. In fact, these two countries simultaneously became independent from Britain in 1947. India, officially the Republic of India (Hindi Bharat), is bounded on the north by China, Nepal, and Bhutan; on the east by Bangladesh, Myanmar (formerly known as Burma), and the Bay of Bengal; on the south by the Palk Strait, the Gulf of Mannar (which separates it from Sri Lanka), and the Indian Ocean; and on the west by the Arabian Sea and Pakistan. New Delhi is the country's capital. The division of India caused tremendous dislocation of populations. Some 3.5 million Hindus and Sikhs moved from Pakistan into India, and about 5 million Muslim refugees (known as Mohajirs) migrated from India to Pakistan. The demographic shift caused an initial bitterness between the two countries that was intensified further by continuous territorial claims.

Two more wars occurred between Pakistan and India following the First Kashmir War in 1947. One of the wars was in 1965, resulting in a stalemate between the two countries. The second war occurred in 1971, triggered by Pakistan trying to pacify the Bengali peasantry by confiscating Hindu land and giving it to the Muslims, an action yielding eight million refugees and creating an immense burden on the Indian government. The Indian Prime Minister, Indira Gandhi, felt that the only way to stop the flow of refugees was to support the Bengali freedom fighters, especially the Muki Bahini. Pakistan then began to attack suspected Muki Bahini camps located inside of India's territory. They later struck nine Indian airfields along the western border. India declared war on Pakistan and defeated them in two weeks. The Second Kashmir War in 1965 marked the beginning of a long-lasting conflict that shaped the rivalry between the two countries (*CIA World Factbook*).

Pakistan, officially the Islamic Republic of Pakistan, marks the area where South Asia converges with Southwest Asia and Central Asia. The capital of Pakistan is Islamabad. The territory was part of the Mughal Empire from 1526 until the 1700s, when it came under British rule. Pakistan gained independence in August 1947. It initially comprised two parts, West

Pakistan and East Pakistan, which were separated by about 1,600 km (1,000 mi) of territory within India. In December 1971, East Pakistan seceded and became the independent republic of Bangladesh (Microsoft Encarta, 2007).

In spite of the vicissitudes of the country's evolution, Pakistan is an important regional arms trader and established itself as a nuclear power with successful nuclear tests in 1998; leading scientists in the program later were accused of selling secrets to Iran, Libya, and North Korea. Defense spending is a high priority, accounting for about a quarter of government expenditures. The United States, once a key arms supplier, imposed sanctions in 1990–2001, and most military hardware now is produced domestically; the long-range Shaheen surface-to-surface missile was tested in 2004 (*World Desk Reference*). Since the founding of Pakistan, the army has been involved highly in politics, even at times when a military regime was not actually in power. Since the late 1970s, the Army has been in control in the Pakistani decision-making process.

However, India, the largest democracy in the world, has the world's third-largest military and produces its own hardware. In 2001, the Agni-II intermediate-range missile, which is able to carry a nuclear warhead anywhere in Pakistan, went into production, whereas the long-delayed Light Combat Aircraft began flight tests. Virtual nuclear tests became possible in 2003 with the construction of the Param Padma supercomputer (*World Desk Reference*). Moreover, India successfully has launched its first mission to the moon. The unmanned Chandrayaan 1 spacecraft blasted off smoothly from a launch pad in southern Andhra Pradesh to embark on a two-year mission of exploration. The robotic probe will orbit the moon, compiling a 3-D atlas of the lunar surface and mapping the distribution of elements and minerals. The launch is regarded as a major step for India as it seeks to keep pace with other space-faring nations in Asia. It also will drop the Indian flag on the surface of the moon. The country's tricolor flag is painted on the side of the probe and, if successful, India will become the fourth country after the United States, Russia, and Japan to place its national flag on the lunar surface (BBC News, October 22, 2008, http://news.bbc.co.uk/2/hi/science/nature/7679818.stm, accessed on August 8, 2009; year; *World Reference Desk*, Microsoft Encarta).

Table 4.5 shows the military balance between India and Pakistan in reference to their army, navy, air force, and nuclear capabilities. It is obvious that Indian capabilities exceed Pakistan in number of personnel and amount of equipment along with all of the aforementioned aspects. Thus, it is no wonder that India defeated Pakistan in three past wars.

Table 4.5. Comparison of India and Pakistan Military Capabilities in 2002.

	Pakistan		India
Army	2,317 Main battle tanks (PRC Type-59/69/85, M-48A5, T-54/55/80) and 550,000 personnel	Army	3,898 Main battle tanks (700 T-72 M1, 1200 Vijayanta, 84-T-90S) and 1.1 million personnel
Navy	10 Submarines, 8 frigates, 9 patrol boats, and 25,000 personnel	Navy	19 Submarines, 1 Carrier, 8 destroyers, 16 frigates, 4 corvettes, 45 patrol boats, and 55,000 personnel
Air Force	347 Combat aircraft (52 Mirage 5, 41 Q-5) and 45,000 personnel	Air Force	744 Combat aircraft (64 jaguar S(I), 407 MIG-21/23/27/29, 40 Mirage 2000H/TH) and 170,000 personnel
Nuclear capability	Capability undisclosed; weapons tested in 1998	Nuclear capability	Capability undisclosed; weapons tested in 1998

The Pakistani Indian dyad is in congruence with Richardson's (1960) action-reaction model. As shown in Table 4.1, the Pakistan–India dyad has 41 observations (from 1960 to 2002). The reaction's parameters for Pakistan and India are significant (0.165 and 4 E-5, respectively); the positive sign of the coefficient is similar to those of Richardson's (1960) model Eqs. (4.1) and (4.2); the fatigue's parameters are significant (+5 E-4 and+0.198); the grievance parameters are significant (+6 E-3 and +6 E-4); and the values of R-squared are 0.95 and 0.98, very high for both countries. Moreover, Figs. 4.2 and 4.3, which represent respectively the trends in Pakistani and Indian military spending, offer additional evidence of the action-reaction relationship between the defense doctrines of the two countries. The trends of both countries represent an in-phase relationship since there is similar movement over many segments of the two graphs.

4.10. GULF STATES

The Persian Arab or the Arab Persian Gulf (PAG) states include Bahrain, Kuwait, Qatar, the United Arab Emirates, Iran, Iraq, Oman, and Saudi Arabia.

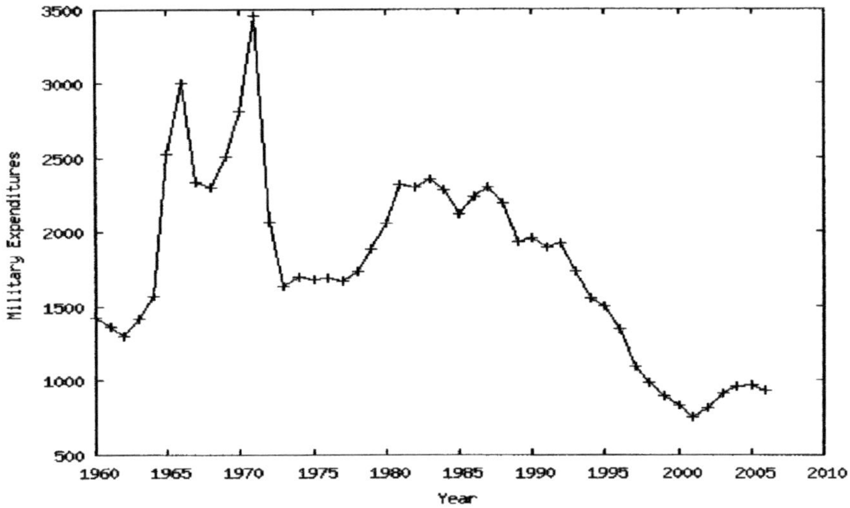

Fig. 4.2. Pakistani Military Expenditures from 1960 to 2006 $US Million (Constant Values).

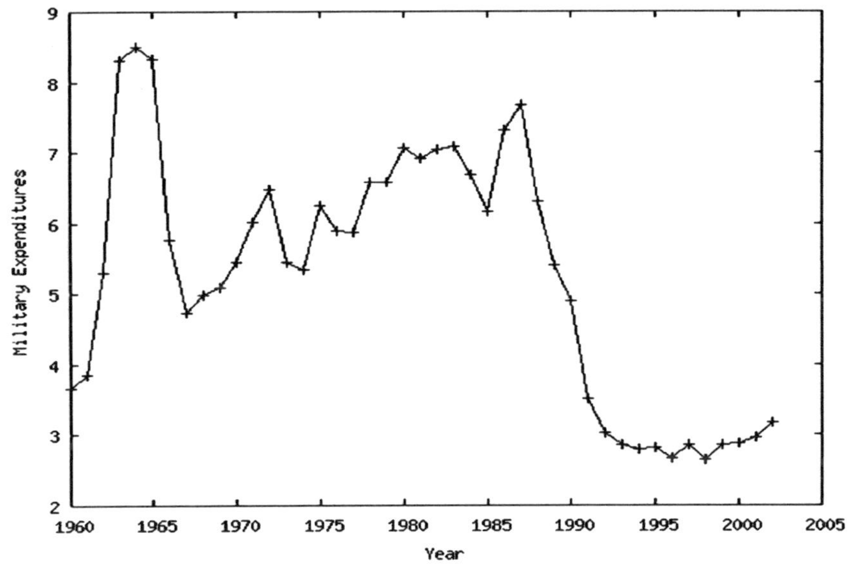

Fig. 4.3. Indian Military Expenditures from 1960 to 2006 $US Billion (Constant Values).

4.10.1. Saudi Arabia

In addition to Iran, Saudi Arabia is a major state in the Gulf region; thus, it is important to understand the structure of its defense to evaluate the strategic balance in the PAG region. In 1902, 63 men led by King Abdulaziz ibn Saud conquered the city of Riyadh. From there, his forces captured other territories and unified them, and he renamed the vast realm Saudi Arabia in 1932. The core of Ibn Saud's military forces was made up of townsmen from Najd as well as a zealous force called the Ikhwan (brotherhood). The Ikhwan, former Bedouins who had taken up Abd al-Wahhab's cause, had a keen thirst for plunder and fought with a blazing ferocity. After the discovery of oil and the meeting between King Ibn Saud and the American President Franklin D. Roosevelt on February 14, 1945, the United States became a new, major ally of the House of Saud.

The pattern of the Saudi military expenditures is best understood by examining four phases: first, the period of Egyptian–Saudi reconciliation (1968–1977); second, the Soviet invasion of Afghanistan (1978–1989) concurrently with the Iranian revolution in 1979 and the Iran–Iraq War (1980–1988); third, Iraq's invasion of Kuwait in August of 1990, which resulted in the First Gulf War, which involved a coalition led by the United States on January 17, 1991; and fourth, the period from the September 11, 2001 attack on the World Trade Center and the Pentagon to the present (Attar, 2009).

The period of Egyptian–Saudi reconciliation (1968–1977) occurred after the stunning defeat of Egypt in the Six-Days War of 1967. After the defeat, President Nassir was in need of financial assistance to rebuild his army and to prepare for another round. King Faisal bin Abdulaziz played a central role in financing the restoration of the Egyptian army to prepare it for another round with Israel. Therefore, the increase in Saudi military spending from 1968 to 1973, as shown in Table 4.6, was not necessarily done to meet Saudi Arabia's needs; rather, it supplied the Egyptian army. King Faisal continued that role during Sadat's rule, and he was a participant in the October (Yom Kippur) 1973 War due to his halting the supply of oil to the United States, which he believed was the main supporter of Israel. King Faisal was assassinated in 1975 by his nephew.

The Soviet invasion of Afghanistan (1978–1989) made Saudi Arabia the main financier of the Mujahedeen in Afghanistan against the Soviet invasion, providing funds for recruitment, weapons, transportation, and training to all Mujahedeen throughout the Afghani war of liberation from the Soviets in 1989. The increase in Saudi Arabian defense spending also was

Table 4.6. Saudi Arabian Military Expenditures from 1968 to 2006 in Constant $US Million.

Year	Military Expenditures	Year	Military Expenditures
1968	2506.45	1988	16487.20
1969	2615.73	1989	14466.46
1970	2979.92	1990	13274.54
1971	3118.90	1991	25518.78
1972	4523.02	1992	12266.03
1973	2876.92	1993	14348.54
1974	3205.38	1994	12327.06
1975	6137.95	1995	10795.12
1976	10191.01	1996	9990.16
1977	11613.98	1997	12930.18
1978	14168.50	1998	17760.68
1979	13822.84	1999	14114.27
1980	13660.72	2000	13741.44
1981	16013.13	2001	14985.35
1982	20637.57	2002	14748.08
1983	21950.18	2003	12244.72
1984	20562.52	2004	12322.79
1985	19875.54	2005	12599.54
1986	20604.40	2006	13844.77
1987	17181.07		

impacted by the victory of the Iranian revolution, which bluntly threatened neighboring countries through the export of their revolutionary ideas. The Saudis feared Iranian support of the Shia Muslims in Saudi Arabia's eastern region. The Iraqi invasion of Kuwait in August 1990 added a huge burden to Saudi Arabia because of its historical responsibilities toward Kuwait. Saudi Arabian defense spending increased sharply, as shown in Table 4.5, because the Kingdom had to pay most of the expenses for the operation to liberate Kuwait, to buy additional weapons and equipment to maintain its security, and to ensure the safety of its citizens from potential chemical attacks.

The September 11, 2001 attacks, which involved 11 Saudi nationals, placed Saudi Arabia at the forefront of War on Terror, which required maintaining a high level of military spending from 2001 to the current day, as can be seen in Table 4.5. Moreover, the dynamic of conflicts had changed in Saudi Arabia. For the first time, the al-Qaeda organization transferred their operations to the Kingdom. Several coordinated destructive attacks have been launched inside the Kingdom, requiring more spending to cope with internal instability.

The size of the Saudi armed forces was 106,500 active personnel as of 2002; the number is distributed among the army, navy, and air force, with 758,000, 15,500, and 16,000 personnel, respectively. The Saudi army has 1,055 main battle tanks (315 M-1A2 Abrams, 290 AMX-30, and 450 M60A3). The navy deploys 4 frigates, 4 corvettes, and 26 patrol boats. The air force has 294 combat aircraft including 29 F-5 s, 158 F-15 s, 85 Tornado IDS, and 22 Tornado ADVs (see *World Desk Reference*). According to (SIPRI, 2008, Appendix 5A), Saudi Arabia ranked eighth among the 15 countries with the highest military expenditures in 2007 at 33.8 $US billion, constituting 3 percent of the world's military expenditures (*World Desk Reference*).

4.10.2. The Islamic Republic of Iran

The strategic balance in this region was lost after the invasion of Iraq, and Iran became the dominant power in the Gulf region. The analysis in Table 4.1 does not show evidence of action-reaction behavior with respect to armament between Iran and the UAE. Also, I did not expect to find evidence of action-reaction behavior between Iran and any of the Gulf states because Iran built a military power that is sufficient to engage Gulf states collectively. Iran's military buildup has not been undertaken in response to a single Gulf state such as the UAE or Bahrain; rather, it has been done to compete with great powers in the Gulf such as the United States and the United Kingdom. Table 4.7 shows the military expenditures of Iran, Bahrain, Kuwait, and the UAE from 1960 to 2004. Evaluating Table 4.7, it is hard to see action-reaction behavior among these states. Moreover, Iran manufactures most weapons domestically and also does not report most of its military activities and transactions.

The Iranian armed forces consist of an army of 350,000, an air force of 18,000, and a navy of 52,000 personnel. The Iranian army possesses 1,565 main battle tanks (M-47/48/60A1, Chieftain MK3/5, and T-54/55/62/72); the navy has 3 submarines, 3 frigates, and 56 patrol boats; and the air force deploys 306 combat aircraft (F-4D/E-F-SE/F, Su-24, F-14, F-7, MIG-29, and Mirage F-1 E). Iran has an ambitious nuclear program that potentially makes it a very dangerous country considering the fact that its leadership has not refrained from constantly announcing to the whole world Iran's intentions of wiping some countries off of the world map (Attar,

Table 4.7. Military Expenditures of Iran, Bahrain, Kuwait, and the UAE from 1960 to 2004 in $US Million (Constant Values).

Year	Iran	Bahrain	Kuwait	UAE	Year	Iran	Bahrain	Kuwait	UAE
1960	1480.19				1983	4625.30	281.29	1501.95	1247.33
1961	1479.36				1984	4208.97	308.83	1537.45	1989.28
1962	1465.96				1985	4997.17	150.53	1559.95	2043.04
1963	1494.69				1986	5210.44	194.44	1991.53	1118.30
1964	1650.36				1987	4218.38	192.84	1657.30	1376.36
1965	2220.68				1988	3752.83	223.98	2030.34	860.23
1966	3063.21				1989	4698.03	226.43	2493.50	430.11
1967	3848.11				1990	5754.69	220.81	7391.93	935.50
1968	4366.29				1991	6054.21	264.81	3764.83	978.51
1969	5135.15				1992	5946.81	293.01	4418.40	784.96
1970	5775.43		670.42		1993	386.03	300.23	4682.12	763.45
1971	7509.33		654.78		1994	379.82	285.37	3408.54	2052.95
1972	7582.95		743.75		1995	281.31	301.92	2682.07	2171.19
1973	10235.01		1710.20	4326.40	1996	317.62	318.85	3040.12	18616.92
1974	22995.08		1256.10	3337.41	1997	355.22	315.94	2655.53	18269.08
1975	29290.07	24.23	1575.71	3366.93	1998	375.15	346.15	2619.59	
1976	30620.18	34.49	2069.59	3018.94	1999	380.11	373.73	3666.96	
1977	24653.92	46.83	2146.46	2117.03	2000	559.52	321.60		
1978	22925.39	124.37	2154.17	1542.14	2001	741.83	328.39		
1979	13667.30	148.14	1609.01	1096.43	2002	118.97	362.65		
1980	10623.38	154.30	1352.29	1107.65	2003	123.33			
1981	10404.23	195.56	1472.97	5129.11	2004	127.07			
1982	5737.72	258.98	1226.69	5430.19					

2009; *World Desk Reference*; Cordesman & Burk, 2008, pp. 1–2). Another concern is transferring Iranian weapons and technology to non-state actors such as Hezbollah and HAMAS, which have expanded the zone of conflicts in the ME.

NOTES

1. For details about military data, see chapter 6.
2. Egypt maintained the official name the United Arab Republic until President Anwar al-Sadat changed it to the Arab Republic of Egypt after the death of President Gamal Abdul Nassir.

CHAPTER 5

THEORIES AND MODELS

There is no single point of view for people considering international politics. Rather, there are several perspectives from which political issues are assessed and different approaches to tackling problems encountered by decision makers at domestic and international levels. There are some fundamental traditions in world politics with which most students of international relations are familiar: realism, liberalism, and radicalism. As the international system has evolved (beginning with the Thirty Years' War that ended with the Treaty of Westphalia in 1648 until the present), the contradictions among those traditions have not centered on pure philosophical grounds. Instead, the core of the debate has always concerned the politics of economics regardless of the philosophical question under consideration. Allocation of resources has been the crucial factor in the continuous struggle among realists, liberals, and radicals. They can agree that there is a relationship between politics and economics, but they disagree on the nature of that relationship or, in other words, the extent of political influence in economic affairs.

According to Frieden and Lake (2000, p. 1), "International political economy is the study of the interplay of economics and politics in the world arena. In the most general sense, the economy can be defined as the system of producing, distributing, and using wealth; politics is the set of institutions and rules by which social and economic interactions are governed." Political economy has a variety of meanings. For some, the term is defined as the study of the political basis of economic actions, the ways in which government policies affect market operations. Others see it as the economic basis of political action, the ways in which economic forces mold government policies (*ibid.*). The purpose of this study is investigating the political basis of economic action, in particular, the effects of political and conflict factors on economic development in the Third World since the contemporary IPE is characterized by increasing political conflicts as individuals, groups, classes, and countries clash over economic transactions.

International political economy (IPE) is a field in which people study those who thrive on the process that Joseph Schumpeter called "creative destruction." The growing prominence of IPE as a field of study is in part a result of the continuing breakdown of disciplinary boundaries between economics and politics in particular and among the social sciences in general. Increasingly, the most pressing and interesting problems are those that can best be understood from a multidisciplinary, interdisciplinary, or trans-disciplinary point of view. The objective of an IPE project is to pull down the fences that restrict intellectual inquiry in the social sciences so that important questions and problems can be examined without reference to disciplinary borders (Veseth, 2007). It is hard to imagine a world without IPE because the mutual interaction of international politics (or international relations) and international economics is widely appreciated today, and scholars studying the subject have plunged into theoretical research and applied policy analysis. The political actions of nation-states clearly affect international trade and monetary flows, which in turn affect the environment in which nation-states make political choices, and entrepreneurs make economic choices. It is probably impossible to consider important questions of international politics or international economics without taking these mutual influences and effects into account (*ibid.*). To place those issues within a broader context, I am going to explain the political traditions of realism, liberalism, and radicalism.

5.1. REALISM

According to Thucydides, writing in 416 BC, when the Melians suggested that the Athenians accept Melian neutrality in the war against Sparta, the Athenians replied, "No, for your enmity doth not so much hurt us as your friendship will be an argument of our weakness and your hatred of our power amongst those we have ruled over" (Vasquez, 1996, p. 16). Realists consider the Melian Dialogue to be an immutable lesson that morality in itself is not sufficient against power (Vasquez, 1996, p. 1). Edward H. Carr (1939) articulates the main tenets of classical realism in *The Twenty Years' Crisis 1919–1939*. According to Carr, "Internationally, it is no longer possible to deduce virtue from right reasoning, because it is no longer seriously possible to believe that every state, by pursuing the greatest good of the whole world, is pursuing the greatest good of its own citizens, and vice versa" (p. 12). Thus, the eternal dispute, as Albert Sorel put it, is "between those who imagine the world to suit their policy, and those who arrange their policy to suit the realities of the world," and the realists resolved it by making policies that suit the world (as cited by Carr, 2001, p. 12).

Central to realist theory are several assumptions that shaped the paradigm that formed the basis for much theoretical development. First, the international system is based on nation-states as the key actors. Second, international politics is essentially confrontational, a struggle for power in an anarchic setting in which nation-states rely on their own capabilities to ensure their survival. Third, states exist under conditions of legal sovereignty, but they have gradations of capabilities. Fourth, states are unitary actors, and domestic politics can be separated from foreign policy. Fifth, states are rational actors characterized by a decision-making process leading to choices based on maximizing their national interests. Finally, power is the most important concept in explaining as well as predicting state behavior (Keohane, 1986, p. 58).

To inject greater rigor into realist theory, neo-realists defined key concepts more clearly and consistently and developed a series of propositions that could be subjected to empirical testing and investigations. The neo-realist approach represents an effort to draw from classical realism those elements of a theory adequate to the world of the late twentieth century but also to link other theoretical efforts conceptually. Thus, the structural realism of Kenneth Waltz draws heavily on system constructs of Kindermann's (Munich school) concept "constellation analysis." While retaining the concept of power as an indispensable variable in explaining change and dynamics, neo-realism, as developed by the Munich school, posits politics, not power, as the key concept, both in domestic politics and at the international level (Keohane, 1986, pp. 80–81).

Kenneth Waltz's (1979) *Theory of International Politics* introduced the structural or neo-realist perspective of international politics. While sharing most of the assumptions of the realists, Waltz moves away from the realist perspective by focusing on the international system as the structure that shapes the political relationships that take place among its members. In developing his structural argument, Waltz stated, "A system theory of international politics deals with the forces that are play at the international, and not the national, level" (cited in Keohane, 1986, p. 60). To generate predictions, a scholar using a structural theory must make assumptions about the nature of structure, the motivations of the agent, and the character of the process that connects them. Waltz conceptualizes the nature of structure along three dimensions. First, ordering principles refer to the standards by which the elements of structure are organized. In domestic politics, system units are organized hierarchically. In the international system, the units (states) are sovereign equals, and the ordering principle is therefore anarchic. In the neo-realistic view, anarchy is a constant, so even though it is thought to have certain consequences, it does not explain variations in outcomes. In Waltz's second dimension of the nature of structure, the character of the units refers to the functions performed by the system elements. In a domestic political system, units perform different functions: some deal with defense, others with welfare, and still others with EG. In the international system, states perform the same function (international order and external defense). The third dimension, which Waltz calls the distribution of capabilities, refers to the extent to which material power resources (especially economic and military) are concentrated in the system. Since anarchy is a constant and functional differentiation has been dropped, it is this dimension that causes a variation in international structure and thereby generates varying outcomes (Wendt, 1999, p. 99).

5.2. LIBERALISM

Like realism, liberalism focuses on rational, self-interested actions by major actors in the international system. Four key assumptions pertain to the liberal traditions. First, world politics is inclusive of non-state actors such as international organizations, institutions, and multi-national corporations. Second, the state is not a unitary actor in the international system. The competition and coalitions within and between state bureaucracies, interest groups, and individuals are the catalysts for foreign policy. The third assumption is different from the realist view; liberals view foreign policies as the product of interaction between actors. Fourth, as opposed to the realist obsession with power, liberals focus on issues other than those that are military-strategic, such as economic and welfare issues and the interdependence among states. Liberal theorists believe that the growing interdependence among nations can bring peace and prevent war. Liberalism allows for interstate interactions. For example, cooperation is a way to preserve peace and promote growth. While cooperation may entail costs, liberal theorists believe that the gains resulting from cooperation make the costs worthwhile (Keohane & Nye, 1977, p. 9).

Liberals suggest that constraints inherent in the complexity of power and other legal restraints on executive power make it difficult for a democratic nation to go to war because the decision is no longer limited to a small group of elites (Mintz & Geva, 1993). According to them, "political systems externalize 'norms of behavior that characterize their domestic political process and institutions' ... Thus, among democratic regimes, the dominant political norms emphasize peaceful competition, persuasion, and compromise" (p. 485). In contrast, non-democratic regimes, according to Maoz and Russett (1992, p. 246), "rest upon the elimination or subjugation of political opponents and the forceful resolution of political conflict."

5.3. RADICALISM

Radicalism, which is better known as Marxism, was founded by Karl Marx and Friedrich Engels in the middle of the nineteenth century. Four basic strands can be discerned in modern Marxism. The first is the evolutionary Marxism of social democracy associated with Eduard Bernstein and Karl Kautsky. At the other extreme is the revolutionary Marxism of Lenin and, in theory at least, of the former Soviet Union. There is, according to Marxists, no inherent social harmony or return to equilibrium as liberals believe. The second strand is a materialist approach to history. Marxists believe that the development of productive forces and economic activities is central to historic change and operates through the class struggle over distribution of the social product. The third strand is a general view of capitalist development. The capitalist mode of production and its destiny are governed by a set of "economic laws of motion of modern society." The fourth is a normative commitment to socialism; all Marxists believe that a socialist society is a path to the necessary and desirable end of historical development.

Marxism characterizes capitalism as the private ownership of the means of production and the existence of wage labor. Marxists argue that capitalism is driven by people striving for profits and capital accumulation in a competitive market economy. The origin, evolution, and eventual demise of the capitalist mode of production are, according to Marx, governed by three inevitable economic laws.

The *law of disproportionality* is a denial of Say's law, which holds that supply creates its own demands. Marx argued that capitalist economies tend to overproduce particular types of goods. There is, Marx argued, an inherent contradiction in capitalism between its capacity to produce goods and the capacity of consumers (wage earners) to purchase those goods, so that the constantly recurring disproportionality between production and consumption due to the "anarchy" of the market causes periodic depressions and economic fluctuations. He predicted that these recurring economic crises would become increasingly severe, and in time, they would impel the suffering proletarian to rebel against the system (Balaam & Veseth, 2008, p. 60; Gilpin, 1987; Russett et al., 2006, pp. 44–46; Frieden & Lake, 2000, pp. 9–13).

The *law of the concentration (or accumulation) of capital* posits that the motivating force of capitalism is the drive for profits, which makes it necessary for the individual capitalist to accumulate and invest. Competition forces the capitalists to increase their efficiency and capital investment or risk extinction. As a result, the evolution of capitalism moves toward increasing concentrations of wealth in the hands of the efficient few and the growing impoverishment of the many. With the petite bourgeoisie being pushed down into the swelling ranks of the impoverished proletariat, the reserve army of the unemployed increases, labor's wages decline, and the capitalist society becomes ripe for social revolution (*ibid.*).

The *law of the falling rate of profit* states that as capital accumulates and becomes more abundant, the rate of return declines, thereby decreasing the incentive to invest. Marx, on the contrary, believed that the tendency for profits to decline was inescapable. As the pressure of competition forces capitalists to increase efficiency and productivity through investment in new labor-saving and more productive technology, the level of unemployment will increase and the rate of profit or surplus value will decrease. Capitalists will thereby lose their incentive to invest in productive ventures and to create employment. This will result in economic stagnation, increasing unemployment, and the "immiserization" of the proletariat. In time, the ever-increasing intensity and depth of the business cycle will cause the workers to rebel and destroy the capitalist economic system (*ibid.*).

5.4. POLITICAL ECONOMY OF CONFLICTS IN DEVELOPING COUNTRIES

It is obvious that Marx could not foresee the dynamic and creative evolution of the capitalist system and the ability of that system to escape the three Marxian laws and "avoid its own destruction." Vladimir I. Lenin (1996) observed that under-consumption led to the accumulation of surplus capital. As a result, industrial and banking interests combine to gain effective control of the state; therefore, the drive to export surplus capital became a competition among countries rather than a competition among corporations, ultimately leading to war among capitalist powers. This phase of capitalist expansionism is called imperialism, which is, according to Lenin, "the highest stage" of capitalism. Therefore, capitalism escapes its own destruction through expanding to other countries and creating captive markets overseas (Russett et al., 2006, p. 207).

Lenin was neither the first nor the last thinker to link conflicts to imperialist competition to gain market outlets for products and capital and new sources of raw materials. The English economist John A. Hobson (1858–1940) argued that "under-consumption" in the domestic market forced capitalists to invest their capital abroad and to compete with others to control foreign markets. Hobson's (1971) *Imperialism: A Study* influenced notable thinkers such as Nikolai Bukharin, Hannah Arendt, and Lenin. Later, Nazli Choucri and Robert North (1975) wrote *Nations in Conflict: National Growth and International Violence* in which they explored in a systematic way the connection between the outbreak of violence in the international system and the population dynamics in the system (Organski, 1997, p. 814; Hobson, 1971; Lenin, 1996; Choucri & North, 1977; Russett et al., 2006, pp. 206–208).

The main objective in reviewing the above literature was to determine the impact of major power expansionism on developing countries' levels of conflict. The conventional wisdom states, "When elephants fight, it is the grass that suffers." While the source of this quote is lost in the distant past, it is as true today as when those words were first spoken. When the large, the strong, the dominant fight, it is the small, the weak, the least powerful who suffer most. Regardless of which elephant wins or loses, the grass beneath their feet will always be trampled and destroyed. Economic issues involving commercial navigation, access to resources, colonial competition, and protection of commercial interests were factors that motivated great powers to compete in the ME and caused conflicts in the countries in that region. For example, the Battle of the Nile (Aboukir Bay) between the British and the French occurred because Napoleon Bonaparte attempted to cut off the land bridge to the Red Sea from the Mediterranean to block the British link to India and ultimately to expel the British from the Indian subcontinent; The Greek civil war that was waged from 1945 to 1947 was a continuation of struggles born during the Second World War; the Soviet Union and Britain's occupation of Iran to establish a supply route from the Arab–Persian Gulf to Russia in August 25, 1941, and the Soviet invasion of Afghanistan in 1979 were part of their attempts to make Cold War strategic gains.

The "elephant-grass" metaphor led some scholars, such as the followers of the dependencia tradition, to suggest that capitalist countries compete with each other over the resources of developing countries. Capitalist countries fight to keep those resources flowing from the periphery to the cores, enriching the latter at the expense of the former. The works of Samir Amin (1977, 2004), *Imperialism and Unequal Development* and *The Liberal Virus: Permanent War and the Americanization of the World*, best represent that theme. There is no single view on the impact of conflicts on EG. Some scholars have postulated that conflicts have a positive effect on growth while others have found negative effects. Our empirical evidence in the Middle Eastern region demonstrates that conflicts have diminished growth.

5.5. NATIONAL SOVEREIGNTY AND DEFENSE

The central principle of the Peace of Westphalia was as follows: He who rules a region determines its religion. Today that principle can be interpreted to mean that major issues of countries must be determined by local rulers, not by an external authority. The key elements of the modern nation-state are a people, a territory in which they live, a government to administer the affairs of the people, and a sovereignty that makes the government independent from external forces. Hudley Bull (1977, p. 8) distinguished two types of sovereignty: internal and external. Bull noted that states assert, in relation to "territory and population, what may be called internal sovereignty, which means supremacy over all other authorities within that territory and population. On the other hand, they assert what may be called external sovereignty, by which is meant not supremacy but independence from outside authorities." European countries fought for thirty years (1618–1648) to assert their external sovereignty from the Catholic Church and for fifteen years (1800–1815) to assert their internal sovereignty from the Napoleonic principle of popular sovereignty.

5.6. MERCANTILISM AND DEFENSE

The main theme of economic policy during the period of mercantilism was to strengthen both external and internal sovereignties of the state. External sovereignty was to be strengthened through the command of strong military forces, which require a strong economy (more exports than imports) to sustain it. Internal sovereignty was to be promoted through controlling and monopolizing all forces of violence in society, abolishing local duties and tolls, improving internal transportation, establishing common weights and measures and business laws, and maintaining other policies that ensure the coherence and unity of the state (Damsgaard, 2001, pp. 61–62; Weatherby, 2009, p. 50).

5.7. THE PHYSIOCRATS AND DEFENSE

François Quesnay (1645–1774) considered agriculture to be the mainspring of economic life and minimized the importance of foreign trade. He also challenged most mercantilist conventions including those pertaining to national defense. In Quesnay's view, an army's strength did not come from its efficiency, and a nation's strength was not dependent on the size of its armies. Indeed, Quesnay suggested that the evolution in the way wars were waged showed that a large number of soldiers is a less decisive factor in victory than the level of incomes that the state could devote to the financing of conflicts (Fanny Coulomb, 2004, pp. 43–46). In his *Hommes (Men)* (1757, p. 520), Quesnay noted, "[It] is good for the soldier and the officer limited to military expedition to believe that the nation's fate only depends on the success of sieges, of battles; to think that a densely populated state is very powerful, because it can provide a high number of combatants [...], but the government which has wider views won't depopulate the country side and won't destroy the source of public income to seek a particular best economy of the general good" (cited in Coulomb, 2004, p. 44).

5.8. ADAM SMITH AND DEFENSE

Adam Smith, the apostle of free trade, proposed in Book V of *The Wealth of Nations* that the first duty of a government was the defense of the country from invasion and violence of other societies. For Smith, "defense was of more importance than opulence"; without the former, you would lose prospects for the latter. The implied question he posed was how much defense was enough. The slope leading from sufficient defense to sufficient war capacity to engage in interventions in the affairs of foreign countries was slippery. And Britain was too easily dragged into such conflicts (partly a product of the prevalence of dynastic kingdoms dominating Europe and their colonies). Smith was not opposed to defense industries, which were necessary to defend the country.

5.9. POLITICAL ECONOMY OF DEFENSE

The PED is a relatively new field in IPE. The main political and economic debate on national defense has focused on the most efficient use of armed forces to maintain political order and protect economic process. Thus, defense was treated by political economists as an extrinsic and instrumental factor when dealing with national economic arrangements, that is, dealing with defense as a controlling factor in relation to the order and function of the sociopolitical and economic process. Prior to the PED, the two main approaches were the arms race model and the incremental or budgetary model.

5.10. ARMS RACE MODEL

The arms race model, proposed by British meteorologist Lewis Frye Richardson (1960), is one of the most widely studied mathematical models in international relations. Richardson began by postulating a hypothetical international system consisting of two nations (or blocks). Next, he postulated the following laws of interaction. He supposed that the rate of growth of the armaments budget of each nation was stimulated in proportion to the already existing size of the rival's armament budget and inhibited in proportion to the nation's own armament budget. A pair of constant terms was added to represent the effects on the rate of change of the budgets, independent of the existing levels. Richardson expressed these assumptions mathematically by the pair of differential equations shown below:

$$dx/dt = ly - \alpha x + g... \tag{5.1}$$

$$dy/dt = kx - \beta y + h... \tag{5.2}$$

The coefficients l and k measure each nation's reaction to its opponent's armaments, which Richardson referred to as a "threat." The coefficients, α and β measure each nation's reaction to its own armaments, which Richardson called "fatigue and expense," and the coefficients g and h are reactions to general "grievances," which are not dependent on the numbers of arms (Rapoport, 1968, pp. 42–43; Schrodt, 1978; Richardson, 1960).

According to Rapoport (1968, p. 44), "the value of this approach is a heuristic one. It *illustrates* a method and so provides a starting point for further more extensive and more sophisticated investigations. Using the same paradigm, future investigators can turn their attention to other possibly more important variables, postulate other possibly more realistic interactions among them, make use of more powerful mathematical machinery (for example, computer simulation, which was not available to Richardson), increase the number of actors, etc." Above all, according to Rapoport, "the value of the approach should not be seen in terms of the answers it provides but in terms of the questions it raises" (*ibid.*).

Rapoport's expectations were actualized by the authors of several articles that exemplified the relevant dimension in Richardson's paradigm (*ibid.*). Philip Schrodt (1978) analyzed two concepts associated with balance of power theory under the assumption that arms levels in the international system change based on Richardson's N-nation arms race model. Schrodt showed that an interpretation of the Richardson model coefficients with respect to alliance and hostility relationships can be used as a compact method of defining alliance structures in a system. Schrodt illustrated that in small systems, symmetric hostility between nations will preserve collective security and, furthermore, that a single nation can serve as a "balancer" to an arms race by setting the values of its own coefficients in the model when "balance" is taken to mean stability of the arms race.

Another usage of Richardson's paradigm stems from the realist-liberal view of relative versus absolute gains, which is one of the fundamental differences between the two theories. Realists argue that states are interested in maximizing their relative gains; therefore, any emerging gaps in capabilities will not be turned against them in the future. But liberals argue that states pursue absolute gains, and arrangements that improve the welfare of society are really what motivate a state's foreign policy, even when those arrangements may be of greater benefit to other societies (Russett et al., 2006, p. 345). This idea resonated in Michael Ward's (1984) "Differential Paths to Parity: A Study of the Contemporary Arms Race." Ward presented a model of arms expenditures and the arms accumulation of the Soviet Union and the United States from 1952 through 1978. He argued that contemporary superpowers do not react solely to each other's military budgets in assessing the potential threat against which they must allocate military resources, that is, in deciding upon their military budgets. Rather, they respond primarily to the relative balance of strategic and conventional military forces. Ward developed a continuous time model of this process and estimated it. He suggested that if one examines only the budgets of these two nations, it will appear that no race is occurring; rather, the Soviets are simply increasing their arms expenditures irrespective of what the United States does. However, when one examines the relative stocks of military capabilities, it appears that the USSR is racing to catch up to the United States.

Mark Irving Lichbach (1989) employed Richardson's paradigm in developing a tit-for-tat (TFT) solution, based on repeated play, to discrete and continuous choice versions of arms rivalries that are iterated (repeated) prisoner's dilemmas (IPDs). Lichbach (1989, p. 1016) justified the utilization of Richardson's paradigm as follows, "Earlier efforts at solving a prisoner's dilemma (PD) arms rivalry with TFT relied on arbitrary payoff functions. The model used here employs Richardson-type utility functions that allow a fascinating result to emerge: given the assumptions behind certain Richardson-type utility functions, the conclusions about the existence and stability of equilibrium in Richardson's arms races, derived from the additional assumptions of non-rationality inherent in Richardson's differential equations, and the conclusions about the emergence of cooperation in IPD arms rivalries, derived from the additional assumptions of rationality inherent in game theory, bear remarkable similarities yet subtle differences."

Moreover, Lichbach (1989, p. 1021) argued that using Richardson-type utility functions in IPD games produces four further improvements over previous treatments of IPD arms rivalries that used arbitrary payoff functions: continuous as well as binary choice versions of the IPD arms rivalry can be studied; more substantive conclusions about arms rivalries can be produced; connections between the conditions for a Richardson-type arms rivalry to be a PD and the conditions for solving a PD arms rivalry with TFT are established; and some fundamental flaws with the TFT solution to a PD arms rivalry are revealed.

5.11. INCREMENTAL APPROACH

The incremental approach posited that since the defense budgetary process must pass over many desks, budgetary policy makers rely heavily on the record of past expenditures, with only marginal adjustments of previous appropriations (Mintz, 1991, p. 6). In the article "A Theory of the Budgetary Process" Davis, Dempster, and Wildavsky (1966, p. 529) noted that "there are striking regularities in the budgetary process. The evidence from more than half of the non-defense agencies indicates that the behavior of the budgetary process of the United States government results in aggregate decisions similar to those produced by a set of simple decision rules that are linear and temporally stable ... Budgets are almost never actively reviewed as a whole in the sense of considering at once the value of all existing programs as compared to all possible alternatives. Instead, this year's budget is based on last year's budget, with special attention given to a narrow range of increases or decreases." In his review of Aaron Wildavsky's (1964) *The Politics of the Budgetary Process*, Stephen K. Bailey (1965, p. 144) stated, "Can something more rigorous be said about the political and social correlates of decisions about incremental changes from previous budgets?" Another critique came from John Wanat (1974, p. 1221) in his assessment of Davis, Dempster, and Wildavsky's *A Theory of the Budgetary Process*. Doubting their theory's explanatory power, Wanat argued that incrementalism must specify not only that the change is a slight modification of the existing state but also must specify why that modification is slight. He attempted to show that the techniques used by Davis, Dempster, and Wildavsky do not allow valid inferences to be made about why budgetary incrementalism occurs.

5.12. DEFENSE SPENDING AND ECONOMIC GROWTH

Mintz and Stevenson (1995, p. 637) noted, "The question of how defense spending affects economic growth has been important to both academicians and the policy community." While many studies of this question have been conducted, a dominant theoretical framework has not emerged. Therefore, in his review article, Chan (1987, p. 35) wrote, "Even though we understand the processes through which military spending can affect economic performance much better now than a decade ago, there remains much that we do not know or that we disagree about."

There is no consensus among scholars on the impact of defense spending on EG. Some scholars such as Emile Benoit (1978) argue that defense programs of most countries help EG, while others such as Nicole Ball (1983) suggest that they do not always promote EG. In a far more systematic classification, Heo's (1996, pp. 4–6) dissertation and an article by Heo and DeRouen (1998, p. 832) illustrate three perspectives concerning the relationship between defense spending and growth. One group of scholars has found that defense spending has a positive impact on EG (Atesoglu & Mueller, 1990; Benoit, 1973, 1978; Biswas, 1993; Kaldor, 1976; Kennedy, 1983; Mueller & Atesoglu, 1993; Weed, 1983). The standard argument of researchers in this group, according to Heo and DeRouen (1998) is that "defense spending may help economic growth by increasing aggregate demand and purchasing power, financing heavy industry such as armaments, as well as producing positive externalities from technology and security spill over."

A second group of scholars has found a negative relationship between defense spending and EG (Deger, 1986; Deger & Sen, 1983; Deger & Smith, 1983; Faini, Annez, & Taylor, 1984; Mintz & Huang, 1990, 1991; Smith, 1980; Ward & Davis, 1992; Heo, 1998). These scholars focus on two disadvantages of spending on defense: the allocation effect (gun vs. butter trade-off) and the growth effect (gun vs. growth trade-off). According to the allocation effect argument, the government expenditures have a dampening effect on investment, which in turn slows down EG. A third group of scholars has been unable to find any relationship between defense spending and EG (Alexander, 1990; Biswas & Rati, 1986; DeRouen, 1993).

To study how defense spending affects EG, Benoit (1973, 1978) conducted an empirical analysis of forty-four developing countries between 1950 and 1965. The first analysis included the whole period while the second analysis covered only the period 1960–1965. Benoit did not find any relationship between defense spending and EG in his first analysis. However, he did find that countries with a heavy defense burden generally had the fastest growth rates, and those with the lowest growth rates spent little on defense. Benoit (1978, p. 276) argued that defense programs in most countries help EG by (1) feeding, clothing, and housing a number of people who would otherwise have to be fed, housed, and clothed by the civilian economy; (2) providing education and medical care and technical training; (3) engaging in a variety of public works such as roads, dams, airports, and communication networks that may serve civilian uses; (4) engaging in scientific and technical specialties such as hydrographic studies, mapping, aerial surveys, meteorology, soil conservation, and forestry projects as well as certain quasi-civilian activities such as disaster relief. Ball (1983) criticized Benoit on the grounds that the utility of the military offering goods and services should be evaluated based on the comparative prices of the same goods and services offered by the civilian sector.

Deger and Sen (1983) argued that military expenditures divert resources from other uses, and therefore, they create direct opportunity costs in terms of investment and consumption. Furthermore, the balance of payment is affected because the weapon systems require importing a great amount of materials. Nevertheless, when the aggregate demand is shorter than the potential supply, military expenditures will increase employment. In their study on less developed countries, Deger and Smith (1983) found that military expenditures have a negative effect on growth and thus hinder development.

The apparent contradiction related to the impact of defense spending on EG led Cappelen, Gleditsch, and Bjerkholt (1984) to attempt overcoming this dilemma by pooling cross-sectional and longitudinal data within the framework of a model of EG. They used data from seventeen countries that were members of the Organization for Economic Cooperation and Development (OECD) for the period 1960–1980. The authors found that military spending has a positive impact on manufacturing output but a negative effect on investment. These two effects had an opposite impact on EG for the whole sample of countries and for the subgroups, except for the Mediterranean countries.

Frederiksen and Looney (1983, 1985, 1986) argued that the critical determinant in the relationship between defense spending and EG depends on the country's financial resources. According to these authors, a country with limited financial resources will always face budget reductions. These reductions will often stop development projects in favor of a defense program. Thus, the authors hypothesized that in countries with constrained resources, defense spending will hinder EG while defense spending will have positive impact on growth in countries with abundant resources. They conducted a cluster analysis on thirty-seven developing countries from 1950 to 1965. Their hypotheses were supported by the analysis.

Lim (1983) examined the relationship between defense and growth for fifty-four developing countries: twenty-one in Africa, thirteen in the Western Hemisphere, eleven in Asia, and nine in the ME and southern Europe for the period 1965–1973. He conducted an OLS analysis for the fifty-four countries and found that defense spending has a significantly negative effect on growth. However, when the author conducted an analysis of the regions, only countries in Africa and the Western Hemisphere experienced a negative relationship between defense spending and EG. Faini et al. (1984) also conducted an empirical test on sixty-nine countries from 1952 to 1970 and concluded that defense spending had a clear negative effect on EG. They also found that export expansion was positively associated with EG. Likewise, population growth, except in Africa, was positively associated with EG.

Kinsella (1990) investigated the relationship between defense spending and economic performance in the United States from 1943 to 1989 using vector auto-regression analysis (VAR). The evidence indicated that there was no substantial relationship, in a causal direction, between defense spending and the price level, the unemployment rate, or the interest rate, nor did there appear to be any substantial gap in the relationship between defense spending and output. Kinsella concluded that attempts to link defense spending to economic performance are not supported empirically.

However, Jeording (1986) argued that although many previous researchers assumed that defense spending preceded economic performance, the opposite seemed to be the case. He conducted a Granger causality test on fifty-seven developing countries from 1962 to 1977 using SIPRI data and from 1967 to 1976 using ACDA data. Joerding found that defense spending did not have any statistically significant causal impact on EG. Contrary to Benoit (1978), he found that EG caused military spending. Concurring with Joerding about the possibility that EG may precede defense spending, Chowdhury (1991) conducted a Granger causality analysis of defense spending and EG in fifty-five developing countries. He did not find a causal relationship between defense spending and EG across countries.

Biswas and Rati (1986) developed a model employing Feder's growth model to examine the relationship between defense spending and EG in fifty-eight developing countries (seventeen low-income and forty one middle-income) from 1960 to 1970 and from 1970 to 1977. The coefficient of the ratio of the military expenditures to GDP for 1960–1970 in the total pooled sample shows that defense spending had a positive impact on EG. However, when the total group was divided into low-income and middle-income groups, only the middle-income group experienced a positive effect. To test the externality effect of defense spending, the authors developed an augmented model, which is a two-sector model: defense and civilian. The model allows the size of defense sector to enter the PF for the civilian sector, which indicates the effect of the former on the latter. The model showed no evidence that defense spending had a statistically significant impact on growth of total output. Alexander (1990, p. 42) criticized Biswas and Rati on the grounds that their model omitted relevant variables, which lead to the omission of important economic linkages.

Heo (1998) investigated how the changes in a country's defense burden will affect EG by testing the economic effects of defense spending on growth in eighty countries using a non-linear defense-growth model that included technological progress. Heo's results revealed that two-thirds of the countries under investigation could possibly expect a "peace dividend" due to the negative relationship between defense spending and EG.

This review of the impact of defense spending on EG leads us to agree with Smith and Georgiou's (1983, p. 15) observation that "if there can be any single conclusion about the effects of military expenditures on the economy, it must be that it depends on the nature of the expenditure, the prevailing circumstances, and the concurrent government policies."

5.13. CONTEXTUAL THEORY OF PRODUCTION FUNCTION DEFENSE-GROWTH MODEL

Standards of living differ greatly in different parts of the world. Although a precise comparison is difficult, the best available estimate suggests that the average real incomes in countries such as the United States, Germany, and Japan exceed those in countries such as Bangladesh and Zaire by a factor of twenty or more. Some countries in the Third World, such as South Korea, Turkey, and Singapore, appear to be making the transition into the group of relatively wealthy industrialized economies. Others, including many in the ME, Latin America, and Africa, have experienced difficulty obtaining positive growth rates of real income per capita. Understanding the problems of EG and development in the Third World is very important because of their impact on people's standards of living (Romer, 1996, pp. 5–7).

This study applies the defense-growth-political model (the H–M model) of Heo and Mintz (2002) to the Third World countries. However, it is hard to learn the insights offered by using the H–M model without investigating the series of augmentations that the PF has gone through. As Romer (1996, p. 7) observed, "The Solow model is the starting point for almost all analyses of growth. Even a model that departs fundamentally from Solow's is often best understood through comparison with the Solow model." The Solow (1988) model focuses on four variables: output (Y), capital (K), labor (L), and "knowledge" or the "effectiveness of labor" (A). At any time, the economy has inputs of capital, labor, and knowledge, and these are combined to produce output. The PF takes the form $Y(t) = F[K(t), A(t), L(t)]$, where t denotes time. Two features of the PF should be noted. First, time does not enter the PF directly but only through K, L, and A. That is, output changes over time only if the inputs into the PF change. In particular, the amount of output obtained from given quantities of capital and labor rises over time only if the amount of knowledge increases. Second, knowledge (A) and labor (L) enter the PF multiplicatively. The product (AL) is referred to as effective labor, and technological progress, which enters in this fashion, is known as *labor-augmenting* or *Harrod-neutral* (Romer, 1996, Chapter 1).

Before the Solow model was available, growth theories succeeded reasonably well in comparing equilibrium paths for the economy. In doing so, however, they failed to come to grips adequately with the right way to deal with deviations from equilibrium growth. Solow (1988, pp. x–xvi) suggested this failure was partially due to the fact that earlier growth theories were mechanical or physical in the sense that they were almost entirely a description of flows and stocks of goods. This mechanical configuration of growth theories kept them from detecting and explaining deviations from the equilibrium paths. Solow's (1957, 1988) advanced use of technology made the PF amenable in explaining deviations from equilibrium paths, which opened up growth theory to a wider variety of real-world facts and to a closer connection with general economic theories. Robert Solow (1957, 1988) and Edward Denison (1967, 1985) are credited with having developed an aggregate PF, which has become widely accepted in growth economics. Based on the neo-classical PF logic, Ram (1986) developed a two-sector (government and private sectors) growth model to examine the relationship between government spending and EG. Ram's equation is as follows:

$$\dot{Y} = \alpha(I/Y) + \beta\dot{L} + (\delta' + C_G)\dot{G}(G/Y) \tag{5.3}$$

In this equation, a dot above the variable indicates its rate of growth, Y represents GNP, I represents investment, L represents labor, and G denotes government spending.

Cornes and Sandler (1986) proposed that there is likely to be an externality effect when government activities influence the private sector's production capacity without being priced on competitive markets. Following Cornes and Sandler, Ram also developed a model incorporating the externality effect of the government sector. Ram's externality equation is as follows:

$$\dot{Y} = \alpha(I/Y) + \beta\dot{L} + \theta\dot{G} \tag{5.4}$$

In this equation, a dot above G indicates the externality effects.

According to Mintz and Huang (1990, 1991), the effect of military expenditures on growth may not be the same as the effect of non-military government spending. Thus, it is theoretically reasonable to separate the military sector from the overall government sector to study how various components of public spending affect economic performance differently (see also Heo, 1999; Heo & Mintz, 2002). Mintz and Huang's equation is (Heo & Mintz, 2002) as follows:

$$\begin{aligned}\dot{Y}/Y = {} & \alpha(I/Y) + \beta(\dot{L}/L) + (\delta_m - \theta_m)[(\dot{M}/M)(M/Y)] \\ & + (\delta_n - \theta_n)[(\dot{N}/N)(N/Y)]\end{aligned} \tag{5.5}$$

In this equation, a dot above the variable indicates its rate of growth, Y represents GNP, I represents investment, L represents labor, and NM denotes non-military government spending.

Huang and Mintz (1991) also examined the externality effects of defense spending on growth but separately from that of the non-military government sector. According to them, "the externality effect generated by the military sector (e.g., technologic spin-offs) may be different from the one generated by the non-military government sector (e.g., regulations)" (p. 1020). Thus, Huang and Mintz specified the separate externality effects of the defense and non-defense government sector. Huang and Mintz's externality equation is (Heo &Mintz, 2002) as follows:

$$\begin{aligned}\dot{Y}/Y &= \alpha(I/Y) + \beta(\dot{L}/L) + (\delta_n - \theta_n)[(\dot{N}/N)(N/Y)] \\ &\quad + \theta_n[(\dot{N}/N)((Y-M)/Y)] + (\delta_m - \theta_m)[(\dot{M}/M)(M/Y)] \\ &\quad + \theta_m[(\dot{M}/M)((Y-N)/Y)] \end{aligned} \tag{5.6}$$

In this equation, a dot above the variable indicates its rate of growth, Y represents GNP, I represents investment, L represents labor, and NM denotes non-military government spending.

Ward and Davis (1992) divided the state activity into two components – military spending and non-military state spending – and tested the externality effects of these expenditures. Ward and Davis's equation is as follows:

$$\begin{aligned}\frac{\Delta Y}{Y_{-1}} &= \alpha_0 + \alpha\frac{I}{Y_{-1}} + \beta\frac{\Delta L}{L_{-1}} + \left(\frac{\delta_M}{1+\delta_M} - \theta_M\right)\frac{\Delta M}{Y_{-1}} \\ &\quad + \left(\frac{\delta_N}{1+\delta_N} - \theta_N\right)\frac{\Delta N}{Y_{-1}} + \theta_M\frac{\Delta M}{S_{-1}} + \theta_N\frac{\Delta N}{S_{-1}} + \varepsilon \end{aligned} \tag{5.7}$$

In this equation, Δ indicates the growth rate; national income is represented by Y, investment by I, labor by L, defense spending by M, non-military government spending by N, and total government spending by S (Heo & Mintz, 2002).

Solow (1988, p. 35) wrote that a "labor augmenting form of technological progress is necessary for steady state growth to be possible." For this reason, Mueller and Atesoglu (1993) included technological progress in their model, utilizing the concept of the Hicks neutral technological change.[1] In other words, this concept will allow us to measure the effects of technological progress separately without affecting the contribution that labor and capital make to the growth (Heo, 1999). By assuming that technological progress develops gradually, Mueller and Atesoglu developed their defense-growth model. Their equation is as follows:

$$dY/Y = \lambda + e^{\lambda t}\psi_l(L/Y)(dL/L) + e^{\lambda t}\psi_k(I/Y) + [\pi_m(M/Y) + e^{\lambda t}\psi_m(M/Y)](dM/M) + \lambda\pi_m(M/Y) \quad (5.8)$$

In this equation, Y indicates GDP; dM/M represents the defense spending growth rate; M/Y is the defense share of GDP; ψ_m denotes the externality effects of defense spending; and λ represents technological progress. The technological change factor, $e^{\lambda t}$, is always positive, even in cases in which λ is negative because technology does not digress (Mueller & Atesoglu, 1993; Heo & Mintz, 2002).

Heo and DeRouen (1998) further augmented Mueller and Atesoglu's (1993) model, suggesting that Mueller and Atesoglu implicitly assumed that technological progress and productivity change in the non-military public sector and that of the private sector are identical. Ward and Davis differed from Mueller and Atesoglu in that they showed that the U.S. government sector had a lower productivity than the civilian sector. Therefore, Heo and DeRouen (1998) argued that it is theoretically more reasonable to separate the private and the non-military government sector while keeping technological change effects in the model (see also Heo, 1999). They asserted that this division of the sectors allows the economic effects of defense spending on growth to be measured more accurately. Heo and DeRouen's equation is as follows:

$$dY/Y = \lambda + e^{\lambda t}\psi_l(dL/L) + e^{\lambda t}\psi_k(I/Y) + [\pi_m(M/Y) + e^{\lambda t}\psi_m](dM/M) + [\pi_n(N/Y) + e^{\lambda t}\psi_n](dN/N) + \lambda\pi_m(M/Y) + \lambda\pi_n(N/Y) \quad (5.9)$$

In this equation, dL/L represents the growth rate of employed labor; I/Y represents the investment share of GDP; dM/M represents the growth rate of defense spending; M/Y indicates the defense share of GDP; dN/N represents the growth rate of non-defense government spending; and N/Y represents the non-defense government spending share of GDP.

According to Heo and Mintz (2002, p. 10), "The defense-growth production function model has thus far been politically neutral. Labor, capital, technology and defense and non-defense elements govern it. No 'political' variable per se has been included in the model. This structure of the model reflects its historical evolution as a supply side economic model of growth." Thus, a political approach to the defense-growth model may add to our understanding of the defense-growth trade-off (Chan, 1995; Mintz, 1991).

The purpose Chapter 6 is to integrate political and conflict variables into the PF defense-growth model and assess the effects of economic and military factors within political contexts to make the PF defense-growth model more realistic and increase its explanatory power.

NOTE

1. Hicks neutral technological change means that changes in technology do not change the share of income going to the factors of production and the factor ratios (Mueller & Atesoglu, 1993, p. 261).

CHAPTER 6

THE MODEL

Although technology provides more flexibility to the PF, the Solow model made it difficult to rationalize deviations from the steady state conditions of economic growth. Ignoring political conditions left the PF operating in isolation from its environment. This dualism of politics and economics hampers any realistic explanation of the problems of economic growth. The realization that the political contexts grow and accompany the PF over time as its shadow led some contemporary political economists to discontinue overlooking the impact of political factors on economic growth.

The political approach to understand deviations from the equilibrium paths emphasizes the impact of internal political configuration on economic growth. It becomes evident that the apparent harmony of political systems does not reflect the internal harmony of domestic forces nor does it reflect the consensus of these forces on economic policies. Accordingly, it is not feasible to offer serious explanations about the problems of economic growth without taking into account the configurations of internal political forces.

In my opinion, the advancement of a political variable (political party) to the PF by Heo and Mintz (2002) was the most important contribution to the research program of economic growth since Solow (1957, 1988) introduced technology to the PF. The worthiness of the Heo-Mintz study derived from the fact that it was the first empirical investigation of the structural political economic impact on growth in the context of the PF. Heo and Mintz tested their model within the American political context by considering a dichotomous variable (1, 0) for the Republican Party and the Democratic Party, respectively. The authors deliberately utilized a dummy variable to capture the effect of politics on economic growth so that they did not destabilize the theoretical construct of the PF. Incorporating the impact of a political party on the economy, the Heo–Mintz (H–M hereafter) augmented PF model becomes:

$$dY/Y = \lambda + e^{\lambda t}\psi_l(dL/L) + e^{\lambda t}\psi_k(I/Y) + [\pi_m(M/Y) + e^{\lambda t}\psi_m](dM/M) + [\pi_n(N/Y) + e^{\lambda t}\psi_n](dN/N) + \lambda\pi_m(M/Y) + \lambda\pi_n(N/Y) + P * D \quad (6.1)$$

In this equation, dL/L represents the growth rate of employed labor; I/Y is the investment share of GDP; dM/M is the growth rate of defense spending; M/Y indicates the defense share of GDP; dN/N is the growth rate of non-defense government spending; N/Y is the non-defense government spending share of GDP; P denotes the coefficient of the political party variable; and D is the dummy variable for a political party.

Incorporating the political context into the PF paved the way to investigating the impact of other political variables on economic growth. I have augmented the H–M model by incorporating into it five political regime variables (political freedom, institutional freedom, regime type, regime stability, and regime ideological base) while controlling with conflict variables. By incorporating political and conflict variables, I extended the applicability of the H–M model to capture most of the fundamental characteristics of political regimes. Moreover, I extended the applicability of the H–M model to the Third World, which has a different level of economic and political development from the First World.

My model extends the H–M model, which basically incorporates a political variable into the PF model. I developed and tested the H–M model in two forms. First, I incorporated separately one of the following eight political and conflict variables: political freedom, institutional freedom, regime type, regime stability, ideological base, external conflicts, internal conflicts, and total conflicts to the PF. Consequently, I tested eight models as shown in Eqs. (6.2–6.9).

$$dY/Y = \lambda + e^{\lambda t}\psi_l(dL/L) + e^{\lambda t}\psi_k(I/Y) + [\pi_m(M/Y) + e^{\lambda t}\psi_m](dM/M) + [\pi_n(N/Y) + e^{\lambda t}\psi_n](dN/N) + \lambda\pi_m(M/Y) + \lambda\pi_n(N/Y) + \eta_1 R_{CONFext} \quad (6.2)$$

$$dY/Y = \lambda + e^{\lambda t}\psi_l(dL/L) + e^{\lambda t}\psi_k(I/Y) + [\pi_m(M/Y) + e^{\lambda t}\psi_m](dM/M) + [\pi_n(N/Y) + e^{\lambda t}\psi_n](dN/N) + \lambda\pi_m(M/Y) + \lambda\pi_n(N/Y) + \eta_2 R_{CONFint} \quad (6.3)$$

$$dY/Y = \lambda + e^{\lambda t}\psi_l(dL/L) + e^{\lambda t}\psi_k(I/Y) + [\pi_m(M/Y) + e^{\lambda t}\psi_m](dM/M) + [\pi_n(N/Y) + e^{\lambda t}\psi_n](dN/N) + \lambda\pi_m(M/Y) + \lambda\pi_n(N/Y) + \eta_3 R_{CONFtot} \quad (6.4)$$

$$dY/Y = \lambda + e^{\lambda t}\psi_l(dL/L) + e^{\lambda t}\psi_k(I/Y) + [\pi_m(M/Y) + e^{\lambda t}\psi_m](dM/M) + [\pi_n(N/Y) + e^{\lambda t}\psi_n](dN/N) + \lambda\pi_m(M/Y) + \lambda\pi_n(N/Y) + \delta R_{FR\text{-}POL} \quad (6.5)$$

$$dY/Y = \lambda + e^{\lambda t}\psi_l(dL/L) + e^{\lambda t}\psi_k(I/Y) + [\pi_m(M/Y) + e^{\lambda t}\psi_m](dM/M) + [\pi_n(N/Y) + e^{\lambda t}\psi_n](dN/N) + \lambda\pi_m(M/Y) + \lambda\pi_n(N/Y) + \delta R_{FR\text{-}INS} \quad (6.6)$$

$$dY/Y = \lambda + e^{\lambda t}\psi_l(dL/L) + e^{\lambda t}\psi_k(I/Y) + [\pi_m(M/Y) + e^{\lambda t}\psi_m](dM/M) + [\pi_n(N/Y) + e^{\lambda t}\psi_n](dN/N) + \lambda\pi_m(M/Y) + \lambda\pi_n(N/Y) + \beta R_{TY} \quad (6.7)$$

$$dY/Y = \lambda + e^{\lambda t}\psi_l(dL/L) + e^{\lambda t}\psi_k(I/Y) + [\pi_m(M/Y) + e^{\lambda t}\psi_m](dM/M) + [\pi_n(N/Y) + e^{\lambda t}\psi_n](dN/N) + \lambda\pi_m(M/Y) + \lambda\pi_n(N/Y) + \tau Rst \quad (6.8)$$

$$dY/Y = \lambda + e^{\lambda t}\psi_l(dL/L) + e^{\lambda t}\psi_k(I/Y) + [\pi_m(M/Y) + e^{\lambda t}\psi_m](dM/M) + [\pi_n(N/Y) + e^{\lambda t}\psi_n](dN/N) + \lambda\pi_m(M/Y) + \lambda\pi_n(N/Y) + \xi R_{IB} \quad (6.9)$$

In these equations, Y represents GDP; λ is technological progress; ψ_k, ψ_l, ψ_m, and ψ_n are the externality effects of capital, labor, and defense spending; π_m and π_n represent the military and non-military sectors; dL/L is the growth rate of employed labor; I/Y is the investment share of GDP; M/Y is the defense share of GDP; dM/M is the defense spending growth rate; and N/Y is the non-defense government spending share of GDP; dN/N is the growth rate of non-defense government spending; $R_{CONFext}$ is external conflicts; $R_{CONFint}$ is the internal conflicts; $R_{CONFtot}$ is total conflicts; $R_{FR\text{-}POL}$ is political freedom; $R_{FR\text{-}INS}$ is institutional freedom; R_{TY} is regime type; R_{ST} is regime stability; and R_{IB} is ideological base.

I developed models 6.10–6.14 by adding two conflict variables – external conflicts and internal conflicts as control variables to the PF – and incorporating a single political variable in each model. Therefore, the general form of this model is: economic growth = PF + internal conflicts + external conflicts + political variable. Below are the models:

$$\begin{aligned} dY/Y = {} & \lambda + e^{\lambda t}\psi_l(dL/L) + e^{\lambda t}\psi_k(I/Y) + [\pi_m(M/Y) + e^{\lambda t}\psi_m](dM/M) \\ & + [\pi_n(N/Y) + e^{\lambda t}\psi_n](dN/N) + \lambda\pi_m(M/Y) \\ & + \lambda\pi_n(N/Y) + \eta_1 R_{CONFext} + \eta_2 R_{CONFint} + \varepsilon R_{FR\text{-}POL} \end{aligned} \quad (6.10)$$

$$\begin{aligned} dY/Y = {} & \lambda + e^{\lambda t}\psi_l(dL/L) + e^{\lambda t}\psi_k(I/Y) + [\pi_m(M/Y) + e^{\lambda t}\psi_m](dM/M) \\ & + [\pi_n(N/Y) + e^{\lambda t}\psi_n](dN/N) + \lambda\pi_m(M/Y) \\ & + \lambda\pi_n(N/Y) + \eta_1 R_{CONFext} + \eta_2 R_{CONFint} + \delta R_{FR\text{-}INS} \end{aligned} \quad (6.11)$$

$$\begin{aligned} dY/Y = {} & \lambda + e^{\lambda t}\psi_l(dL/L) + e^{\lambda t}\psi_k(I/Y) + [\pi_m(M/Y) + e^{\lambda t}\psi_m](dM/M) \\ & + [\pi_n(N/Y) + e^{\lambda t}\psi_n](dN/N) + \lambda\pi_m(M/Y) \\ & + \lambda\pi_n(N/Y) + \eta_1 R_{CONFext} + \eta_2 R_{CONFint} + \beta R_{TY} \end{aligned} \quad (6.12)$$

$$\begin{aligned} dY/Y = {} & \lambda + e^{\lambda t}\psi_l(dL/L) + e^{\lambda t}\psi_k(I/Y) + [\pi_m(M/Y) + e^{\lambda t}\psi_m](dM/M) \\ & + [\pi_n(N/Y) + e^{\lambda t}\psi_n](dN/N) + \lambda\pi_m(M/Y) + \lambda\pi_n(N/Y) \\ & + \eta_1 R_{CONFext} + \eta_2 R_{CONFint} + \tau R_{ST} \end{aligned} \quad (6.13)$$

$$\begin{aligned} dY/Y = {} & \lambda + e^{\lambda t}\psi_l(dL/L) + e^{\lambda t}\psi_k(I/Y) + [\pi_m(M/Y) + e^{\lambda t}\psi_m](dM/M) \\ & + [\pi_n(N/Y) + e^{\lambda t}\psi_n](dN/N) + \lambda\pi_m(M/Y) + \lambda\pi_n(N/Y) \\ & + \eta_1 R_{CONFext} + \eta_2 R_{CONFint} + \xi R_{IB} \end{aligned} \quad (6.14)$$

In these equations, Y represents GDP; λ is technological progress; ψ_k, ψ_l, and ψ_m are the externality effects of capital, labor, and defense spending; π_m and π_n represent the military and non-military sectors; dL/L is the growth rate of employed labor; I/Y is the investment share of GDP; M/Y is the defense share of GDP; dM/M is the defense spending growth rate; N/Y is the non-defense government spending share of GDP; dN/N is the growth rate of non-defense government spending; $R_{CONFext}$ is external conflicts; $R_{CONFint}$ is internal conflicts; $R_{FR\text{-}POL}$ is political freedom; $R_{FR\text{-}INS}$ is institutional freedom; R_{TY} is regime type; R_{ST} is regime stability; and R_{IB} is ideological base.

HYPOTHESES

I developed eight hypotheses concerning the impact of political factors on economic growth. The hypotheses are valid for the NLS analysis as well as for the CNTS analysis.

H1. Interstate conflict has a negative effect on economic growth in developing countries.

H2. Intra-state conflict has a negative effect on economic growth in developing countries.

H3. The effect of total conflict on economic growth in developing countries is negative.

H4. The effect of political freedom on economic growth in developing countries is positive.

H5. Institutional freedom has a positive effect on economic growth in developing countries.

H6. A democratic political regime has a positive effect on economic growth in developing countries.

H7. A stable political regime has a positive effect on economic growth in developing countries.

H8. There is a positive relationship between a liberal ideological base and economic growth in developing countries.

I tested Eqs. (6.2–6.9) using the NLS method on sixty individual developing countries, using time-series data from 1960 to 2002. I tested Eqs. (6.10–6.14) by using CNTS analysis on 69 countries from 1960 to 2002. I conducted the CNTS tests on eight regions and the entire sample, which encompasses a total of 69 countries. The subsystems are: MENA, oil-producing countries, non–oil producing countries, the Arab World, Latin America, Africa, Asia, the Caribbean region, and the entire sample of the 69 countries.

The following are the groups of countries included in each region: *The Middle East and North African region* consists of Jordan, Morocco, Saudi Arabia, Algeria, Bahrain, Egypt, Kuwait, Mauritania, Tunisia, United Arab Emirates, Sudan, Pakistan, Turkey, and Iran; the *Asian countries* consist of the Philippines, India, Indonesia, Korea, Malaysia, Nepal, Singapore, Sri Lanka, and Thailand; the *African region* consists of Benin, Burundi,

Cameroon, Ethiopia, Gabon, Kenya, Liberia, Mauritius, Malawi, Niger, Nigeria, Rwanda, Senegal, Sierra Leon, Tanzania, Togo, Uganda, Zaire, Zambia, Zimbabwe, and the Sudan; the *Latin American countries* consist of Argentina, Bolivia, Mexico, Brazil, Chile, Colombia, Cost Rica, El Salvador, Guatemala, Guyana, and Honduras, Nicaragua, Panama, Paraguay, Peru, Venezuela, and Uruguay; and the *Caribbean region* consists of Dominican Republic, Ecuador, Guatemala, Haiti, Jamaica, and Trinidad.

The *Total Model* (the entire sample) includes Algeria, Argentina, Benin, Bahrain, Bangladesh, Bolivia, Brazil, Burundi, Cameroon, Chile, Colombia, Costa Rica, Dominican Republic, Ecuador, Egypt, El Salvador, Ethiopia, Gabon, Ghana, Guatemala, Guyana, Haiti, Honduras, India, Indonesia, Iran, Jamaica, Jordan, Kenya, Korea, Kuwait, Liberia, Mauritania, Madagascar, Malawi, Malaysia, Mauritius, Mexico, Mali, Morocco, Nepal, Nicaragua, Nigeria, Niger, Pakistan, Panama, Peru, Paraguay, Philippines, Rwanda, Saudi Arabia, Senegal, Sierra Leon, Singapore, Sri Lanka, Sudan, Tanzania, Thailand, Togo, Trinidad, Tunisia, Turkey, United Arab Emirates, Uganda, Uruguay, Venezuela, Zaire, Zambia, and Zimbabwe.

Iraq, Syria, and Libya were excluded from the dataset because their data may not be reliable. Syria and Libya were the most-favored clients of the former Soviet Union among Middle Eastern countries, and this relationship required its leaders to be secretive, especially concerning military spending. Moreover, Iraq and Libya were under United Nations sanctions from the early 1990s to early 2003. I also did not include Lebanon in my dataset because it has been considered a failing state since 1975. The real power in Lebanon until 1982 belonged to the PLO and its allies in the Lebanese parties. Since the early 1980s, the real power in Lebanon has transferred to Syria and its allies in the Lebanese parties, mainly Hezbollah (Party of God) and the Amal movement (Afwaj al Muqawamah al Lubnaniyyah).

Likewise, Somalia was excluded from my dataset because it has had no central government since 1991. Fighting erupted in Somalia in November 1991 between forces of the Hawiye clan led by Ali Mahdi Mohamed and the Abgal subclan led by General Muhammed Farah Aidid. The two clans continue to fight for supremacy. Fighting in Somalia continues among different Islamic factions, including al-Qaeda, for the control of the country. On the other hand, Eritrea and Djibouti were excluded from the data analysis because they obtained their independence in 1993 and 1977, respectively – too short a time frame to produce meaningful statistical results (Derbyshire & Derbyshire, 1996; Microsoft Encarta, 2007).

I elected to analyze data from 1960 to 2002 because the majority of countries in the MENA, Africa, and Asia began the process of state formation after the 1960s: Algeria, 1962; Benin, 1960; Bahrain, 1971; Bangladesh, 1971; Burundi, 1962; Cameroon, 1960; Gabon, 1960; Kenya, 1963; Kuwait, 1961; Mauritania, 1960; Madagascar, 1960; Malawi, 1964; Mauritius, 1968; Malim, 1960; Nigeria, 1960; Niger, 1960; Rwanda, 1962; Senegal, 1960; Sierra Leon, 1961; Singapore, 1970; Tanzania, 1961; Togo, 1960; United Arab Emirates, 1971; Uganda, 1962; Zaire, 1960; Zambia, 1964; Zimbabwe, 1980 (Derbyshire & Derbyshire, 1996).

CHAPTER 7

DATA AND ESTIMATION AND RESULTS

This research utilizes time series data on sixty-nine developing countries in Asia:[1] the ME, Africa, Latin America, and the Caribbean region from 1960 to 2002. The data used for this research consist of four types: economic, military, political, and conflict data.

7.1. ECONOMIC DATA

Data on economic variables are drawn from the *International Financial Statistics* (IFS) *Yearbook* (Edward, 2008; Carson, 2000, 2002, 2004; McLenaghan, 1992, 1995) published by the International Monetary Fund (IMF) Statistics Department (1964, 1973, 1981, 1983). The economic variables that I obtained from the IFS are GDP, gross domestic investment, and government expenditures. The IMF values for the variables are in current prices. The current values are non-comparable across countries due to the different amounts of inflation across nations over time. I converted all data to constant values with the year 1985 as a base year using the GDP deflator provided by the IFS. For countries that do not have GDP deflators for the period (1960–2002), I used the consumer price index (CPI)[2] provided by the same source. In addition, the values for the variables are converted from their respective national currencies to U.S. dollars. Some countries in Latin America posed problems when I conducted the conversion process because they arbitrarily changed their national currencies several times from 1960 to 2002. These currency changes made it very difficult in the cases of Argentina, Brazil, Bolivia, and Mexico to draw reliable conclusions from the empirical analysis. Several countries – Chile, Indonesia, Liberia, Mauritius, Madagascar, the Sudan, Tanzania, Zaire, and Zambia – have numerous missing values that made their time series fall below the required span for appropriate time series analysis. These nine countries were dropped from the

NLS analysis, which reduced the number of countries involved in the NLS analysis to sixty countries. However, these nine countries were included in the CNTS analysis.

For labor data, following Ram (1986), Alexander (1990), DeRouen (1993), Mintz and Stevenson (1995), Ward and Davis (1992), Lebovic and Ishaq (1987), and Heo (1998), population growth rate data are used as proxy. Ram (1986) pointed out that these data are reliable but are not a good proxy in some areas. However, there are two reasons for using population as a proxy to labor: (1) time series data on the labor force are available only for very few countries and plagued with many missing values; and (2) the quality of the labor force variable in developing countries is questionable due to inaccurate reporting for political reasons. Nevertheless, Lebovic and Ishaq (1987, p. 118) suggested that "because labor participation rates show little volatility in the short run, the population growth rate may be used instead."

7.2. MILITARY DATA

The military expenditure values can be found in the *SIPRI Yearbook: World Armament and Disarmament* (1969, 1974, 1983, 1992, 1996, and 2004) published annually by the SIPRI. The SIPRI publishes long-term annual data of three different types: military expenditures in current prices (local currencies); military expenditure in constant U.S. dollars; and military expenditures as a percentage share of GDP. Although for the purpose of this research I am interested in the constant U.S. dollar values, it is not possible to use the constant U.S. dollar values of military expenditures of *SIPRI* "as is." It is possible to convert data to the same base year since the base year changes several times over the period (1960–2002).

Many scholars have criticized the quality of military expenditure data, suggesting that they may not by comparable across countries (Brzoska, 1981). All three major sources of military expenditure data (SIPRI, U.S. ACDA, and International Institute of Strategic Studies (IISS)) rely, at least in part, on definitions of military expenditures that are different for different countries or groups of countries. Thus, the comparability of data from countries using different definitions is highly questionable (Mintz & Stevenson, 1995, p. 290; Lebovic & Ishaq, 1987, p. 683). Therefore, I have used *SIPRI* definitions for values across countries and across groups of countries.

The *SIPRI* data have many comparative characteristics that cause researchers to prefer using them over other datasets. Deger and Smith (1983,

p. 348) preferred using *SIPRI* data over *ACDA* data because, on one hand, *SIPRI* reveals its data sources clearly, uses publicly available information, gives details of military expenditures in national currencies as well as constant U.S. dollars, and also supplies data on military burden. On the other hand, according to Deger and Smith (1983), *ACDA* data have some major problems such as the lack of detailed information regarding sources of data collection and methods of data preparation; thus, it is difficult to have any independent checks on the accuracy of the figures. Consequently, Deger and Smith (1983) concluded that *SIPRI* provides the most consistent data for this type of analysis. Non-military government expenditures are obtained by subtracting defense spending from the total government expenditures for each year. Since the data for government and military expenditures are obtained from different sources (from IFS and SIPRI), respectively, the comparability of the data may not be perfect (Alexander, 1990).

7.3. POLITICAL DATA

The political variables – political freedom, institutional freedom, regime type, regime stability, and regime ideological base – are drawn from *The Polity IV: Political Regime Characteristics and Transitions, 1800–2002*. The *Polity* data originally were developed by Eckstein & Gurr (1975) and recently investigated and updated by Marshall, Jaggers, and Gurr (2007).[3] They contain coded annual information on regime and authority characteristics for all independent states (with total populations greater than 500,000) in the global state system and cover the years 1800–2002.

7.4. INSTITUTIONAL AND POLITICAL FREEDOMS

Sen (1999, p. 3) admitted that the growth of GNP or of individual incomes can be very important as a means of expanding the freedoms enjoyed by members of the society. However, Sen (1999) emphasized that freedoms depend also on other determinants, such as social and economic arrangements (e.g., facilities for education and health care) as well as political and civil rights (e.g., the liberty to participate in public discussion and scrutiny). In other words, development requires institutional freedom as well as political freedom.

Two distinctive types of freedoms are investigated in this empirical study: political freedom and institutional freedom. The operational indicators of these two types of freedoms as derived from *Polity IV* dataset are as follows:

1. Institutional freedom: the variable PARREG (regulation of participation) means the development of institutional structures for political expression.
2. Political freedom is a composite of institutional freedom (PARREG) and competitiveness of participation (PARCOMP). The variable PARCOMP is an indicator of the extent to which the non-elite are able to access institutional structures for political expression.

7.5. REGIME TYPE

In an attempt to make the *Polity* data more compatible with other measure of democracy, it is useful to establish a single, summary measure of the institutional characteristics of the political regimes by subtracting a state's autocracy score from its democracy score (DEMOC-AUTOC) (Jaggers & Gurr, 1995, p. 473). Jaggers and Gurr's (1995) approach has three empirical advantages over treating democracy and autocracy as separate indicators. First, it makes the *Polity* data more easily compatible with other measures of democracy that conceptualize regime type along a single analytic continuum in which democratic and autocratic systems are assumed to occupy its two extreme ends. Second, DEMOC-AUTO is easily interpretable, ranging from positive ten for states that are purely democratic to negative ten for those that are purely autocratic. The zero to ten scores for both DEMOC and AUTOC are not so easily interpretable, especially in situations with "mixed" authority characteristics. Third, this summary measure of regime type helps lessen the bimodal nature of the democracy and autocracy indicators found in the policy datasets.

The operational indicator of institutionalized democracy (DEMOC) is conceived as three essential elements. One is the presence of institutions and procedures through which citizens can express effective preferences about alternative policies and leaders. Second is the existence of institutionalized constraints on the exercise of power by the executive. Third is the guarantee of civil liberties to all citizens in their daily lives and in acts of political participation. The democracy indicator is an additive eleven-point scale (0–10).

In contrast, "authoritarian regime" in Western political discourse is a pejorative term whose common properties are a lack of regularized political competition and concern with respect to political freedoms. In the *Polity IV* dataset, the authors used the term "autocracy" as a more neutral term and defined it operationally in terms of the presence of a distinctive set of political participation: the chief executives are chosen in a regularized process of selection within the political elite, and once in office, they exercise power with few institutional constraints.

What distinguishes the *Polity* dataset from other datasets are the scholarly efforts to update it, the longer period of time it covers, and the consistency of measuring the variables. Furthermore, the *Polity* dataset's measurements for democracy are more dynamic and more applicable than other data to different levels of political development. Other datasets such as Vanhanen's (2003)[4] *Democratization and Power Resources 1850–2000* measure of democracy is constructed exclusively from electoral data, which makes it difficult to measure political development in the Third World. The Bollen (2001) dataset[5] in *Cross-National Indicators of Liberal Democracy 1950–1990* relies on a combination of objective and subjective data in the construction of the indices, which makes the measurement inconsistent (see also Bollen, 1980, 1991, 1993; Jaggers & Gurr, 1995; Vanhanen, 2000).

7.6. REGIME STABILITY

A stable political system, according to *Polity VI* dataset, is one whose authority patterns remain similar over a long period of time and demonstrates a capacity to adapt more or less gradually in response to internal and environmental stress. "Durability" is the term used here for the distinguished property of systems that both persist and adapt (Gurr, 1974, p. 1484). The indicator of stability in the *Polity* dataset is the variable DURABLE, which is coded from the year of the first regime transition or the first year of independence for all years since 1949.

7.7. IDEOLOGICAL BASE

Derbyshire and Derbyshire (1996, p. 23) noted, "Identifying the ideology on which a political system is based, or influenced by, will help us penetrate the façade of institutions and slogans, but we must first clarify what we mean by ideology." The meaning depends on how we construct ideology since the word "ideology" "is a much overused, word." To lessen the tautological confusion of the word "ideology," I checked Derbyshire and Derbyshire's (1996, p. 21) definition against the *Polity* variables that I think meet the requirements of their definition of liberal ideology.

Derbyshire and Derbyshire (1996) compiled a list of markers of liberal ideology, identifying it as one that has evidence of a constitutionally elected government for assemblies and executives, the active presence of more than one political party, protection of personal liberties, an independent judiciary, and checks and balances between three elements of government. Parallel to these elements, I found that the variable Executive Recruitment (EXREC) in the *Polity IV* dataset is the closest to Derbyshire and Derbyshire's (1996) definition. EXREC is a concept variable that combines information presented in three component variables: XRREG (Regulation of Executive Recruitment) indicates institutionalized procedures regarding the transfer of executive power; XCOMP (Competitiveness of Executive Recruitment) indicates the extent to which executives are chosen through competitive elections; and XROPEN (Openness of Executive Recruitment) indicates opportunity for non-elites to attain executive office. A political system that exhibits opposing characteristics to these elements, such as communism, national socialism, authoritarian socialism, military authoritarianism, religious nationalism, and absolutism, has conservative ideologies (Derbyshire & Derbyshire, 1996, pp. 23–38).

7.8. CONFLICT VARIABLES

External conflicts, internal conflicts, and total conflicts are drawn from Singer and Small's (last update 2006) *The Correlates of War Project: International and Civil War Data, 1816–1992 (COW).*[6] The *COW* provides the most thorough and influential quantitative dataset on international conflicts. The *COW* dataset was developed by Singer and Small (1992) in their effort to understand the root causes of war. The data collected describes international and civil wars for the years 1816–1992, and they are divided into two parts: international and extra-systemic wars and civil wars (see also Singer, Bremmer, & Stuckey, 1972; Singer & Small, 1992; Small & Singer, 1982).

7.9. INTERNATIONAL AND EXTRA-SYSTEMIC WARS

This part contains 1,278 logical records for 426 cases. Each case contains the values for 40 variables describing the experience of one participant in an international war. The participants are nation-states with total populations of at least 500,000 and either diplomatic recognition by at least two major powers or membership in the United Nations. This part of the dataset describes two types of international wars: interstate wars, in which a nation-sate engages in a war with another member of the interstate system, and extra-systemic wars, in which a nation-state engages in a war with a political entity that is not an interstate system member. The extra-systemic wars are divided further into two sub-types. First, imperial wars involve an independent political entity but do not qualify it as a member of the interstate system. Second, colonial wars include international wars in which the adversary was a colony.

7.10. CIVIL WARS

According to Meredith and Schafer (2000, p. 124), "In 1994 the *COW* began the process of slightly modifying its classification of wars as they originally appear in *The Wages of War 1816–1965: A Statistical Handbook* and *Resort to Arms: International and Civil War, 1816–1980*." A continuation of this process by Meredith and Schafer (2000) added a new, expanded war typology, resulting in an update of the *COW* in 1997. The period 1998–2002 is covered by *The International Crisis Behavior Project* (*ICB*) (see Eralp, Hewitt, Jonas, Quinn, & Wilkenfeld, 2006). I included conflict based on the *ICB* that meet the criteria of the *COW*. The conflicts of Algeria, Ethiopia, Rwanda, the Sudan, Turkey, Uganda, and Zaire/Congo were coded based on the *ICB* for only a few events.

7.11. METHODS

This study is a continuation, expansion, and application of the Heo and Mintz (2002) PF defense-growth political model, which aims at testing the impact of politics on EG. Since the PF model is derived theoretically, I used dummy variables to capture the effects of politics on EG without affecting the theoretical logic of the PF approach (see Heo & Mintz, 2002, p. 11). I tested the impacts of dichotomous political and conflict variables with the PF to avoid any deformation of its theoretical structure. This study involves NLS analysis, CNTS analysis, and an in-depth case study of the ME based on the empirical results.

Each analytical method has relative advantages and disadvantages. There is no singular method that can explain all social phenomena and illuminate all their sides due to the complexity of the political economic world. A method that might be appropriate at a certain level of analysis is not necessarily appropriate at another level of analysis. To illuminate different sides of the phenomenon, it is necessary to look from different directions, or at different levels of analysis. As Przeworski and Teune (1970, p. 36) noted, "comparative research is an inquiry in which more than one level of analysis is possible."

Thus, I employed different methods to investigate EG in developing countries, using a longitudinal design in which comparison of the same unit at different times is employed. Lijphart (1971, p. 689) argued that the longitudinal analysis offers a solution to the control problem. Dogan and Pelassy (1984, p. 19) suggested that only by examining multiple cases can we locate, rank, and build a hierarchy. The in-depth analysis of the ME is not intended to form a theory on its own; rather, the intent is to serve the general research question of this book. As Eckstein (1963, p. 15) pointed out, "case studies never 'prove' anything; their purpose is to illustrate generalizations which are established elsewhere, or to direct attention toward generalizations."

After Solow (1957, 1988) incorporated technological progress into the PF, the EG model became more reflective of the dynamic of industrial capitalism. Consequently, it was natural to think of an aggregate model from long-run time series for a real economy. Sartori (1970, p. 103) criticized the cross-sectional design as being the province of "overconscious thinkers," arguing that cross-sectional units are not comparable – the apple and orange argument. Macridis and Brown (1986) argued that cross-sectional design represents an oversimplified and arbitrary approach. Likewise, Rostow (1960) argued that this type of research makes it impossible to formulate causal inferences.

Similarly, Ball (1983) and Chan (1985) have argued that statistical analysis of a cross-sectional sample is not equipped to deal with the diversity that is present in different countries in terms of the structural variations of economic and political systems. Moreover, many scholars (Brzoska, 1981) have suggested that military expenditure data may not be comparable across countries. Therefore, I will use time series data for individual countries and CNTS for regionally based analysis. Following Heo (1998), Heo and Mintz (2002), and Heo and DeRouen (1998), I will employ the NLS regression method to test for individual countries.

The time series properties of the data were investigated using Dickey–Fuller tests, accounting for both drift and deterministic time trends. All variables that exhibited non-stationary behaviors were differenced and rendered stationary before using them in the analysis. The t-ratio level of significance at 0.01 and 0.05 levels is calculated. The Durbin–Watson (DW) values calculated by NLS analysis are not reliable indicators for the presence or absence of autocorrelation. According to White (1992, p. 370), "Durbin-Watson distribution theory assumes a linear model so the exact F(d) test cannot be used with a nonlinear model." Thus, White (1992) suggested the approximate non-linear Durbin–Watson (AND) test to deal with this problem. White (1992, p. 370) claimed that "many researchers who continue to compute the d statistic in nonlinear models would like to use this test" because the proposed AND test has good size and power when compared to other alternatives, especially with currently available econometric software (White, 1992, p. 372). The White method is shown in the context of estimation of a constant elasticity substitution (CES) by developing a z-matrix, which is described in Judge, Griffiths, Hill, Lutkepohl, and Lee (1985, Equation 6.2.3). The z-matrix is used to store the derivatives of the non-linear function with respect to each parameter (see Durbin & Watson, 1950, 1951, 1971).

Following Heo (1998) and Heo and Mintz (2002), I utilized the AND test to verify the presence or absence of autocorrelation. I found autocorrelation in eleven countries: Iran with external conflicts; Gabon with political freedom; Haiti with external conflicts, internal conflicts, total conflicts, and political freedom variables; Jordan, Trinidad, and Benin with all political and conflict variables; Algeria with external and internal conflicts; and Uganda with external conflicts (see Appendix A found on pages 191–239). For these countries, the generalized non-linear least squares (GNLS) method suggested by Pagan (1974) is utilized to correct the problem of autocorrelation.

7.12. RESULTS

The results of the empirical analysis contain estimation of thirteen regression models. Eight models (Eqs. (6.2)–(6.9)) consist of the PF in addition to a political or conflict variable. The remaining five models (Eqs. (6.10)–(6.14)) were tested using CNTS analysis. I tested models Eqs. (6.2)–(6.9) using NLS analysis method. Appendix A on pages 191–239 contains the NLS estimation of models given in Eqs. (6.2)–(6.9) for sixty countries. Each page of appendix A has the estimates of the PF with one of the political or conflict variables: political freedom, institutional freedom, regime type, regime stability, ideological base, external conflicts, internal conflicts, and total conflicts. The coefficients of the PF variables that appear in Appendix A – ψ_l (PSIL), ψ_k (PSIK), ψ_m (PSIM), and

ψ_n (PSIN) – represent the externality effects of labor, capital, military expenditures, and non-military expenditures, respectively; π_m (PIEM) and π_n (PIEN) are the coefficients of military and non-military sectors, respectively; and λ (Lambda) is a constant representing technological progress.

I conducted the CNTS analysis in two forms:

1. *Form 1:* The PF defense-growth model with a single political or conflict variable of eight regions in addition to the entire model (ALL STATES): ME (451 observations), ME non-oil-producing countries (251 observations), ME oil-producing countries (200 observations), the Arab world (351 observations), Latin America (649 observations), Africa (649 observations), Asia (346 observations), the Caribbean region (178 observations), and all states (full model) (2,349 observations). The results of this form are shown in Appendix B on pages 241–248.
2. *Form 2:* The PF defense-growth model with external and internal conflicts as control variables with individual political variables over five regions, in addition to the entire model (ALL STATES): the ME (451 observations), Latin America (649 observations), Asia (347 observations), Africa (718 observations), the Caribbean region (178 observations), and the full model (2,349 observations). The results of this form are shown in Appendix C on pages 249–252. In Appendices A, B, and C, I reported the number of cases (N), DW statistics, and the goodness of fit (R^2).

7.13. SUMMARY OF NLS RESULTS

I report a summary of the NLS empirical results of Appendix A in Table 7.1. In this table, information on the impact of economic and military variables as well as their externality effects on EG with respect to political and conflict variables is given. In each group of Table 7.1, the numbers of countries that have significant and positive impact on EG (+Sig) and their percentages (%+Sig) are indicated. Likewise, the numbers of countries that have significant and negative impact (–Sig) and their percentages (%–Sig) are also indicated. Also, the numbers of countries that do not show a positive or negative significant impact on EG (NonSig) and their percentages (%NonSig) are also indicated. Each group in Table 7.1 represents a summary of the PF estimates with the influence of one of the political or conflict variables as elaborated below.

Table 7.1. Summary of the Non-Linear Least Squares Empirical Analysis Results.

	+Sig	%+Sig	−Sig	% −Sig	NonSig	%NonSig
Technology	13.00	21.00	24.00	40.00	23.00	38.33
Labor	13.00	21.00	11.00	18.00	36.00	60.00
Investment	11.00	18.33	9.00	15.00	40.00	66.00
Military sector	19.00	31.00	10.00	16.67	31.00	51.67
Military externalities	13.00	21.00	6.00	10.00	41.00	68.33
Non-military sector	21.00	35.00	16.00	21.00	23.00	38.33
Non-military externalities	30.00	50.00	5.00	8.33	25.00	41.67
External conflict	6.00	10.00	2.00	3.33	52.00	66.00
Technology	15.00	25.00	16.00	26.67	29.00	48.33
Labor	13.00	21.00	8.00	13.33	39.00	65.00
Investment	10.00	16.67	9.00	15.00	41.00	68.33
Military sector	9.00	15.00	10	16.67	41.00	68.33
Military externalities	12.00	20.00	5.00	8.33	43.00	71.67
Non-military sector	18.00	30.00	20.00	33.33	22.00	36.67
Non-military externalities	41.00	68.33	1.00	1.67	18.00	30.00
Internal conflict	15.00	25.00	6.00	10.00	39.00	65.00
Technology	17.00	28.00	17.00	28.00	26.00	43.00
Labor	11.00	18.33	11.00	18.33	38.00	63.33
Investment	11.00	18.33	8.00	13.33	41.00	68.33
Military sector	7.00	11.67	13.00	21.67	40.00	66.67
Military externalities	19.00	31.67	3.00	5.00	38.00	63.33
Non-military sector	16.00	26.67	19.00	31.67	25.00	41.67
Non-military externalities	25.00	41.67	2.00	3.33	33.00	55.00
Total conflict	19.00	31.67	7.00	11.67	34.00	56.00
Technology	15.00	25.00	24.00	40.00	21.00	35.00
Labor	19.00	31.67	5.00	8.33	36.00	60.00
Investment	5.00	8.33	15.00	25.00	40.00	66.67
Military sector	8.00	13.33	12.00	20.00	40.00	66.67
Military externalities	12.00	20.00	4.00	6.67	44.00	73.33
Non-military sector	11.00	18.33	20.00	33.33	29.00	48.33
Non-military externalities	32.00	53.00	3.00	5.00	25.00	41.67
Political freedom	11.00	18.33	4.00	6.67	45.00	75.00
Technology	14.00	23.00	29.00	48.33	17.00	28.33
Labor	10.00	16.67	7.00	11.67	43.00	71.67
Investment	5.00	8.33	8.00	13.67	47.00	78.33
Military sector	12.00	20.00	8.00	13.33	39.00	65.00
Military externalities	11.00	18.33	3.00	5.00	46.00	76.00
Non-military sector	8.00	13.33	25.00	41.67	27.00	45.00
Non-military externalities	29.00	48.33	2.00	3.33	29.00	48.33
Institutional freedom	13.00	21.33	10.00	16.67	37	61.67

Table 7.1. (*Continued*)

	+Sig	%+Sig	−Sig	% −Sig	NonSig	%NonSig
Technology	15.00	25.00	20.00	33.00	25.00	33.00
Labor	19.00	31.67	6.00	10.00	35.00	38.00
Investment	8.00	13.67	12.00	20.00	40.00	66.33
Military sector	8.00	13.33	13.00	21.67	39.00	38.33
Military externalities	13.00	21.67	6.00	10.00	41 00	38.33
Non-military sector	13.00	21.67	14.00	23.33	33.00	38.33
Non military externalities	32.00	53.33	2.00	3.33	53.33	38.33
Regime type	9.00	15.00	10.00	16.67	38.33	38.33
Technology	19.00	31.67	18.00	30.00	23.00	38.33
Labor	16.00	26.67	5.00	8.33	39.00	65.00
Investment	9.00	15.00	9.00	15.00	42.00	70.00
Military sector	11.00	18.33	9.00	15.00	40.00	66.67
Military externalities	13.00	21.67	2.00	3.33	45.00	75.00
Non-military sector	18.00	30.00	17.00	28.33	25.00	41.67
Non-military externalities	30.00	50.00	5.00	8.33	25.00	41.67
Stability	12.00	20.00	12.00	20.00	36.00	60.00
Technology	17.00	28.33	19.00	31.67	24.00	40.00
Labor	15.00	25.00	5.00	8.33	40.00	66.67
Investment	11.00	18.33	12.00	20.00	37.00	61.67
Military sector	7.00	11.67	12.00	20.00	41.00	68.33
Military externalities	8.00	13.33	6.00	10.00	46.00	76.00
Non-military sector	15.00	25.00	17.00	28.33	28.00	46.67
Non-military externalities	32.00	53.33	2.00	3.33	26.00	43.33
Ideology	16.00	26.67	8.00	13.33	36.00	60.00

7.13.1. The Production Function with Political Freedom

As indicated in Table 7.1 and displayed in Fig. 7.1, *political freedom* exerts a positive and significant impact on EG in eleven countries (25 percent), while it has a negative and significant impact in four countries (6.67 percent). The estimates of the PF for political freedom in Table 7.1 are as follows:

- Technological progress has a positive and significant impact on EG in fifteen out of sixty countries (25 percent), while it hinders EG in twenty-four of sixty countries (40 percent).
- Changes in labor growth have a positive and significant impact on EG in nineteen countries (31.67 percent), while they significantly hinder EG in five countries (8.33 percent).

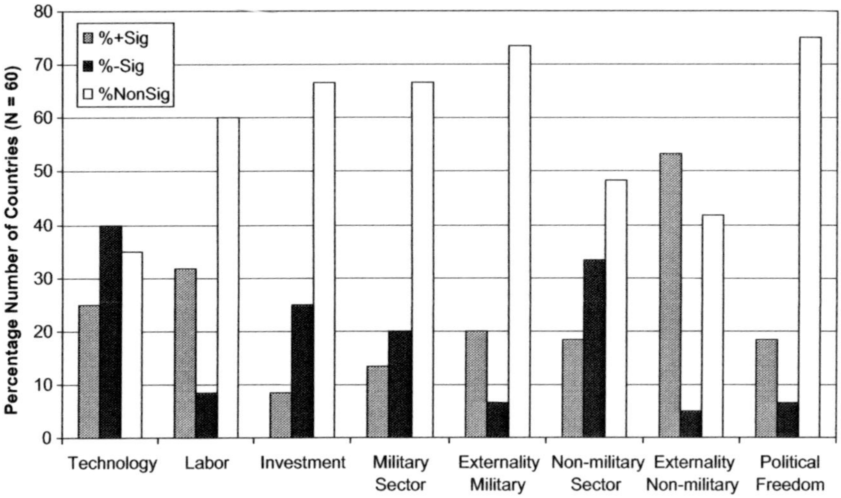

Fig. 7.1. The Impact of Political Freedom, Economic, Military, and Non-Military Factors and Their Externalities on Economic Growth.

- Investment has a positive and significant impact on EG in five countries (8.33 percent), while it has a negative and significant impact in fifteen countries (25 percent).
- The combined effects of technological progress and productivity of the military sectors have a positive and significant impact on EG in eight countries (13.33 percent), while they have a negative and significant impact in twelve countries (20 percent).
- The EEDS have a positive and significant impact in twelve countries (20 percent), while they have a negative and significant impact in four countries (6.67 percent).
- The combined effects of technological progress and productivity of the non-military sectors have a positive and significant impact in eleven countries (18.33 percent), while they show a negative and significant impact in twenty countries (33.33 percent).
- The externality effects of non-military government spending show an overwhelming positive and significant impact in thirty-two countries (53.33 percent), while they significantly hinder EG in three countries (5 percent).

7.13.2. The Production Function with Institutional Freedom

As indicated in Table 7.1 and displayed in Fig. 7.2, *institutional freedom* has a positive and significant impact on EG in thirteen countries (21.67 percent), while it has a negative and significant impact on EG in ten countries (16.67 percent). The estimates of the PF with institutional freedom are as follows:

- Technological progress has a positive and significant impact on (EG) in fourteen of sixty countries (23.33 percent), while it significantly hinders EG in twenty-nine of sixty countries (48.33 percent).
- Changes in labor growth have a positive and significant impact on EG in ten countries (16.67 percent), while they hinder EG in seven countries (11.67 percent).
- Investment has a positive and significant impact on EG in five countries (8.33 percent), while it has a negative and significant impact in eight countries (13.33 percent).
- The combined effects of technological progress and productivity of the military sectors have a positive impact on EG in twelve countries (20 percent), while they have a negative and significant impact in nine countries (15 percent).

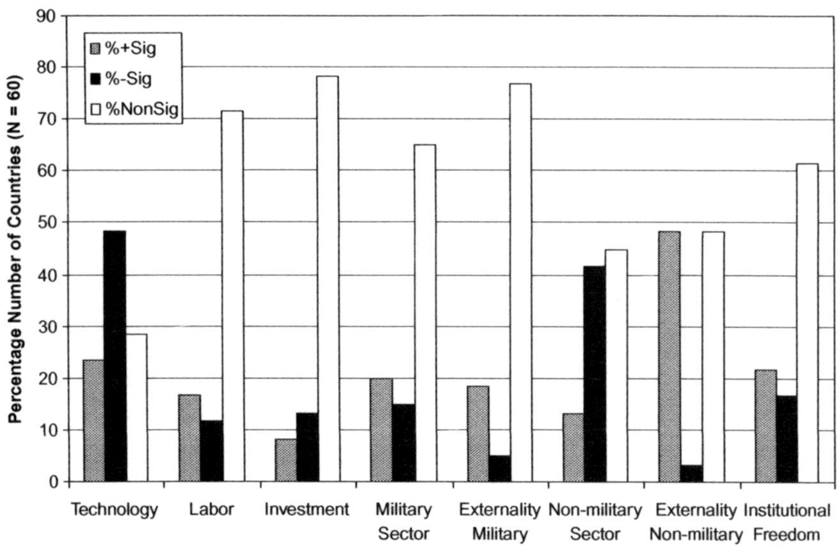

Fig. 7.2. The Impact of Institutional Freedom, Economic, Military, and Non-Military Factors and Their Externalities on Economic Growth.

- The EEDS have a positive and significant impact in eleven countries (18.33 percent), while they have a negative and significant impact in three countries (5 percent).
- The combined effects of technological progress and productivity of the non-military sectors have a positive and significant impact in eight countries (13.33 percent), while they show a negative and significant impact in twenty-five countries (41.67 percent).
- The externality effects of non-military government spending show a positive and significant impact in twenty-nine countries (48.33 percent), while they significantly hinder EG in two countries (3.33 percent).

7.13.3. The Production Function with Regime Type

As indicated in Table 7.1 and displayed in Fig. 7.3, *regime type* has a positive and significant impact on EG in nine countries (15 percent), while it has a negative and significant impact on EG in ten countries (16.33 percent). The estimates of the PF with political freedom are as follows:

- Technological progress has a positive and significant impact on EG in fifteen of sixty countries (25 percent), while it significantly hinders EG in twenty of sixty countries (38.33 percent).

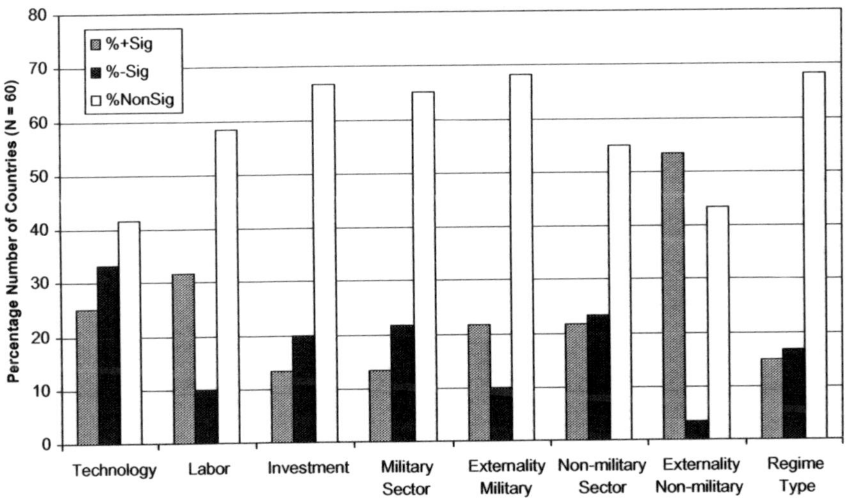

Fig. 7.3. The Impact of Regime Type, Economic, Military, and Non-Military Factors and Their Externalities on Economic Growth.

- Changes in labor growth have a positive and significant impact on EG in nineteen countries (31.67 percent), while they significantly hinder EG in six countries (10 percent).
- Investment has a positive impact on EG in eight countries (13.33 percent), while it has a negative impact in twelve countries (20 percent).
- The combined effects of technological progress and productivity of the military sectors have a positive and significant impact on EG in eight countries (13.33 percent), while they have a negative and significant impact in thirteen countries (21.67 percent).
- The EEDS have a positive and significant impact in thirteen countries (21.67 percent), while they have a negative and significant impact in six countries (10 percent); the combined effects of technological progress and productivity of the non-military sectors have a positive and significant impact in thirteen countries (21.67 percent), while they show a negative and significant impact in fourteen countries (23.33 percent).
- The externality effects of non-military government spending show a positive and significant impact in thirty-two countries (53.33 percent), while they significantly hinder EG in two countries (3.33 percent).

7.13.4. The Production Function with Political Stability

As indicated in Table 7.1 and displayed in Fig. 7.4, *political stability* has a positive and significant impact in twelve countries (20 percent), while it has a negative and significant impact in five countries (8.33 percent). The estimates of the PF with political stability are as follows:

- Technological progress has a positive and significant impact on EG in nineteen of sixty countries (31.67 percent), while it significantly hinders EG in eighteen of sixty countries (30 percent).
- Changes in the labor growth have a positive and significant impact on EG in sixteen countries (26.67 percent), while they significantly hinder EG in five countries (8.33 percent).
- Investment has a positive and significant impact on EG in nine countries (15 percent), while it has a negative and significant impact in nine countries (15 percent).
- The combined effects of technological progress and productivity of the military sectors have a positive and significant impact on EG in eleven countries (18.33 percent), while they have a negative and significant impact in nine countries (15 percent).

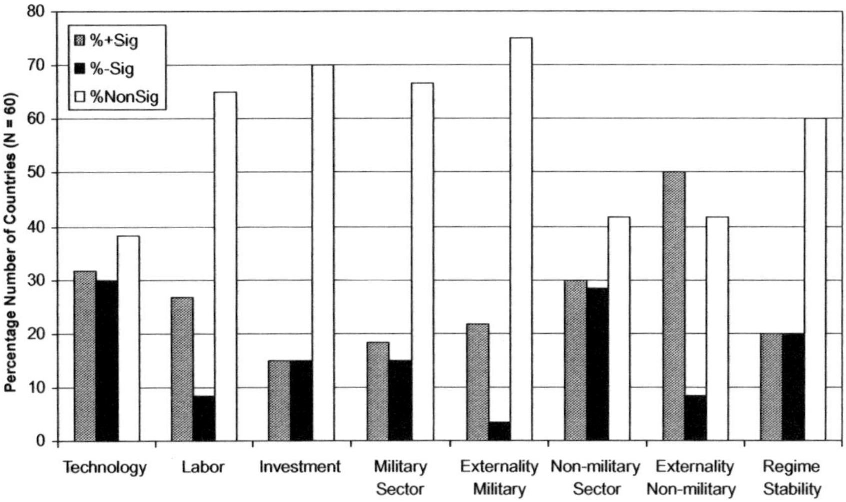

Fig. 7.4. The Impact of Regime Stability, Economic, Military, and Non-Military Factors and Their Externalities on Economic Growth.

- The EEDS have a positive and significant impact in thirteen countries (21.67 percent), while they have a negative and significant impact in two countries (3.33 percent).
- The combined effects of technological progress and productivity of the non-military sectors have a positive and significant impact in eighteen countries (30 percent), while they show a negative and significant impact in seventeen countries (28.33 percent).
- The externality effects of non-military government spending show a positive and significant impact in thirty countries (50 percent), while they significantly hinder EG in five countries (8.33 percent).

7.13.5. The Production Function with Ideological Base

As indicated in Table 7.1 and displayed in Fig. 7.5, *regime ideological base* has a positive and significant impact on EG in sixteen countries (26.67 percent), while it has a negative and significant impact in eight countries (13.33 percent). The estimates of the PF with ideological base are as follows:

- Technological progress has a positive and significant impact on EG in seventeen of sixty countries (28.33 percent), while it significantly hinders EG in nineteen of sixty countries (31.67 percent).

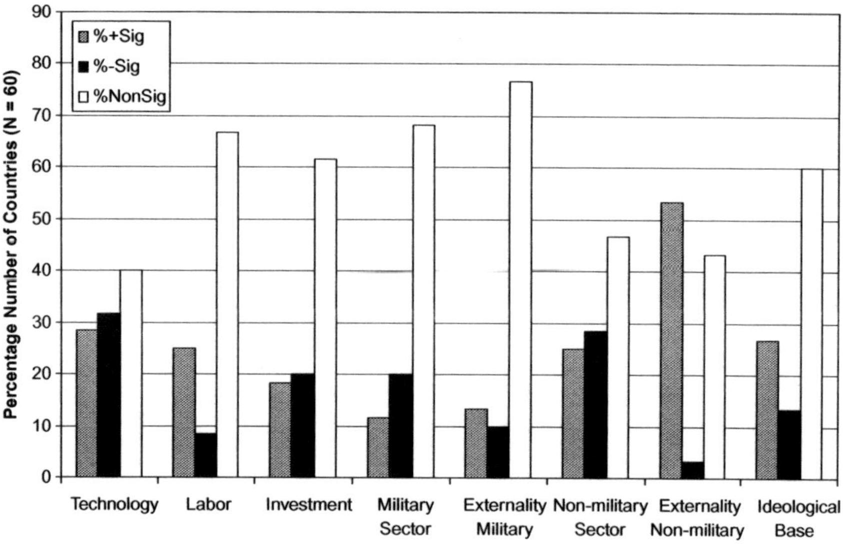

Fig. 7.5. The Impact of Regime Ideological Base, Economic, Military, and Non-Military Factors and Their Externalities on Economic Growth.

- Changes in labor growth have a positive and significant impact on EG in fifteen countries (25 percent), while they significantly hinder EG in five countries (8.33 percent).
- Investment has a positive and significant impact on EG in eleven countries (18.33 percent), while it has a negative and significant impact in twelve countries (20 percent).
- The combined effects of technological progress and productivity of the military sectors have a positive and significant impact on EG in seven countries (11.67 percent), while they have a negative and significant impact in twelve countries (20 percent).
- The EEDS have a positive and significant impact in eight countries (13.33 percent), while they have a negative and significant impact in six countries (10 percent).
- The combined effects of technological progress and productivity of the non-military sectors have a positive and significant impact in fifteen countries (25 percent), while they show a negative and significant impact in seventeen countries (28.33 percent).
- The externality effects of non-military government spending show a positive and significant impact in thirty-two countries (53.33 percent), while they significantly hinder EG in two countries (3.33 percent).

7.13.6. The Production Function with Internal Conflicts

As indicated in Table 7.1 and displayed in Fig. 7.6, *internal conflicts* have a positive and significant impact in fifteen countries (25 percent), while they have a negative and significant impact in six countries (10 percent). The estimates of the PF with internal conflicts are as follows:

- Technological progress has a positive and significant impact on EG in fifteen of sixty countries (25 percent), while it significantly hinders EG in sixteen of sixty countries (26.67 percent).
- Changes in labor growth have a positive and significant impact on EG in thirteen countries (21 percent), while they significantly hinder EG in eight countries (13.33 percent).
- Investment has a positive and significant impact on EG in ten countries (16.67 percent), while it has a negative and significant impact in nine countries (15 percent).
- The combined effects of technological progress and productivity of the military sectors have a positive and significant impact on EG in nine countries (11.67 percent), while they have a negative and significant impact in ten countries (16.67 percent).

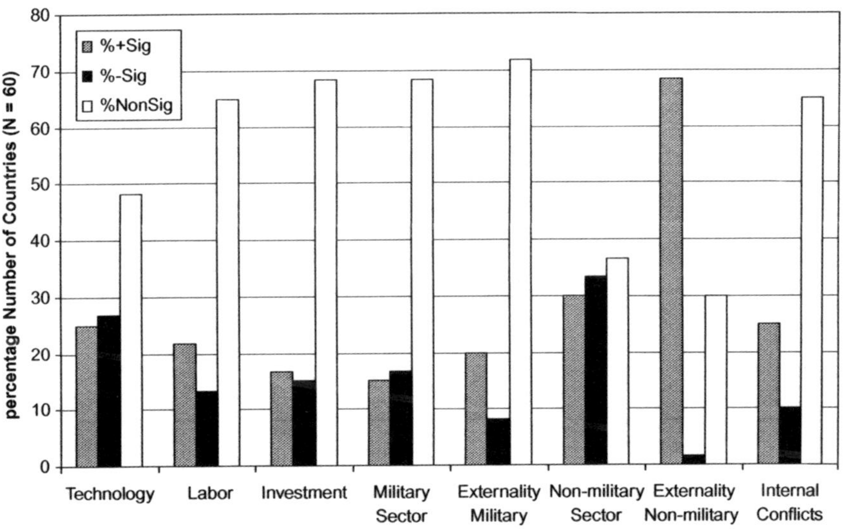

Fig. 7.6. The Impact of Internal Conflicts, Economic, Military, and Non-Military Factors and Their Externalities on Economic Growth.

- The EEDS have a positive and significant impact in twelve countries (20 percent), while they have a negative and significant impact in five countries (8.33 percent).
- Technological progress and productivity of the non-military sectors have a positive impact in eighteen countries (30 percent), while they show a negative and significant impact in twenty countries (33.33 percent).
- The externality effects of non-military government spending show an overwhelming positive and significant impact in forty-one countries (68.33 percent), while they hinder EG in a single country (1.67 percent).

7.13.7. The Production Function with External Conflicts

As indicated in Table 7.1 and displayed in Fig. 7.7, *external conflicts* have a positive and significant impact on EG in only six countries (10 percent), while only two countries (3.33 percent) show a negative and significant impact on EG. The estimates of the PF with internal conflicts are as follows:

- Thirteen of sixty countries (21.67 percent) show a positive and significant impact of technological progress on EG, while twenty-four of sixty countries (40 percent) show a negative and significant impact on EG.

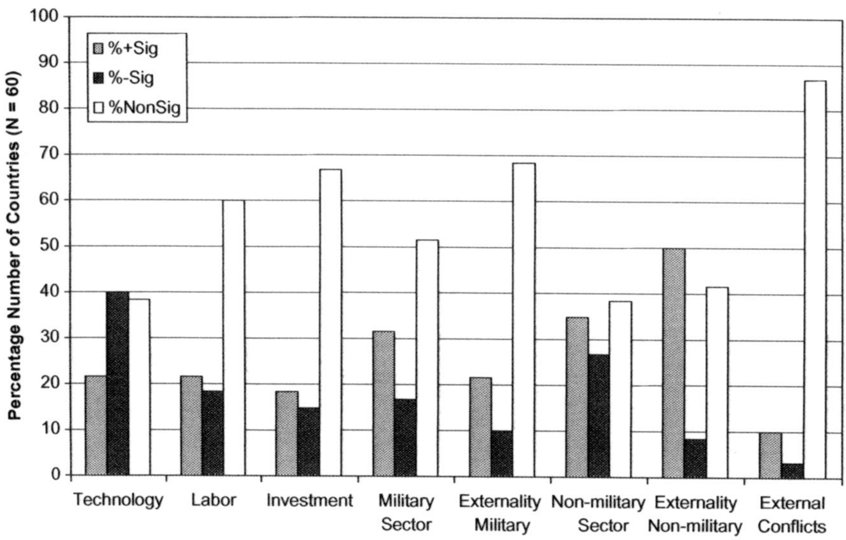

Fig. 7.7. The Impact of External Conflicts, Economic, Military, and Non-Military Factors and Their Externalities on Economic Growth.

- Changes in labor growth show a positive and significant impact in thirteen countries (21.67 percent), while they show a negative and significant impact in eleven countries (18.33 percent).
- Investment has a positive and significant impact on EG in eleven countries (18.33 percent), while it has a negative and significant impact on EG in nine countries (15 percent).
- The combined effects of technological progress and productivity of the military sector have a positive and significant impact on EG in nineteen countries (31.67 percent), while it hampers EG in ten countries (16.67 percent).
- The EEDS show a positive and significant impact on EG in thirteen countries (21.67 percent), while they show a negative and significant impact on EG in six countries (10 percent).
- The combined effects of technological progress and productivity of the non-military sectors show a positive and significant impact in twenty-one countries (35 percent), while sixteen countries (26.67 percent) incur a negative and significant impact on EG.
- The externality effects of non-military government spending show an overwhelming positive and significant impact in thirty countries (50 percent) on EG, while only five countries (8.33 percent) incur a negative and significant impact on EG.

7.13.8. The Production Function with Total Conflicts

As indicated in Table 7.1 and displayed in Fig. 7.8, *total conflicts* have a positive and significant impact in nineteen countries (31.67 percent), while they have a negative and significant impact in seven countries (56.67 percent). The estimates of the PF with total conflicts are as follows:

- Technological progress has a positive and significant impact on EG in seventeen of sixty countries (28 percent), while it significantly hinders EG in seventeen of sixty countries (28 percent).
- Changes in labor growth have a positive and significant impact on EG in eleven countries (18.33 percent), while they significantly hinder EG in eleven countries (18.33 percent).
- Investment has a positive and significant impact on EG in eleven countries (18.33 percent), while it has a negative and significant impact in eleven countries (13.33 percent).

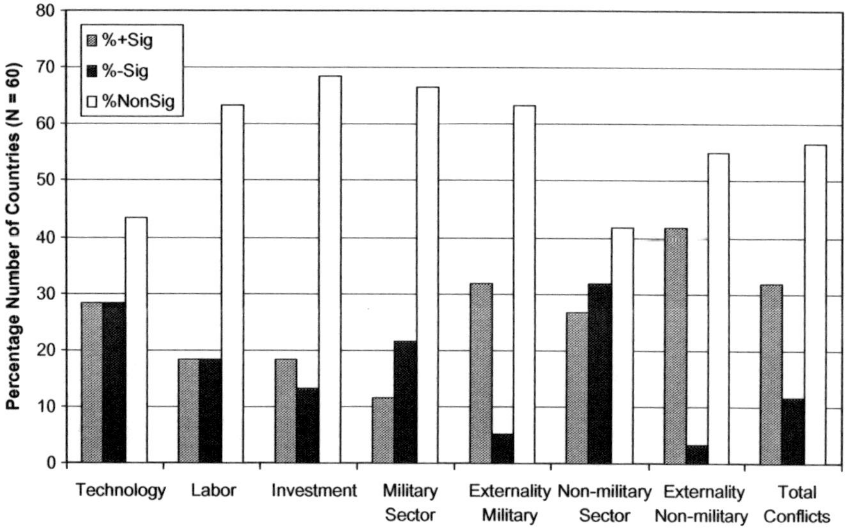

Fig. 7.8. The Impact of Total Conflicts, Economic, Military, and Non-Military Factors and Their Externalities on Economic Growth.

- The combined effects of technological progress and productivity of the military sectors have a positive and significant impact on EG in seven countries (11.67 percent), while they have a negative impact in thirteen countries (21.67 percent).
- The EEDS have a positive and significant impact in nineteen countries (31.67 percent), while they have a negative impact in three countries (5 percent).
- The combined effects of technological progress and productivity of the non-military sectors have a positive and significant impact in sixteen countries (26.67 percent), while they show a negative and significant impact in nineteen countries (31.67 percent).
- The externality effects of non-military government spending show a positive and significant impact in twenty-five countries (41.67 percent), while they significantly hinder EG in two countries (3.33 percent).

7.14. RESULTS OF THE CROSS-NATIONAL TIME SERIES ANALYSIS

A summary of the CNTS empirical results of Appendix B in Table 7.2, demonstrating the direction and significance of the relationships between

Table 7.2. Summary of the Cross-National Time Series of the Production Function with a Single Political or Conflict Variable.

	Labor	Investment	Military	Military Externalities	Non-Military	Non-Military Externalities
All states	(+)*	(+)	(+)*	(+)*	(−)*	(−)
Non-oil	(+)*	(−)	(−)*	(+)*	(−)	(−)
Oil	(+)*	(−)*	(−)*	(+)*	(−)*	(−)*
Arabia	(+)*	(−)*	(+)*	(+)*	(+)	(−)
ME	(+)*	(−)	(+)	(+)*	(+)	(−)
Latinos	(+)*	(+)	(+)*	(+)*	(+)	(+)
Africa	(+)*	(+)	(+)*	(+)*	(−)*	(+)
Asia	(NA)	(NA)	(NA)	(NA)	(NA)	(NA)
Caribbean	(NA)	(NA)	(NA)	(NA)	(NA)	(NA)
External conflict	(−)	(−)	(+)	(+)	(−)*	
	(+)	(+)	(NA)	(NA)		
All states	(+)*	(+)	(+)*	(+)*	(−)*	(−)
Non-oil	(+)*	(−)	(−)*	(+)*	(+)	(−)
Oil	(+)*	(−)*	(−)*	(+)*	(−)*	(−)
Arabia	(+)*	(−)*	(+)*	(+)*	(+)	(−)
ME	(+)*	(−)	(+)	(+)*	(+)	(−)
Latinos	(+)*	(+)	(+)	(+)*	(+)	(−)
Africa	(+)*	(+)	(+)	(+)*	(−)*	(−)
Asia	(+)*	(−)	(−)*	(+)*	(−)	(−)
Caribbean	(+)*	(−)*	(−)*	(+)*	(+)	(−)
Internal conflict	(−)*	(−)*	(+)	(−)	(−)*	
	(−)	(+)	(+)	(−)		
All states	(+)*	(+)	(+)*	(+)*	(−)*	(−)
Non-oil	(+)*	(−)	(−)*	(+)*	(+)	(+)
Oil	(+)	(−)*	(−)*	(+)*	(−)*	(−)*
Arabia	(+)*	(−)*	(+)	(+)*	(+)	(−)
ME	(+)*	(−)	(+)	(+)*	(+)	(−)
Latinos	(+)*	(+)	(+)*	(+)*	(+)	(+)
Africa	(+)*	(+)	(+)*	(+)*	(−)*	(+)
Asia	(+)*	(+)	(+)	(+)	(−)	(+)
Caribbean	(+)*	(−)	(+)*	(+)*	(+)	(+)
Total conflict	(−)*	(−)*	(+)	(−)	(−)	
	(−)	(+)*	(+)	(+)		
All states	(+)*	(+)	(+)*	(+)*	(−)*	(−)
Non-oil	(+)*	(−)	(−)*	(+)*	(+)	(−)
Oil	(+)*	(−)*	(−)*	(+)*	(−)*	(−)*
Arabia	(+)*	(−)*	(+)*	(+)*	(+)	(−)
ME	(+)*	(−)	(−)	(+)*	(+)	(−)
Latinos	(+)	(+)	(+)*	(+)*	(+)	(+)
Africa	(+)*	(+)	(+)	(+)	(−)*	(+)
Asia	(+)*	(−)*	(+)*	(+)*	(−)	(−)*
Caribbean	(+)*	(−)*	(+)*	(+)*	(+)	(+)
Political freedom	(+)	(−)	(+)	(−)	(−)	
	(+)	(−)	(−)	(−)		

***Table** 7.2.* (*Continued*)

	Labor	Investment	Military	Military Externalities	Non-Military	Non-Military Externalities
All states	(+)*	(+)	(+)*	(+)*	(−)*	(−)
Non-oil	(+)*	(−)	(−)*	(+)*	(+)	(−)
Oil	(+)*	(−)	(−)*	(+)*	(−)*	(−)
Arabia	(+)*	(−)	(+)*	(+)*	(+)	(−)
ME	(+)*	(−)	(+)	(+)*	(+)	(−)
Latinos	(+)*	(+)	(+)*	(+)*	(+)	(+)
Africa	(+)*	(+)	(+)*	(+)	(−)*	(+)
Asia	(+)*	(−)	(+)	(+)*	(−)	(−)
Caribbean	(+)*	(−)	(+)*	(+)*	(+)	(+)
Institutional freedom	(+)*	(+)	(−)	(+)	(+)	
	(+)	(+)	(−)	(−)		
All states	(+)*	(+)	(+)*	(+)*	()	()
Non-oil	(+)*	(−)	(−)*	(+)*	()	()
Oil	(+)*	(−)*	(−)*	(+)*	()	()
Arabia	(+)*	(−)*	(+)*	(+)*	()	()
ME	(+)*	(−)*	(+)	(+)*	()	()
Latinos	(+)*	(+)	(+)*	(+)*	()	()
Africa	(+)*	(+)	(+)*	(+)*	()	()
Asia	(+)*	(−)	(+)	(+)	()	()
Caribbean	(+)*	(−)*	(+)	(+)*	()	()
Type	(−)	(−)	(−)	(−)	(−)	
	(−)	(−)	(−)	(−)		
All states	(+)	(+)	(+)*	(+)*	(−)*	(−)
Non-oil	(+)*	(−)	(−)*	(+)*	(+)	(−)
Oil	(+)*	(−)*	(−)*	(+)*	(−)*	(−)
Arabia	(+)*	(−)*	(+)*	(+)*	(+)	(−)
ME	(+)*	(−)	(+)*	(+)*	(+)	(−)
Latinos	(+)	(+)	(+)*	(+)*	(+)	(+)
Africa	(+)*	(+)	(+)*	(+)*	(−)*	(+)
Asia	(+)*	(−)	(+)	(+)*	(−)	(−)
Caribbean	(+)*	(−)*	(+)*	(+)*	(+)	(+)
Stability	(−)	(+)	(−)	(+)	(+)	
	(−)	(+)	(+)	(−)		
All states	(+)*	(+)	(+)*	(+)*	(−)*	(−)
Non-oil	(+)*	(−)	(−)*	(+)*	(+)	(−)
Oil	(+)*	(−)*	(−)*	(+)*	(−)*	(−)*
Arabia	(+)*	(−)*	(+)*	(+)*	(+)	(−)*
ME	(+*)	(−)	(+)	(+)*	(+)	(−)*
Latinos	(+)*	(+)	(+)*	(+)*	(+)	(+)
Africa	(+)*	(+)	(+)*	(+)*	(−)*	(+)
Asia	(+)*	(−)*	(+)	(+)*	(−)	(−)*
Caribbean	(+)*	(−)*	(+)*	(+)*	(−)	(+)
Ideology	(−)	(−)	(−)	(−)	(−)	
	(−)	(−)	(−)	(−)		

* Significant at 0.05 level.

economic and military variables as well as EG under the influence of a single political variable or conflict variable for nine regions including the full model, ME non-oil-producing countries, ME oil-producing countries, the Arab world, the ME, Latin America, Africa, Asia, the Caribbean region, and all states (full model), is reported.

Also, summary of the CNTS empirical results of Appendix C in Table 7.3, demonstrating the direction and significance of the relationships between economic and military variables as well as EG while controlling for internal and external conflicts under the influence of a single political variable for six regions, the ME, Latin America, Asia, Africa, the Caribbean region, and all states (full model), is reported.

7.14.1. The CNTS Analysis with a Single Political Variable

Below are the results of the CNTS analysis organized regionally and showing the influence of political variables on EG as given in Table 7.2.

7.14.1.1. All States

In reference to Table 7.2, the *political freedom* full model (entire sample) exerts an insignificant positive impact on EG. The estimates of the PF with political freedom are as follows:

- Changes in labor growth have a positive and significant impact on EG.
- The combined effects of technological progress and productivity of the military sectors show a positive and significant impact on EG.
- The EEDS have a positive and significant impact on EG.
- The combined effects of technological progress and productivity of the non-military sectors have a negative and significant impact on EG.

7.14.1.1.1. Institutional Freedom. As indicated in Table 7.2, *institutional freedom* exerts an insignificant positive impact on EG. The estimates of the PF with institutional freedom are as follows:

- Changes in labor growth have a positive and significant impact on EG.
- The combined effects of technological progress and productivity of the military sectors show a positive and significant impact on EG.
- The EEDS have a positive and significant impact on EG.
- The combined effects of technological progress and productivity of the non-military sectors have a negative and significant impact on EG.

Table 7.3. Summary of the CNTS Results with External and Internal Conflicts as Control Variables.

	Political Freedom	Institutional Freedom	Type	Stability	Ideology
All states					
Labor	(+)*	(+)*	(+)*	(+)*	(+)*
Investment	(+)	(+)	(+)	(+)	(+)
Military sector	(+)*	(+)*	(+)*	(+)*	(+)*
Military externalities	(+)*	(+)*	(+)*	(+)*	(−)*
Non-military sector	(−)*	(−)*	(−)*	(−)*	(−)*
Non-military externalities	(−)	(−)	(−)	(−)	(−)
Political variable	(+)	(+)	(−)	(−)	(−)
External conflict	(−)	(−)	(−)	(−)	(−)
Internal conflict	(−)*	(−)*	(−)*	(−)*	(−)*
Africa					
Labor	(+)*	(+)*	(+)*	(+)*	(+)*
Investment	(+)	(+)	(+)	(+)	(+)
Military sector	(+)*	(+)*	(+)*	(+)*	(+)*
Military externalities	(+)*	(+)*	(+)*	(+)*	(+)*
Non-military sector	(+)*	(+)*	(+)*	(+)*	(+)*
Non-military externalities	(+)	(+)	(+)	(+)	(+)
Political variable	(−)	(+)	(−)	(+)	(−)
External conflict	(−)	(−)	(+)	(−)	(−)
Internal conflict	(−)	(+)	(−)	(+)	(−)
Asia					
Labor	(+)*	(+)*	(+)*	(+)*	(+)*
Investment	(−)*	(−)*	(−)*	(−)*	(−)*
Military sector	(+)	(+)	(+)	(+)	(+)
Military externalities	(+)*	(+)*	(+)*	(+)*	(+)*
Non-military sector	(−)	(−)	(−)	(−)	(−)
Non-military externalities	(−)*	(−)*	(−)*	(−)*	(−)*
Political variable	(−)	(+)	(−)	(+)	(−)
External conflict	(−)	(−)	(−)	(−)	(−)
Internal conflict	(−)	(+)	(−)	(+)	(−)
ME					
Labor	(+)*	(+)*	(+)*	(+)*	(+)*
Investment	(−)	(−)	(−)	(−)	(−)
Military sector	(−)	(+)	(+)	(+)	(+)
Military externalities	(+)*	(+)*	(+)*	(+)*	(+)*
Non-military sector	(+)	(+)	(+)	(+)	(+)
Non-military externalities	(−)	(−)	(−)	(−)	(−)
Political variable	(−)	(+)	(−)	(+)	(−)
External conflict	(−)*	(−)*	(−)*	(−)*	(−)*
Internal conflict	(−)*	(−)*	(−)*	(−)*	(−)*
Latin America					
Labor	(+)*	(+)*	(+)*	(+)*	(+)*
Investment	(+)*	(+)*	(+)*	(+)*	(+)*
Military sector	(+)	(+)	(+)	(+)	(+)

Table 7.3. *(Continued)*

	Political Freedom	Institutional Freedom	Type	Stability	Ideology
Military externalities	(+)*	(+)*	(+)*	(+)*	(+)*
Non-military sector	(+)	(+)	(+)	(+)	(+)
Non-military externalities	(+)	(+)	(+)	(+)	(+)
Political variable	(+)	(+)	(−)	(−)	(−)
External conflict	(−)	(−)	(−)	(−)	(−)
Internal conflict	(−)	(−)	(−)	(−)	(−)
The Caribbean					
Labor	(+)*	(+)*	(+)*	(+)*	(+)*
Investment	(−)*	(−)*	(−)*	(−)*	(−)*
Military sector	(−)*	(−)*	(−)*	(−)*	(−)*
Military externalities	(+)*	(+)*	(+)*	(+)*	(+)*
Non-military sector	(+)	(+)	(+)	(+)	(+)
Non-military externalities	(+)*	(+)*	(+)*	(+)*	(+)*
Political variable	(−)	(−)	(−)	(−)	(−)
External conflict	(−)	(−)	(−)	(−)	(−)
Internal conflict	(−)	(−)	(−)	(−)	(−)

* Significant at 0.05 level.

7.14.1.1.2. Regime Type. As indicated in Table 7.2, *regime type* exerts an insignificant negative impact on EG. The estimates of the PF with regime type are as follows:

- Changes in labor growth have a positive and significant impact on EG.
- The combined effects of technological progress and productivity of the military sectors show a positive and significant impact on EG.
- The EEDS have a positive and significant impact on EG.

7.14.1.1.3. Regime Stability. As indicated in Table 7.2, *regime stability* exerts a insignificant negative impact on EG. The estimates of the PF with regime stability are as follows:

- The combined effects of technological progress and productivity of the military sectors show a positive and significant impact on EG.
- The EEDS have a positive and significant impact on EG.
- The combined effects of technological progress and productivity of the non-military sectors have a negative and significant impact on EG.

7.14.1.1.4. Regime Ideological Base. As indicated in Table 7.2, *regime ideological base* exerts an insignificant negative impact on EG. The estimates of the PF with ideological base are as follows:

- Changes in labor growth have a positive and significant impact on EG.
- The combined effects of technological progress and productivity of the military sectors show a positive and significant impact on EG.
- The EEDS have a positive and significant impact on EG.
- The combined effects of technological progress and productivity of the non-military sectors have a negative and significant impact on EG.

7.14.1.1.5. Internal Conflicts. As indicated in Table 7.2, *internal conflicts* show a negative and significant impact on EG. The estimates of the PF with internal conflicts are as follows:

- Changes in labor growth have a positive and significant impact on EG.
- The combined effects of technological progress and productivity of the military sectors show a positive and significant impact on EG.
- The EEDS have a positive and significant impact on EG.
- The combined effects of technological progress and productivity of the non-military sectors have a negative and significant impact on EG.

7.14.1.1.6. External Conflicts. As indicated in Table 7.2, *external conflicts* have insignificant negative impact on EG. The estimates of the PF with external conflicts are as follows:

- Changes in labor growth have a positive and significant impact on EG.
- The combined effects of technological progress and productivity of the military sectors show a positive and significant impact on EG.
- The EEDS have a positive and significant impact on EG.
- The combined effects of technological progress and productivity of the non-military sectors have a negative and significant impact on EG.

7.14.1.1.7. Total Conflicts. As indicated in Table 7.2, *total conflicts* have a negative and significant impact on EG. The estimates of the PF with total conflicts are as follows:

- Changes in labor growth have a positive and significant impact on EG.
- The combined effects of technological progress and productivity of the military sectors show a positive and significant impact on EG.
- The EEDS have a positive and significant impact on EG.

- The combined effects of technological progress and productivity of the non-military sectors have a negative and significant impact on EG.

7.14.1.2. ME Non-Oil-Producing Countries

In reference to Table 7.2, *political freedom* shows an insignificant positive impact on EG. The estimates of the PF with political freedom are as follows:

- Changes in labor growth have a positive and significant impact on EG.
- The combined effects of technological progress and productivity of the military sectors show a positive and significant impact on EG.
- The EEDS have a positive and significant impact on EG.

Institutional freedom shows an insignificant positive impact on EG. The estimates of the PF with institutional freedom are as follows:

- Changes in labor growth have a positive and significant impact on EG.
- The combined effects of technological progress and productivity of the military sectors show a positive and significant impact on EG.
- The EEDS have a positive and significant impact on EG.

Regime type shows an insignificant positive impact on EG. The estimates of the PF with regime type are as follows:

- Changes in labor growth have a positive and significant impact on EG.
- The combined effects of technological progress and productivity of the military sectors show a positive and significant impact on EG.
- The EEDS have a positive and significant impact on EG.

Regime stability shows an insignificant positive impact on EG. The estimates of the PF with regime type are as follows:

- Changes in labor growth have a positive and significant impact on EG.
- The combined effects of technological progress and productivity of the military sectors show a positive and significant impact on EG.
- The EEDS have a positive and significant impact on EG.

Ideological base shows an insignificant negative impact on EG. The estimates of the PF with ideological base are as follows:

- Changes in labor growth have a positive and significant impact on EG.
- The combined effects of technological progress and productivity of the military sectors show a positive and significant impact on EG.
- The EEDS have a positive and significant impact on EG.

Internal conflicts show a negative and significant impact on EG. The estimates of the PF with internal conflicts are as follows:

- Changes in labor growth have a positive and significant impact on EG.
- The combined effects of technological progress and productivity of the military sectors show a positive and significant impact on EG.
- The EEDS have a positive and significant impact on EG.
- The combined effects of technological progress and productivity of the non-military sectors have a negative and significant impact on EG.

External conflicts show an insignificant negative impact on EG. The estimates of the PF with external conflicts are as follows:

- Changes in labor growth have a positive and significant impact on EG.
- The combined effects of technological progress and productivity of the military sectors show a positive and significant impact on EG.
- The EEDS have a positive and significant impact on EG.

Total conflicts show a negative and significant impact on EG. The estimates of the PF with total conflicts are as follows:

- Changes in labor growth have a positive and significant impact on EG.
- The combined effects of technological progress and productivity of the military sectors show a positive and significant impact on EG.
- The EEDS have a positive and significant impact on EG.
- The combined effects of technological progress and productivity of the non-military sectors have a positive and significant impact on EG.

7.14.1.3. ME Oil-Producing Countries

In reference to Table 7.2, *political freedom* shows an insignificant positive impact on EG. The estimates of the PF with political freedom are as follows:

- Changes in labor growth have a positive and significant impact on EG.
- Investment shows a negative and significant impact on EG.
- The combined effects of technological progress and productivity of the military sectors show a negative and significant impact on EG.
- The EEDS have a positive and significant impact on EG.
- The combined effects of technological progress and productivity of the non-military sectors have a negative and significant impact on EG.
- The externality effects of non-military government spending have a negative and significant impact on EG.

Institutional freedom shows an insignificant positive impact on EG. The estimates of the PF with institutional freedom are as follows:

- Changes in labor growth have a positive and significant impact on EG.
- Investment shows a negative and significant impact on EG.
- The combined effects of technological progress and productivity of the military sectors show a negative and significant impact on EG.
- The EEDS have a positive and significant impact on EG.
- The combined effects of technological progress and productivity of the non-military sectors have a negative and significant impact on EG.
- The externality effects of non-military government spending have a negative and significant impact on EG.

Regime type shows an insignificant negative impact on EG. The estimates of the PF with regime type are as follows:

- Changes in labor growth have a positive and significant impact on EG.
- Investment shows a negative and significant impact on EG.
- The combined effects of technological progress and productivity of the military sectors show a negative and significant impact on EG.
- The EEDS have a positive and significant impact on EG.

Regime stability shows an insignificant positive impact on EG. The estimates of the PF with political stability are as follows:

- Changes in labor growth have a positive and significant impact on EG.
- Investment shows a negative and significant impact on EG.
- The combined effects of technological progress and productivity of the military sectors show a negative and significant impact on EG.
- The EEDS have a negative and significant impact on EG.

Ideological base shows an insignificant negative impact on EG. The estimates of the PF with ideological base are as follows:

- Changes in labor growth have a positive and significant impact on EG.
- Investment shows a negative and significant impact on EG.
- The combined effects of technological progress and productivity of the military sectors show a negative and significant impact on EG.
- The EEDS have a positive and significant impact on EG.
- The combined effects of technological progress and productivity of the non-military sectors have a negative and significant impact on EG.
- The externality effects of non-military government spending have a negative and significant impact on EG.

Internal conflicts show an insignificant positive impact on EG. The estimates of the PF with internal conflicts are as follows:

- Changes in labor growth have a positive and significant impact on EG.
- Investment shows a negative and significant impact on EG.
- The combined effects of technological progress and productivity of the military sectors show a negative and significant impact on EG.
- The EEDS have a positive and significant impact on EG.
- The combined effects of technological progress and productivity of the non-military sectors have a negative and significant impact on EG.

External conflicts show an insignificant positive impact on EG. The estimates of the PF with external conflicts are as follows:

- Changes in labor growth have a positive and significant impact on EG.
- Investment shows a negative and significant impact on EG.
- The combined effects of technological progress and productivity of the military sectors show a negative and significant impact on EG.
- The EEDS have a positive and significant impact on EG.
- The combined effects of technological progress and productivity of the non-military sectors have a negative and significant impact on EG.
- The externality effects of non-military government spending have a negative and significant impact on EG.

Total conflicts show an insignificant positive impact on EG. The estimates of the PF with total conflicts are as follows:

- Investment shows a negative and significant impact on EG.
- The combined effects of technological progress and productivity of the military sectors show a negative and significant impact on EG.
- The EEDS have a positive and significant impact on EG.
- The combined effects of technological progress and productivity of the non-military sectors have a negative and significant impact on EG.
- The externality effects of non-military government spending have a negative and significant impact on EG.

7.14.1.4. Arab World

In reference to Table 7.2, *political freedom* shows an insignificant negative impact on EG. The estimates of the PF with political freedom are as follows:

- Changes in labor growth have a positive and significant impact on EG.
- Investment shows a negative and significant impact on EG.

- The combined effects of technological progress and productivity of the military sectors show a positive and significant impact on EG.
- The EEDS have a positive and significant impact on EG.
- The combined effects of technological progress and productivity of the non-military sectors have a negative and significant impact on EG.

Institutional freedom shows an insignificant positive impact on EG. The estimates of the PF with institutional freedom are as follows:

- Changes in labor growth have a positive and significant impact on EG.
- The combined effects of technological progress and productivity of the military sectors show a positive and significant impact on EG.
- The EEDS have a positive and significant impact on EG.

Regime type shows an insignificant negative impact on EG. The estimates of the PF with regime type are as follows:

- Changes in labor growth have a positive and significant impact on EG.
- Investment shows a negative and significant impact on EG.
- The combined effects of technological progress and productivity of the military sectors show a positive and significant impact on EG.
- The EEDS have a positive and significant impact on EG.

Regime stability shows an insignificant positive impact on EG. The estimates of the PF with political stability are as follows:

- Changes in labor growth have a positive and significant impact on EG.
- Investment shows a negative and significant impact on EG.
- The combined effects of technological progress and productivity of the military sectors show a positive and significant impact on EG.
- The EEDS have a positive and significant impact on EG.

Ideological base shows an insignificant negative impact on EG. The estimates of the PF with ideological base are as follows:

- Changes in labor growth have a positive and significant impact on EG.
- Investment shows a negative and significant impact on EG.
- The combined effects of technological progress and productivity of the military sectors show a positive and significant impact on EG.
- The EEDS have a positive and significant impact on EG.
- The externality effects of non-military government spending have a negative and significant impact on EG.

Internal conflicts show an insignificant negative impact on EG. The estimates of the PF with internal conflicts are as follows:

- Changes in labor growth have a positive and significant impact on EG.
- Investment shows a negative and significant impact on EG.
- The combined effects of technological progress and productivity of the military sectors show a positive and significant impact on EG.
- The EEDS have a positive and significant impact on EG.

External conflicts show an insignificant positive impact on EG. The estimates of the PF with external conflicts are as follows:

- Changes in labor growth have a positive and significant impact on EG.
- Investment shows a negative and significant impact on EG.
- The combined effects of technological progress and productivity of the military sectors show a positive and significant impact on EG.

Total conflicts show an insignificant negative impact on EG. The estimates of the PF with total conflicts are as follows:

- Changes in labor growth have a positive and significant impact on EG.
- Investment shows a negative and significant impact on EG.
- The EEDS have a positive and significant impact on EG.

7.14.1.5. The Middle East

In reference to Table 7.2, *political freedom* shows an insignificant negative impact on EG. The estimates of the PF with political freedom are as follows:

- Changes in labor growth have a positive and significant impact on EG.
- The EEDS have a positive and significant impact on EG.

Institutional freedom shows an insignificant positive impact on EG. The estimates of the PF with total conflicts are as follows:

- Changes in labor growth have a positive and significant impact on EG.
- The EEDS have a positive and significant impact on EG.

Regime type shows an insignificant negative impact on EG. The estimates of the PF with regime type are as follows:

- Changes in labor growth have a positive and significant impact on EG.
- Investment shows a negative and significant impact on EG.
- The EEDS have a positive and significant impact on EG.

Regime stability shows an insignificant positive impact on EG. The estimates of the PF with political stability are as follows:

- Changes in labor growth have a positive and significant impact on EG.
- The combined effects of technological progress and productivity of the military sectors show a positive and significant impact on EG.
- The EEDS have a positive and significant impact on EG.

Ideological base shows an insignificant negative impact on EG. The estimates of the PF with ideological base are as follows:

- Changes in labor growth have a positive and significant impact on EG.
- The externality effects of non-military government spending have a negative and significant impact on EG.

Internal conflicts show a negative and significant impact on EG. The estimates of the PF with internal conflicts are as follows:

- Changes in labor growth have a positive and significant impact on EG.
- The EEDS have a positive and significant impact on EG.

External conflicts show a negative and significant impact on EG. The estimates of the PF with external conflicts are as follows:

- Changes in labor growth have a positive and significant impact on EG.
- The EEDS have a positive and significant impact on EG.

Total conflicts show an insignificant negative impact on EG. The estimates of the PF with total conflicts are as follows:

- Changes in labor growth have a positive and significant impact on EG.
- The EEDS have a positive and significant impact on EG.

7.14.1.6. Latin America

In reference to Table 7.2, *political freedom* shows positive impact on EG. The estimates of the PF with political freedom are as follows:

- The combined effects of technological progress and productivity of the military sectors show a positive and significant impact on EG.
- The EEDS have a positive and significant impact on EG.

Institutional freedom shows an insignificant positive impact on EG. The estimates of the PF with institutional freedom are as follows:

- Changes in labor growth have a positive and significant impact on EG.

- The combined effects of technological progress and productivity of the military sectors show a positive and significant impact on EG.
- The EEDS have a positive and significant impact on EG.

Regime type shows an insignificant negative impact on EG. The estimates of the PF with regime type are as follows:

- Changes in labor growth have a positive and significant impact on EG.
- The combined effects of technological progress and productivity of the military sector show a positive and significant impact on EG.
- The EEDS have a positive and significant impact on EG.

Regime stability shows a positive impact on EG. The estimates of the PF with political stability are as follows:

- The combined effects of technological progress and productivity of the military sector show a positive and significant impact on EG.
- The EEDS have a positive and significant impact on EG.

Ideological base shows an insignificant negative impact on EG. The estimates of the PF with ideological base are as follows:

- Changes in labor growth have a positive and significant impact on EG.
- The combined effects of technological progress and productivity of the military sector show a positive and significant impact on EG.
- The externality effects of non-military government spending have a negative and significant impact on EG.

Internal conflicts show a negative and significant impact on EG. The estimates of the PF with internal conflicts are as follows:

- Changes in labor growth have a positive and significant impact on EG.
- The EEDS have a positive and significant impact on EG.

External conflicts show an insignificant negative impact on EG. The estimates of the PF with external conflicts are as follows:

- Changes in labor growth have a positive and significant impact on EG.
- The combined effects of technological progress and productivity of the military sector show a positive and significant impact on EG.
- The EEDS have a positive and significant impact on EG.

Total conflicts show an insignificant negative impact on EG. The estimates of the PF with total conflicts are as follows:

- Changes in labor growth have a positive and significant impact on EG.

- The combined effects of technological progress and productivity of the military sectors show a positive and significant impact on EG.
- The EEDS have a positive and significant impact on EG.

7.14.1.7. Africa

In reference to Table 7.2, *political freedom* shows an insignificant negative impact on EG. The estimates of the PF with political freedom are as follows:

- Changes in labor growth have a positive and significant impact on EG.
- The combined effects of technological progress and productivity of the military sectors show a positive and significant impact on EG.
- The externality effects of non-military spending have a negative and significant impact on EG.

Institutional freedom shows an insignificant positive impact on EG. The estimates of the PF with institutional freedom are as follows:

- Changes in labor growth have a positive and significant impact on EG.
- The combined effects of technological progress and productivity of the military sector show a positive and significant impact on EG.
- The externality effects of non-military spending have a positive and significant impact on EG.

Regime type shows an insignificant negative impact on EG. The estimates of the PF with regime type are as follows:

- Changes in labor growth have a positive and significant impact on EG.
- The combined effects of technological progress and productivity of the military sectors show a positive and significant impact on EG.
- The EEDS have a positive and significant impact on EG.

Regime stability shows an insignificant positive impact on EG. The estimates of the PF with regime stability are as follows:

- The combined effects of technological progress and productivity of the military sector show a positive and significant impact on EG.
- The combined effects of technological progress and productivity of the military sectors show a positive and significant impact on EG.
- The EEDS have a positive and significant impact on EG.
- The combined effects of technological progress and productivity of the non-military sectors have a positive and significant impact on EG.

Ideological base shows an insignificant negative impact on EG. The estimates of the PF with ideological base are as follows:

- Changes in labor growth have a positive and significant impact on EG.
- The combined effects of technological progress and productivity of the military sector shows a positive and significant impact on EG.
- The EEDS have a positive and significant impact on EG.
- The combined effects of technological progress and productivity of the non-military sectors have a positive and significant impact on EG.
- The externality effects of non-military spending have a negative and significant impact on EG.

Internal conflicts show a positive and significant impact on EG. The estimates of the PF with internal conflicts are as follows:

- Changes in labor growth have a positive and significant impact on EG.
- The EEDS have a positive and significant impact on EG.
- The combined effects of technological progress and productivity of the non-military sectors have a negative and significant impact on EG.

There are no results for *external conflicts*.

Total conflicts show a positive and significant impact on EG. The estimates of the PF with total conflicts are as follows:

- Changes in labor growth have a positive and significant impact on EG.
- The combined effects of technological progress and productivity of the military sectors show a positive and significant impact on EG.
- The EEDS have a positive and significant impact on EG.
- The combined effects of technological progress and productivity of the non-military sectors have a negative and significant impact on EG.

7.14.1.8. Asia

In reference to Table 7.2, *political freedom* shows an insignificant negative impact on EG. The estimates of the PF with political freedom are as follows:

- Changes in labor growth have a positive and significant impact on EG.
- Investment has a negative and significant impact on EG.
- The combined effects of technological progress and productivity of the military sector show a positive and significant impact on EG.
- The EEDS have a positive and significant impact on EG.
- The combined effects of technological progress and productivity of the non-military sectors have a negative and significant impact on EG.

Institutional freedom shows an insignificant negative impact on EG. The estimates of the PF with institutional freedom are as follows:

- Changes in labor growth have a positive and significant impact on EG.
- The combined effects of technological progress and productivity of the military sectors have a positive and significant impact on EG.

Regime type shows an insignificant negative impact on EG. Labor growth is the only significant variable among the estimates of the PF. Changes in labor growth have a positive and significant impact on EG.

Regime stability shows an insignificant positive impact on EG. The estimates of the PF with regime stability are as follows:

- The combined effects of technological progress and productivity of the military sectors show a positive and significant impact on EG.
- The EEDS have a positive and significant impact on EG.

Ideological base shows an insignificant negative impact on EG. The estimates of the PF with ideological base are as follows:

- Changes in labor growth have a positive and significant impact on EG.
- Investment has a negative and significant impact on EG.
- The combined effects of technological progress and productivity of the military sectors show a positive and significant impact on EG.

Internal conflicts show a positive and significant impact on EG. The estimates of the PF with internal conflicts are as follows:

- Changes in labor growth have a positive and significant impact on EG.
- The combined effects of technological progress and productivity of the military sectors show a negative and significant impact on EG.
- The EEDS have a positive and significant impact on EG.

There are no results for *external conflicts*.

Total conflicts show an insignificant positive impact on EG. Labor growth is the only significant variable among the estimates of the PF with total conflicts. Changes in labor growth have a positive and significant impact on EG.

7.14.1.9. The Caribbean Region

In reference to Table 7.2, *political freedom* shows an insignificant negative impact on EG. The estimates of the PF with political freedom are as follows:

- Changes in labor growth have a positive and significant impact on EG.
- Investment has a negative and significant impact on EG.

- The combined effects of technological progress and productivity of the military sectors show a positive and significant impact on EG.
- The EEDS have a positive and significant impact on EG.

Institutional freedom shows an insignificant negative impact on EG. The estimates of the PF with institutional freedom are as follows:

- Changes in labor growth have a positive and significant impact on EG.
- The combined effects of technological progress and productivity of the military sectors have a positive and significant impact on EG.
- The EEDS have a positive and significant impact on EG.

Regime type shows an insignificant negative impact on EG. The estimates of the PF with regime type are as follows:

- Changes in labor growth have a positive and significant impact on EG.
- The combined effects of technological progress and productivity of the military sectors have a negative and significant impact on EG.
- The EEDS have a positive and significant impact on EG.

Regime stability shows an insignificant negative impact on EG. The estimates of the PF with regime stability are as follows:

- Changes in labor growth have a positive and significant impact on EG.
- Investment has a negative and significant impact on EG.
- The combined effects of technological progress and productivity of the military sector show a positive and significant impact on EG.
- The EEDS have a positive and significant impact on EG.

Ideological base shows an insignificant negative impact on EG. The estimates of the PF with ideological base are as follows:

- Changes in labor growth have a positive and significant impact on EG.
- Investment has a negative and significant impact on EG.
- The combined effects of technological progress and productivity of the military sectors show a positive and significant impact on EG.
- The EEDS have a positive and significant impact on EG.

Internal conflicts show an insignificant negative impact on EG. The estimates of the PF with internal conflicts are as follows:

- Changes in labor growth have a positive and significant impact on EG.
- Investment has a negative and significant impact on EG.

- The combined effects of technological progress and productivity of the military sectors show a negative and significant impact on EG.
- The EEDS have a positive and significant impact on EG.

There are no results for *external conflicts.*

Total conflicts show an insignificant negative impact on EG. The estimates of the PF with total conflicts are as follows:

- Changes in labor growth have a positive and significant impact on EG.
- The combined effects of technological progress and productivity of the military sector shows a positive and significant impact on EG.
- The EEDS have a positive and significant impact on EG.

7.14.2. The CNTA Analysis with Conflicts as Control Variables

The results below are in reference to Table 7.3, demonstrating the direction and significance of the relationships between economic and military variables as well as EG while controlling for internal and external conflicts under the influence of a single political variable for six regions: the ME, Latin America, Asia, Africa, the Caribbean region, and all states (full model).

7.14.2.1. All States

In reference to Table 7.3, all political variables in the full model (entire sample) show insignificant (positive or negative) impact on EG; internal conflicts show a significant negative impact on EG; and external conflicts show an insignificant negative impact on EG. The estimates of the PF with political freedom and conflicts as control variables show the same impact with all political contexts:

- Changes in labor growth have a positive and significant impact on EG.
- The combined effects of technological progress and productivity of the military sectors show a positive and significant impact on EG.
- The EEDS have a positive and significant impact on EG.

7.14.2.2. Africa

In reference to Table 7.3, political and conflict variables show an insignificant impact on EG. The estimates of the PF with the political variables and conflicts as control variables show the same impact with all political contexts:

- Changes in labor growth have a positive and significant impact on EG.
- The combined effects of technological progress and productivity of the military sector show a positive and significant impact on EG.
- The EEDS have a positive and significant impact on EG.

7.14.2.3. Asia

- In reference to Table 7.3, political and conflict variables show an insignificant impact on EG. The estimates of the PF with conflicts as control variables show the same impact with all political contexts:
- Changes in labor growth have a positive and significant impact on EG.
- Investment shows a negative and significant impact on EG.
- The EEDS have a positive and significant impact on EG.
- The externality effects of non-military spending have a negative and significant impact on EG.

7.14.2.4. Middle East

In reference to Table 7.3, political variables show an insignificant impact on EG; internal conflicts show a negative and significant impact on EG; and internal conflicts show a negative and significant impact on EG. The estimates of the PF with conflicts as control variables show the same impact with all political contexts:

- Changes in labor growth have a positive and significant impact on EG.
- The EEDS have a positive and significant impact on EG.

7.14.2.5. Latin America

In reference to Table 7.3, both political and conflict variables show an insignificant impact on EG. The estimates of the PF with conflicts as control variables show the same impacts with all political contexts:

- Changes in labor growth have a positive and significant impact on EG.
- Investment shows a positive and significant impact on EG.
- The EEDS have a positive and significant impact on EG.

7.14.2.6. The Caribbean Region

In reference to Table 7.3, both political and conflict variables show an insignificant impact on EG. The estimates of the PF with conflicts as control variables show the same impact with all political contexts:

- Changes in labor growth have a positive and significant impact on EG.
- Investment shows a negative and significant impact on EG.
- The combined effects of technological progress and productivity of the military sector show a negative and significant impact on EG.
- The EEDS have a positive and significant impact on EG.
- The externality effects of non-military spending have a positive and significant impact on EG.

The main findings of this study are as follows: first, the externality of non-military spending is positive and significant in a majority of countries. Second, political variables – political freedom, institutional freedom, regime type, political stability, and ideological base – are at least as significant as the economic variables. Third, the defense sector has a more significant impact than the private sector on EG. Finally, the positive and significant impact of labor on EG reaches its peak with institutionalized and stable political regimes.

NOTES

1. I utilized similar logic of Heo (1996, 1998) and Heo and Mintz (2002) in developing military and economic data because this study is a continuation and application to their research program.
2. I used the CPI for the following countries: Jordan, Morocco, Turkey, Colombia, Egypt, Ecuador, Gabon, Haiti, Kenya, Malaysia, Mali, Niger, Nigeria, Sir Lanka, Tanzania, Trinidad, UAE, and Zimbabwe.
3. http://www.systemicpeace.org/polity/polity4.htm (accessed on August 9, 2009).
4. http://www.fsd.uta.fi/english/data/catalogue/FSD1216/meF1216e.html (accessed on August, 8, 2009).
5. http://www.nd.edu/~mcoppedg/QPA/BollenCodebook.pdf (accessed on October 8, 2005).
6. http://webapp.icpsr.umich.edu/cocoon/ICPSR-STUDY/09905.xml (accessed on August 9, 2009).

CHAPTER 8

CONCLUSION

Underdevelopment and poverty continue to plague a large number of nations. According to the United Nations Human Development (UNDP) Program 2003 Report, more than 50 countries are poorer in that year than they were in 1990. Human development indicators such as hunger, child mortality, and primary school enrollment show that conditions are now worse in some countries, and extreme poverty affects one fifth of humankind. Needless to say, the majority of poor nations are located in Africa, Asia, Latin America, the Caribbean, and the Middle East.

Researching and writing about the economic growth of developing nations is not done merely to satisfy intellectual curiosity but because it relates to human survival and freedom. Any nation that develops economically enhances the living conditions of its people and frees them from poverty and ignorance, improves their health and education, and gains the respect of other nations. No wonder the Nobel laureate economist Robert Lucas (1988) [as cited in Cock & McKenzie, 1998, p. 1] said, "Once you start thinking about economic growth, it is hard to think about anything else." However, any researcher who looks at the evolution of studies on IPE will attest that there used to be rigid limits that constrained the way one thinks about economic growth such as isolating economics from politics and the denial of contradictions in society. The former sets of beliefs ensured that the production function was governed by pure economic factors such as capital, labor, and investment. The second dogma led to perfunctory simplification of the relationship between economics and politics. It was not surprising then that many people perceived the Keynesian remedy to the cruel Great Depression to be a form of heresy. Nevertheless, the Great Depression provided scientific legitimacy to political economists that they should break away from those dogmas and narrow the gap between theoretical economic constructs and social reality.

Robert Solow's (1957, 1988) incorporation of technology into the production function was a remarkable contribution allowing a linking of the forces of production to the forces of knowledge that made the production function more reflective of real human life. However, Solow's contribution was parochial in that it applied only to the industrially advanced societies. Obviously, Solow's contribution did not make a significant difference in understanding the problems of growth and development in technologically underdeveloped countries. On the contrary, the incorporation of military and non-military variables and their externalities to the production function improved our understanding of the problems of economic development in the world at large because armies have been the most important components of the developing states' structures.

Although the production function defense growth model reflected economic forces at play in any country, one could not use it to link these forces to specific sociopolitical realities. Therefore, economic and military factors were directionless because they were operating in isolation from their sociopolitical contexts. The dualism of economics and politics was caused by economic orthodoxy that emphasized the conclusive role of economic factors in shaping financial growth in isolation from politics. The rigid walls of economic dogmatism were torn down by Heo and Mintz's (2002) seminal article "Bringing Politics In: The Political Economy of the Defense Growth Trade-Off in the United States." The Heo–Mintz (2002) model established a new paradigm in the production function research program because it was the first empirical study that integrated political context with the equation of economic growth. The current study is a generalization of the H–M model and transforms its applicability from the First World to the Third World. The current study made the following contributions to the production function research program:

(1) It incorporated the main political regime variables (political freedom, institutional freedom, regime type, regime stability, and ideological base) into the equation of economic growth. Incorporating those variables transformed the impacts of economic and military and non-military variables on economic growth in the Third World context.
(2) It incorporated conflict variables (interstate and intrastate conflicts) to the production function defense growth political models and tested economic, military and non-military, and political variables with interstate and interstate conflicts as control variables.
(3) It determined the differential influence of internal (intrastate) versus external (interstate) conflicts in relation to economic growth.
(4) It provided a preponderance of empirical evidence that the impact of political and conflict variables are at least as important as economic variables.

(5) It determined the conditions needed for enduring peace in the Middle East.
(6) It determined the processes that led to a more effective and productive economy in the Middle East.

The findings of the statistical analysis can be summarized as follows:

(1) Comparatively, the economic growth of more countries is positively and significantly affected by non-military spending than by military spending within all political contexts.
(2) The impact of non-military sector externalities is positive and significant in the great majority of countries and within all political contexts while the impact of the military sector externalities are positive and significant in only a minority of countries.
(3) Both types of conflicts (interstate and intrastate) have damaging effects on economic growth; however, the damaging effects of internal (intrastate) conflicts have far more damaging effects on economic growth than interstate (external) conflicts.
(4) Investment has a positive and significant impact on economic growth only in a very few number of developing countries while it has no impact on economic growth on the great majority of developing countries.
(5) In general economic performance in the Third World is very poor, and rentier "conquestal" economies pervades most developing nations.

There are several problems concerning my empirical analysis that might be potential sources of estimation bias. First, the impact of technological progress on economic growth within the parameters of developing countries is different from its impact on economic growth in developed countries. In the developed countries, the advancement of technology made the production function amenable in explaining deviations from equilibrium paths because technology is an intrinsic factor in advanced societies. On the contrary, technology has not accompanied the evolution of developing countries and yields its effects on their modes of production over time. Instead, it was added to developing countries as ready-made products. Thus, replicating the effects of technology experienced in industrially advanced societies in those of the Third World might cause estimation bias.

Another source of estimation bias is the high number of sub-economies and shadow economies. Those two types of economies in the Middle East may hinder the accuracy of measuring economic growth because they bypass the converting mechanism (the production function) and create dislocation in the outputs of national economies.

8.1. POLICY IMPLICATIONS OF THE STUDY

Despite the poor economic conditions and the low standards of living, the military expenditures in the developing countries continue to rise and pose great burdens on their respective budgets. Thus, the interplay of resources between defense and civilian sectors is crucial to national economic development because unmanaged military expenditures may divert the resources necessary to attain the developmental objectives, especially in countries with scarce resources.

8.2. EFFECTS OF MILITARY AND NONMILITARY SPENDING ON ECONOMIC GROWTH

Despite decades of discussions and proposals related to diverting resources from the military sector for developmental purposes, the international community has not been able to agree on reducing military expenditures or establishing a ratio of military spending to national development. One of the main sources of disagreement on that issue emanates from the fact that there has been no conclusive empirical evidence that determines the directional impact of defense spending on economic growth. As explained in Chapter 5, one group of scholars has found that defense spending has positive effects on economic growth; a second group of scholars has found negative effects; and a third group of scholars has not been able to find a positive or negative relationship between defense spending and economic growth. Those contradictory findings did not motivate PDMs to limit their defense spending.

The findings of this study provide PDMs in developing countries with a preponderance of empirical evidence concerning the detrimental effects of defense spending on economic growth, thus offering them the motivations to curtail military spending. The results of the NLS analysis of sixty developing countries shown in Table 7.1 demonstrate unequivocally that military expenditures and their externalities hinder economic growth in the majority of developing countries while non-military expenditures and their externalities promote economic growth in the majority of developing countries. Those findings stand in all political and conflict contexts. In addition, as Mintz asserts in many places not only does military spending divert resources from other priorities, but it can also affect the countries' economy, including investment. The NLS results shown in Table 7.1

demonstrate that investments in developing countries are imperceptible and need special attention from PDMs to enhance their performances. Investment is the Achilles' heel of the economies of the developing world; thus, decision makers should develop creative and realistic mechanisms to patch up this economic deficiency.

8.3. DISPARITY BETWEEN DEFENSE SPENDING AND EXTERNALITIES

Although developing countries allocate enormous resources to defense, the positive impact of military externalities on economic growth are very much smaller than the positive impact of nonmilitary externalities (see Table 7.1 and Figs. 7.1–7.8). This finding is fundamental to determine economic factors that caused the ups and downs of the economy. This fundamental finding should lead PDMs to reevaluate military spending and distinguish resources that are necessary for protecting and defending their nations from unnecessary military expenditures. Those unnecessary expenditures should be reallocated to serve a national development economic plan that has positive effects on the whole society. Moreover, PDMs should ensure that resources that leave the national coffers are spent productively. Therefore, it is important to select a group of bureaucrats who have profound experience, integrity, and nuanced understanding of public programs in order to direct government spending to areas that contribute more effectively to the advancement of the national economy.

8.4. THE STRUCTURAL APPROACH AND POLICY ADJUSTMENT

The task of determining the practical application of any study is as important as the theoretical task because it affects the lives of individuals and their standards of living. Furthermore, studies gain additional validity as their findings are successfully applied to real-world situations and resolve controversial issues such as the controversial impact of defense spending on economic growth. The structural approach to defense spending as developed by Mintz (1989) provided me with the appropriate backup to tackle the impact of military and nonmilitary expenditures based on the disaggregate impact of their components. Prior analysis has centered on trade-offs between total defense spending and specific kinds of welfare spending (e.g., health, education, housing). In contrast, Mintz (1989) examined trade-offs between welfare spending and specific kinds of defense expenditures. Mintz's (1989) structural approach to defense spending (focused on the components not the totality of defense spending) provides a powerful procedural tool in shaping the policy recommendations that come from my empirical findings. As Mintz (1989, p. 1290) argues about 20% of the total department of defense administration has not only raised military expenditures substantially but also changed priorities in the department of defense by putting much more emphasis on the purchase of equipment and material (i.e., the capital- and technology-intensive procurement and research and development (R&D) programs than on the so-called operating and maintenance programs (O&M) (i.e., the labor-intensive military personnel and O&M programs). Mintz (1989, p. 1287) explained the logic behind changing the priorities in defense spending: "While allocations to Department of Defense capital-intensive programs are hypothesized to take resources away from welfare programs, allocations to labor-intensive programs may ease the task of government's health and education sector rather than lead to trade-offs." Therefore, it is a great task for the military establishment to redistribute defense spending so that it targets the components that ease the task of government and contributes to ameliorating the people's standard of living.

The purpose of this study is not to attack the military establishments in developing nations or to negate their rights to a portion of the national budget. Rather, it is to offer recommendations that maximize the contributions of military spending externalities to economic development and to social welfare programs. Marfels (1978) correctly pointed out that the bulk of military expenditures for the procurement of military equipment go to large unionized "monopoly sector" firms. Galbraith (1967, p. 316) similarly pointed out that much of the military research and development budget goes largely to oligopolistic corporations that need R&D for "technical and scientific" advances. Perroff and Podolak (1979, p. 24) argued that the cost of weapon systems is therefore carried to a great extent by lower-income groups who have a greater need for welfare programs and "could use additional income for 'necessities' such as health services." Wildavsky (1988, p. 380) similarly concluded that more spending for weapons came to be viewed as "an in-egalitarian taking from the worst-off elements of the population." Given an upper limit to the federal budget, an increase in allocations to weapons systems could come at the expense of welfare spending (Mintz, 1989).

Military expenditures are not necessarily evil, rather, the management of these expenditures may make them useful or harmful to the lives of the citizens, and a good manager may turn them into assets that contribute to the enhancement of economic growth. According to Mintz (1989), military expenditure (and part of the O&M budget) "may alleviate the demand for health, education, and housing programs. Military personnel expenditures may help equalize the contribution of benefits, education, and medical care." Similarly, Binkin, Eitelberg, Schexnider, and Smith (1982) argued that the armed forces provide those in the lower income group with their only chance to escape from the underclass. Military service became an extension of welfare polity for those who could not make it in the larger society. Since the armed forces are providing health and education services to many who might otherwise be in need of government support, there may be a lesser need for the government to spend additional amounts of money on the programs. Diverting military expenditures to military sectors that contribute to the general enhancement of social welfare programs is one of the keys to making the expenditures less harmful to the national economy. The benefits in a single component (e.g., health) might not have a significant impact on the general state of the economy, but the aggregation of the diverted expenditures along all dimensions will make a difference in the general performance of the national economy.

On the one hand, my empirical results provide a general direction to PDMs to redirect national resources from the military sectors to nonmilitary sectors since the externalities of the military sectors have significantly negative impacts on economic growth. Therefore, the general national economic policy should aim at giving priority to non-military expenditures and carefully calculating the defense expenditures so that policy makers know their purpose and specific objectives. Managing defense spending is the golden rule for political development in the Third World regardless of the type of political regime running a country, its institutional or levels of political development, or the nature of its ideological base. The bulk of resources that are spent on defense in the Third World impede national development and hinder the life of individuals in those nations. Nevertheless, the PDM can mitigate the harmful impact of military expenditures through focusing on the components that are more beneficial to the general public.

8.5. THE TRAGIC STATE OF INVESTMENTS IN DEVELOPING COUNTRIES

The state of investments in developing countries is staggeringly poor. The positive impact of investment on economic growth is very weak, thus need a remedy. The recovery period may vary from one nation to another, depending on the cultural and political characteristics of each nation. The poor performance of investments might not be due to lack of capital, labor, or knowledge; rather, it might be a structural problem that requires serious remedial effort from PDMs. The NLS empirical results manifest the depth of the crisis of investment in developing countries. In the majority of developing countries, investment has no significant impact on economic growth. The NLS results for sixty countries as shown in Table 7.1 and Figs. 7.1–7.8 attest to the fact that PDMs should focus on improving investments through supporting the private sector and making non-military spending a priority.

It is worth mentioning that countries where investment still has positive influence on EG will not be secure in the future as long as their high military spending continues increasing. The effect of military spending on investment doesn't appear immediately but has an aggregate impact over time as Mintz and Huang (1991) demonstrated. The two researchers examined the effect of the timing and magnitude of potential defense spending cuts on economic growth in the United States by investigating the direct and the indirect impact of military spending (through investment) on growth, using data from the U.S. economy in the years 1953–1987. The findings reported in their study reveal the existence of an indirect, delayed effect of military spending on growth. To be more specific, they found that in the long run, lower military spending encourages investment, which in turn promotes economic growth. This effect is not immediate, however. Their analysis shows that it takes about five years for such an indirect trade-off to appear; thus, PDMs should be farsighted in managing government spending. The reallocation of resources to non-military activities is essential to economic growth in developing countries. The apparent and short-term progress in the state of the national economy due to the increase in military spending should not lead a PDM to draw the wrong conclusion about the state of the economy; he must weigh priorities based on multidimensional plans and consider all related aspects of the economy, particularly investment.

National security should be sought primarily through efforts to meet the political, economic, social, and cultural rights and needs of the citizens of developing nations and through efforts to promote and maintain regional security. However, security must be understood in a broad perspective: social, economic, ecological, and human. Thus, when governments spend resources on unnecessary and dubious programs such as nuclear or chemical weapons stockpiles, leaders must weigh their impacts on the general situation of their citizens. President Dwight D. Eisenhower (Cock &

McKenzie, 1998, p. 1) correctly pointed out, "Every gun that is made, every warship launched, every rocket fired, represents, in the final analysis, a theft from those that hunger and are not fed, are cold and are not clothed." Unnecessary military expenditures might be avoided when developing countries pursue peaceful relations and seek a high level of political, economic, and military cooperation on regional and international levels.

The relationship between disarmament and development is manifested in different situations, depending on the security and development priorities and conditions in each specific country or region. Every case must be examined on its own merits, especially with regard to the long-held expectation that expenditures withdrawn from military and defense budgets would or should be automatically transferred to financial development programs. The relationships among development, defense, and security should be studied in light of their implications for regional and international affairs. As an example, one can look at the impact of the Iranian nuclear program and military buildup on the stability of the Middle East and the world. Needless to say, in addition to the Iranian nuclear program's devastating economic impact on the life of the Iranian people, it also creates insecurity in the entire Middle East, including Iran.

It is imperative that Iran think of its security beyond narrow nationalistic terms because the Iranian nuclear activities will encourage other countries in the region to follow its lead. As a result, misery and social upheaval in the Middle East will be exacerbated for the sake of useless nuclear programs, especially if such programs are preceded by bombastic pronouncements about wiping other states off the map. Of course, any state that does not follow the Iranian regime's theocratic model might be a legitimate target for elimination. Do military programs, nuclear and biological in particular, make the Middle East safer? Do nuclear programs enhance the quality of life of the Iranian or Pakistani people? To the contrary, the economies of those countries retreated, human rights declined, the quality of life deteriorated, investment levels were abysmal, and most countries in the region and in the world are alarmed by the militaristic and antagonistic rhetoric of the Iranian leadership and by the extremist movements in the Middle East.

Decision makers should look realistically at the sources of domestic conflict to develop specific strategies to overcome them and reduce defense spending. There are a number of ways in which disarmament can release or increase financial, human, or physical resources available for development. The following are some notable examples: reducing military expenditures; strengthening security by building confidence; creating conditions for economic, scientific and technological cooperation; and preventing conflicts and building peace. Moreover, institutions representing the international community must verify how economic assistance and loans to developing countries are spent and investigate instances of corruption and mismanagement. The United Nations, the World Bank, and the International Monetary Fund have established clear and operational conditions under which they grant loans and economic assistance to developing countries. They are based on the recommendations of the United Nations' Department for Disarmament Affairs (UNDDA) (2005), which must be applied strictly and uniformly by all international organizations. Some of the rules and guidelines are explained below.

- Member states should implement with transparency their 1987 commitments to assess their political and security requirements and the level of military spending, taking into account the need to keep their expenditures at the lowest possible level as well as to carry out regular evaluations of the economic and social consequences of their military spending and to inform the public and the United Nations about them. Member states should periodically publish defense white papers and defense policy reviews.
- Developing countries must take into account disarmament and security concerns when preparing their poverty reduction strategy papers with the donor community, and the donor community should link the approval of loans to the disarmament behavior that countries exhibit.
- The donor community is invited to examine the feasibility of new concepts for providing specific assistance in relation to weapons destruction, conversion, and mine action and unexploded ordnance activities, including the idea of debt-for-disarmament swaps, with a view to increasing development opportunities.
- Non-governmental organizations are encouraged to continue to be engaged in the disarmament-development relationship. The UN should encourage support for non-governmental organizations working in this field.
- The Department for Disarmament Affairs affirms the importance of continued progress towards achieving universal participation in the United Nations System for the Standardized Reporting of Military Expenditures and recognizes the value of providing it with more comprehensive data.
- Member states should enhance and support arms control verification regimes through the relevant treaty bodies, and states should pursue policies that strengthen mutual confidence and friendship.

- All states must announce their commitment to Article 26 of the Charter of the United Nations: "Member States have undertaken to promote the establishment and maintenance of international peace and security with the least diversion for armament of the world's human and economic resources."

It is crucial that the ideology of militarism, which views violence as a legitimate solution to conflict and problems, be changed. Unfortunately, militaristic ideology remains intact and is growing stronger in most developing countries. Demilitarization needs to go beyond decreasing spending on defense; rather, it should recast social relations, employing a much broader plan aimed at social transformation. The ideological conversion must focus on a new understanding of security that emphasizes development, human security, international cooperation, acceptance of others, and religious coexistence.

8.6. THE CULTURE OF DEATH AND ECONOMIC GROWTH IN THE MIDDLE EAST

Political scientists and decision makers have been occupied with the organization of world politics in order to achieve certain specific values and objectives, such as international peace and political economic development. Unfortunately, there are some countries in the world that obstruct the implementation of these objectives through diverting a prodigious amount of resources from social developmental programs to fund activities that create instability in the world. The Middle East has suffered from its participation in the lion's share of these destructive activities, especially because of the promulgation of the culture of death.

The culture of death that manifested itself ubiquitously in the form of men, women, and children acting as suicide bombers not only impedes economic development but also shuts the doors on potential development in the region. The tragedy of the culture of death in the Middle East was created not only by some maverick organizations but also by some heavyweight Middle Eastern governments. The proliferation of conflicts in the Middle East has become one of the most damaging factors impeding regional economic growth. Internal conflicts, particularly in Algeria, Lebanon, Somalia, the Sudan, Kashmir, Afghanistan, and Iraq, squander the bulk of the region's resources that could contribute to its economic development.

What is to be done? Courageous Middle Eastern leaders must challenge the culture of death and defeat it. Education must be carefully restructured on all levels in light of openness to world culture, peace and cooperation, and acceptance of others. Secular educators should be employed to lead the process based on specific goals and objectives that meet world standards. Respect and inclusion of other peoples' religions, cultures, and ways of life must be an integral part of the teaching process. Moreover, security should be broadly defined to encompass social, environmental, and human well-being within the context of international order. Considering the broad meaning of security, decision makers in the Middle East should work to implement the following objectives:

- Redirect some of the unnecessary military spending to social welfare programs
- Abandon nuclear weapons programs to offer strong evidence of their commitment to the objectives and goals of the international community
- Establish peace, negotiations, and mutual understanding within the Middle East and between the Middle East and the rest of the world as the norm for conflict resolution
- Reform political systems so they are based on plurality and democratic participation.

REFERENCES

Abadie, A., & Gardeazabal, J. (2003). The economic costs of conflict a case study of the Basque country. *The American Economic Review* (March), 113–132.

Abu-Qarn, A. S., & Abu-Bader, S. (2008). Structural break in military expenditures: Evidence for Egypt, Israel, Jordan and Syria. *Peace Economics, Peace Science and Public Policy, 14*(1), 1–23.

Alexander, R. (1990). The impact of defense spending on economic growth. *Defense Economics, 2*, 39–45.

Alexander, R. W. (1990). The impact of defense spending on economic growth. *Defense Economics, 2*, 39–55.

Al-Jabiri, A. (1982). *Group solidarity and the state: Khaldunian theoretical features of Islamic history*. Casablanca: Dar al-Nashr al-Magribiyya.

Amin, S. (1977). *Imperialism and unequal development*. Columbus, OH: Harvest.

Amin, S. (2004). *The liberal virus: Permanent war and the Americanization of the world*. New York: Monthly Review Press.

Anderson, R. R., Seibert, R. F., & Wagner, J. G. (2009). *Politics and change in the Middle East* (9th ed.). New York: Longman.

Arrow, K. (1963). In: *Social Choice and Individual Values* (2nd ed.). New Haven, CT, and London: Yale University Press.

Atesoglu, S. S., & Mueller, M. J. (1990). Defense spending and economic growth. *Defense Economics, 2*(1), 19–27.

Attar, A. R. (2009). In: Tan, A. T. H. (Ed.), *The global arms trade*. New York: Routledge, Forthcoming.

Attar, R. A. (2007). Egypt. In: K. DeRouen & P. Bellamy (Eds), *International security and the United States: An encyclopedia* (Vol. 1, pp. 225–244). Westport, CT: Praeger Security International.

Ayubi, N. (1999). *Over-stating the Arab state: Politics and society in the Middle East*. London: I.B. Tauris Publishers.

Bailey, S. K. (1965). The politics of the budgetary process by Aaron Wildavsk (reviewed work). *The American Political Science Review, 59*(1), 143–144.

Balaam, D. N., & Veseth, M. (2008). *Introduction to international political economy* (4th ed.). Upper Saddle River, NJ: Person Prentice Hall.

Ball, N. (1983). Defense and development: A critique of the Benoit study. *Economic Development and Cultural Change, 31*, 507–524.

Barro, R. J. (1999). *Economic growth*. Cambridge, MA: MIT Press.

BBC News. October 22, 2008. Available at http://news.bbc.co.uk/2/hi/science/nature/7679818.stm. Retrieved on August 8, 2009.

Benoit, E. (1973). *Defense and economic growth in developing countries*. Lexington, MA: Lexington Books.

Benoit, E. (1978). Growth and defense in developing countries. *Economic Development and Cultural Change, 26*, 270–280.

Binkin, M., Eitelberg, M. J., Schexnider, A. J., & Smith, M. M. (1982). *Blacks and the military*. Washington, DC: Brooking Institution.

Biswas, B. (1993). Defense spending and economic growth in developing countries. In: J. Payne & P. Anandi (Eds), *Defense spending and economic growth* (pp. 224–235). Boulder, CO: Westview Press.

Biswas, B., & Rati, R. (1986). Military expenditures and economic growth in less developed countries: An augmented model and further evidence. *Economic Development and Cultural Change, 34*, 361–372.

Bollen, K. A. (1980). Issues in the comparative measurement of political democracy. *American Sociological Review, 45*, 370–390.

Bollen, K. A. (1991). Political democracy: Conceptual and methodological traps. In: A. Inkeles (Ed.), *On measuring democracy: Its consequences and concomitants* (pp. 1–20). New Brunswick, NJ: Transactions Publishers.

Bollen, K. A. (1993). Liberal democracy: Validity and method factors in cross-national measures. *American Journal of Political Science, 37*, 1207–1230.

Bollen, K. A. (2001). *Cross-national indicators of liberal democracy 1950–1990*. Ann Arbor, MI: ICPSR. Available at http://www.nd.edu/~mcoppedg/QPA/BollenCodebook.pdf. Retrieved on October, 23, 2009.

Borrow, D. (1992). Conclusions: If the times A'changing. In: A. Mintz (Ed.), *The political economy of military spending in the United States* (pp. 3305–3316). London: Routledge.

Borton, H. (1941). War and the rise of industrialization in Japan. In: J. Clarkson & T. Cochran (Eds), *War as a social institution*. (pp. 224–234). New York: Columbia University Press.

Brzoska, M. (1981). The reporting of military expenditures. *Journal of Peace Research, 18*, 260–277.

Bull, H. (1977). *The anarchical society: A study of order in world politics*. New York: Columbia University Press.

Cappelen, Å., Gleditsch, N. P., & Bjerkholt, O. (1984). *Military Spending and Economic Growth in the OECD Countries Journal of Peace Research, 21*(4), 361–373.

Carson, C. S. (2000). *International financial statistics yearbook* (Vol. 54). Washington, DC: International Monetary Fund.

Carson, C. S. (2002). *International financial statistics yearbook* (Vol. 54). Washington, DC: International Monetary Fund.

Carson, C. S. (2004). *International financial statistics yearbook* (Vol. 57). Washington, DC: International Monetary Fund.

Carr, E. H. (1961). *What is history?* New York: Vintage Books.

Carr, E. H. (2001). *The twenty years' crisis, 1919–1939* (2nd ed.). Palgrave Mcmillan.

Carr, H. E. (1939). *The twenty years' crisis, 1919–1939*. London: McMillan and Company Limited.

Chan, S. (1985). The impact of defense spending on economic performance: A survey of evidence and problems. *Orbis, 29*(2), 403–434.

Chan, S. (1987). Military expenditures and economic performance. *World Military Expenditures and Arm Transfers, 1986*, Arms Control and Disarmament Agency.

Chan, S. (1995). Grasping the peace dividend: Some propositions on the conversion of swords into plowshares. *Mershon International Studies Review*, *39*(1), 53–95.
Childe, G. V. (1936). *Man makes himself.* New York: The New American Library.
Childe, G. V. (1942). *What happened in history*. Baltimore, MD: Penguin Books.
Choucri, N., & North, C. R. (1977). *Nations in conflicts: National growth and international violence*. San Francisco: Freeman.
Choucri, N., & North, R. (1975). *Nations in conflict: National growth and international violence*. New York: W H Freeman & Co.
Chowdhury, A. R. (1991). A causal analysis of defense spending and economic growth. *Journal of Conflict Resolution*, *35*, 80–97.
CIA World Factbook. (2009). Available at https://www.cia.gov/library/publications/the-world-factbook/. Retrieved on July 25, 2009.
Clausewitz, C. V. (1968). In: A. Rapoport (Ed.), *On war*. Baltimore, MD: Penguin Books.
Cleveland, W. (2000). *A history of the modern Middle East*. Boulder, CO: Westview Press.
Cock, J., & McKenzie, P. (1998). In: D. Philip (Ed.), *From defense to development: Redirecting military resources in South Africa*. Ottawa, Canada: International Development Research Center.
Cordesman, A. (2000). *Saudi Arabia enters the twenty-first century: The military and international security dimensions*. Westport, CT: Praeger Publisher.
Cordesman, A. H. (2002). *A tragedy of arms: Military and security developments in the Maghreb*. Westport, CT: Praeger.
Cornes, R., & Sandler, T. (1986). *The theory of externalities, public goods, and club goods*. Cambridge: Cambridge University Press.
Coulomb, F. (2004). *Economic theories of peace and war* (1st ed.). London and New York: Routledge.
Damsgaard, H. (2001). *European economic history: From mercantilism to Maastricht and beyond.* Copenhagen: Copenhagen Business School Press.
Dann, U. (1999). *King Hussein and the challenge of Arab radicalism, 1955–1967*. New York: Oxford University Press.
Davis, O. A., Dempster, M. A. H., & Wildavsky, A. (1966). A theory of the budgetary process. *The American Political Science Review*, *LX*(3), 529–549.
Deane, P. (1978). *The evolution of economic ideas*. Cambridge: Cambridge University Press.
Deger, S. (1986). *Military expenditures in third world countries*. London: Routledge and Kegan Paul.
Deger, S., & Sen, S. (1983). Military expenditure, spin-off and economic development. *Journal of Development Economics*, *13*, 67–83.
Deger, S., & Smith, R. (1983). Military expenditures and development: The economic linkages. *IDS Bulletin*, *16*, 49–54.
Denison, E. F. (1967). *Why growth rates differ*. Washington, DC: Brookings Institution.
Denison, E. F. (1985). *Trends in American economic growth, 1929–1982*. Washington, DC: Brookings Institution.
Denoon, D. B. (Ed.) (1986). *Constraints on strategy*. Mclean, VA: Pergamon – Brassey.
Derbyshire, D. J., & Derbyshire, I. (1996). *Political system of the world.* New York: St. Martin's Press.
DeRouen, K. (1993). Defense spending and economic growth in Latin America: The externalities effects. *International Interactions*, *19*, 193–221.

DeRouen, K. (2000). Presidents and the discovery use of force: A research note. *International Studies Quarterly*, *44*(2), 317–328.
Diehl, P. F., & Goertz, G. (1985). Trends in military allocations since 1816: What goes up does not always go down. *Armed Forces and Society*, *12*(1), 134–144.
Dillard, D. (1946). The pragmatic basis of Keynes's political economy. *The Journal of Economic History*, *1*(2), 121–152.
Dogan, M., & Pelassy, D. (1984). *How to compare nations: Strategies in comparative politics*. London: Chatham House Publishers.
Domar, E. (1946). Capital expansion, rate of growth, and employment. *Econometrica*, *14*(2), 137–147.
Domke, W. (1992). Do leaders make a difference? Posture and politics in the defense budget. In: A. Mintz (Ed.), *The political economy of military spending in the United States*. (pp. 33–50). London: Routledge.
Dorn, W. L. (1940). *Competition for empire, 1740–1763*. New York: Harper & Brothers.
Dulles, E. (1942). War and investment opportunities: A historic analysis. *American Economic Review (Part 2: Supplement)*, *32*(1), 112–128.
Durbin, J., & Watson, G. S. (1950). Testing for serial correlation in least squares regression I, II, III. *Biometrica*, *37*, 409–428.
Durbin, J., & Watson, G. S. (1951). Testing for serial correlation in least squares regression I, II, III. *Biometrica*, *38*, 159–178.
Durbin, J., & Watson, G. S. (1971). Testing for serial correlation in least squares regression I, II, III. *Biometrica*, *58*, 1–42.
Easton, D. (1965). *A framework of political analysis*. Englewood Cliffs, NJ: Prentice-Hall, Inc.
Easton, D. (1967). *A system analysis of political life*. New York: Wiley.
Easton, D. (1990). *The analysis of political structure*. New York: Chapman and Hall, Inc.
Eckstein, H. (1963). A perspective on comparative politics, past and present. In: H. Eckstein & D. Apter (Eds), *Comparative politics: A Reader* (pp. 3–22). New York: The Free Press.
Eckstein, H., & Gurr, T. (1975). *Patterns of authority: A structural basis for political inquiry*. New York: Wiley.
Edward, W. R. (2008). *International financial statistics yearbook*. Washington, DC: International Monetary Fund.
Eltis, W. (1988). The contrasting theories of industrialization of François Quesnay and Adam Smith. *Oxford Economic Papers*, *40*, 269–288.
Eralp, P., Hewitt, J., Jonas, A., Quinn, D., & Wilkenfeld, J. (2006). International crisis behavior project. Available at http://www.cidcm.umd.edu/icb/. Retrieved on November 6, 2009.
Faini, R., Annez, P., & Taylor, L. (1984). Defense spending, economic structure and growth: Evidence among countries and over time. *Economic Development and Cultural Change*, *32*, 487–498.
Feder, G. (1982). On export and economic growth. *Journal of Development Economics*, *12*(1), 59–73.
Feldman, S., & Shapir, Y. (Eds). (2001). *The Middle East military balance, 2000–2001, BCSIA Studies in International Securities*. Tel Aviv: Jaffee Center for Strategic Studies.
Foch, F. (1918). *The principles of war*. London: Chapman & Hall.
Fordham, B. (1998). The politics of threat perception and the use of force: A political economy model of U.S. use of force, 1949–1994. *International Studies Quarterly*, *42*, 267–590.
Fraser, H. (1926). *Foreign trade and world politics*. New York: Alfred A. Knopf.

Frederiksen, P. C., & Looney, R. E. (1983). Defense expenditures and economic growth in developing countries. *Armed Forces and Society*, *9*, 633–645.

Frederiksen, P. C., & Looney, R. E. (1985). Another look at defense spending and development hypothesis. *Defense Analysis*, *3*, 205–210.

Frederiksen, P. C., & Looney, R. E. (1986). Defense expenditures, external public debt and growth in developing countries. *Journal of Peace Research*, *23*, 329–337.

Frieden, J. A., & Lake, D. A. (2000). *International political economy: Perspective on global power and wealth* (4th ed.). Belmont, CA: Thomoson Wadsworth.

Fromkin, D. (1989). *A peace to end all peace: The fall of the Ottoman Empire and the creation of the modern Middle East*. New York: Henry Holt and Company.

Gadhafi, M. (1977). *The green book*. Available at http://www.geocities.com/Athens/8744/readgb.htm. Retrieved on October 21, 2009.

Galbraith, J. K. (1967). *The new industrial state*. Boston: Houghton Mifflin.

Gilpin, R. (1987). *The political economy of international relations*. Princeton, NJ: Princeton University Press.

Global Security. (2008). Libyan nuclear weapons [online]. Available at http://www.globalsecurity.org/wmd/world/libya/nuclear.htm. Retrieved on June 5, 2009.

Gould, J. D. (1972). *Economic growth in history: Survey and analysis*. London: Methuen.

Gurr, T. R. (1974). Persistence and change in political systems, 1800–1971. *The American Political Science Review*, *68*, 1482–1504.

Harrod, R. (1939). An essay in dynamic theory. *Economic Journal*, pp. 14–33, Errata, (June): p. 377.

Heo, U. K. (1996). *Modeling the security-prosperity dilemma around the world*. Texas: Ph.D. College Station, A&M University.

Heo, U. K. (1998). Modeling the defense-growth relationship around the globe. *Journal of Conflict Resolution*, *42*(5), 637–657.

Heo, U. K. (1999). *The political economy of defense spending around the world*. Lewiston, NY: Edwin Mellen Press.

Heo, U. K. (2000). The defense growth nexus in the United States revisited. *American Politics Quarterly*, *28*(1), 110–127.

Heo, U. K., & DeRouen, K. (1998). Military expenditures, technological change, and economic growth in the east Asian NICS. *The Journal of Politics*, *60*(3), 830–846.

Heo, U. K., & Mintz, A. (2002). *Bringing politics in: The political economy of the defense growth trade-off in the United States*. New Orleans, LA: International Studies Association.

Herring, E. B. (1941). *The impact of war: Our American democracy under arms*. New York: Farrar and Rinehart.

Hibbs, D. (1977). Political parties and macroeconomic policy. *American Political Science Review*, *71*(4), 1467–1488.

Hirshleifer, J., Boldrin, M., & Levine, D. K. (2009). The slippery slope of concession. *Economic Inquiry*, *47*(2), 197–205.

Hobson, J. A. (1971). *Imperialism: A Study*. Ann Arbor: University of Michigan Press.

Hollist, W. L. (1977). Alternative explanations of competitive arms processes: Tests on four Pairs of nations. *American Journal of Political Science*, *21*(2), 313–340.

Huang, C., & Mintz, A. (1990). Ridge regression analysis of the defense-growth tradeoff in the United States. *Defence Economics*, *2*, 29–37.

Huang, C., & Mintz, A. (1991). Defense expenditures and economic growth: The externality effect. *Defence Economics*, *3*(1), 35–40.

Hudson, M. C. (1977). *Arab politics: The search for legitimacy*. New Haven, CT: Yale University Press.

Ibn Khaldoun, A. (1967). *The muqaddimah: An introduction to history*. Princeton, NJ: Princeton University Press.

International Monetary Fund Statistics Department. (1964). *International financial statistics yearbook*. Washington, DC: International Monetary Fund.

International Monetary Fund Statistics Department. (1973). *International financial statistics yearbook*. Washington, DC: International Monetary Fund.

International Monetary Fund Statistics Department. (1981). *International financial statistics*. Washington, DC: International Monetary Fund.

International Monetary Fund Statistics Department. (1983). *International financial statistics yearbook* (Vol. 36, No. 4). Washington, DC: Brennan Press.

Isacoff, J. B. (2005). Writing the Arab-Israeli conflict: Historical bias and the use of history in political science. *Perspectives on Politics*, *3*(1), 71–88.

Jaggers, K. K., & Gurr, T. R. (1995). Tracking democracy's third wave with the polity III data. *Journal of Peace Research*, *32*(4), 469–482.

Janis, M. W. (2003). *An introduction to international law* (4th ed.). New York: Aspen.

Jeording, W. (1986). Economic growth and defense spending. *Journal of Development Economics*, *21*, 35–40.

Jewish Virtual Library. (1994). Treaty of peace between the State of Israel and the Hashemite Kingdom of Jordan. Available at http://www.jewishvirtuallibrary.org/jsource/Peace/isrjor.html. Retrieved on May 20, 2009.

Jimmy Carter Library and Museum. (2001). Camp David accords: The framework for peace in the Middle East. Available at http://www.jimmycarterlibrary.org/documents/campdavid/. Retrieved on May 30, 2009.

Judge, G., Griffiths, W., Hill, R., Lutkepohl, H., & Lee, T. (1985). *The theory and practice of econometrics*. New York: Wiley.

Kaldor, M. (1976). The military in development. *World Development*, *4*, 459–482.

Kennedy, G. (1983). *Defense economics*. New York: St. Martin's Press.

Keohane, R. (1986). *Neo-realism and its critics*. New York: Columbia University Press.

Keohane, R., & Nye, J. (1977). Power and interdependence: World politics in transition, co- (Boston: Little Brownand Company, 1977; 3rd edition with additional material, New York: Longman, 2000).

Keynes, J. M. (1930). *A treatise on money*. New York: Harcourt, Brace, and Company.

Keynes, J. M. (1935). *The general theory of employment, interests, and money*. New York: Harcourt, Brace, and World.

Keynes, J. M. (1940). *How to pay for war: A radical plan for the chancellor of the exchequer*. New York: Harcourt Brace.

Khaldoun, A. I. (1967). *The muqaddimah: An introduction to history*. Princeton: Princeton University Press.

King Hussein. (1962). *Uneasy lies the head: The autobiography of His Majesty King Hussein I of the Hashemite Kingdom of Jordan* (distributed by Random House). New York: B. Geis Associates.

Kinsella, D. (1990). Defense spending and economic performance in the United States. *Defence Economics*, *1*(3), 295–309.

Lebovic, J., & Ishaq, A. (1987). Military burden, security needs, and economic growth in the Middle East. *Journal of Conflict Resolution*, *31*, 106–138.

Lenin, V. I. (1996). *Imperialism: The highest stage of capitalism*. London: Junius.

Lichbach, M. I. (1989). Stability in Richardson's arms races and cooperation in prisoner's dilemma arms rivalries. *American Journal of Political Science*, *33*(4), 1016–1047.

Lijphart, A. (1971). Comparative politics and the comparative method. *American Political Science Review*, *65*(3), 682–693.

Lim, D. (1983). Another look at growth and defense in less developed countries. *Economic and Cultural Change*, *31*, 377–384.

Lindgren, G. (1984). Armaments and economic performance in industrialized market economies. *Journal of Peace Research*, *21*, 4.

Lucas, R. (1988). On the mechanics of economic development. *Journal of Monetary Economics*, *22*(1), 3–42.

Mackeod, S. (2006). The new Arab peace plan. *Time*. Available at http://www.time.com/time/world/article/0,8599,1533384,00.html. Retrieved on November 4, 2009.

MacMillan, M. (2002). *Paris 1919: Six months that changed the world*. New York: Random House Trade Paperbacks.

Macridis, R., & Brown, B. (1986). *Comparative politics: Notes and readings*. Homewood, IL: Dorsey Press.

Maoz, Z., & Russett, B. (1992). Alliance, contiguity, wealth, and political stability: Is the lack of conflict among democracies a statistical artifact? *International Interactions*, *17*(3), 245–267.

Marfels, C. (1978). The structure of military industrial complex in the United States and its impacts on industrial concentration. *Kyklos*, *31*, 409–423.

Marshall, G., Jaggers, K., & Gurr, T. (2007). Polity IV project: Political regime characteristics and transitions, 1800–2002. Available at http://www.systemicpeace.org/polity/polity4.htm. Retrieved on August 9, 2009.

McLenaghan, J. B. (1992). *International financial statistics yearbook* (Vol. 45). Washington, DC: International Monetary Fund.

McLenaghan, J. B. (1995). *International financial statistics yearbook* (Vol. 18). Washington, DC: International Monetary Fund.

Mendershausen, H. (1943). *The economics of war*. New York: Prentice-Hall.

Meredith, S., & Schafer, P. (2000). The correlates of war data on war: An update to 1997. *Conflict Management and Peace Science*, *18*(1), 123–143.

Merom, G. (1999). Israel's national security and the myth of exceptionalism. *Political Science Quarterly*, *114*(3), 409–434.

Michels, R. (1962). *Political parties: A sociological study of the oligarchical tendencies of modern democracy*. London: Collier Macmillan Publishers.

Microsoft Encarta. (2007). *Encyclopedia*. Redmond, WA: Microsoft Corporation.

Mideast Mirror. (2000). Available at http://www.mideastmirror.com. UK/England: http://worldpress.org. Retrieved on May 2, 2009.

Milton, D. S. (2009). Call to memory: Muslims, Christians, and Jews. Available at http://www.redroom.com/articlestory/call-memory-muslims-christians-and-jews. Retrieved on October 21, 2009.

Mintz, A. (1986). International interactions: Empirical and theoretical research in international relations. *International Interactions*, *12*(3), 229–243.

Mintz, A. (1988). *The politics of resource allocation in the U.S. Department of Defense: International crises and domestic constraints*. Boulder, CO: Westview Press.

Mintz, A. (1989). Guns versus butter. *The American Economic Review*, *83*(4), 1285–1293.

Mintz, A. (1991). Introduction-political economy and national security. In: A. Mintz (Ed.), *The political economy of military spending*. London: Harper Collins.
Mintz, A., & Geva, N. (1993). Why don't democracies fight each other? An experimental study. *Journal of Conflict Resolution, 37*(3), 484–503.
Mintz, A., & Huang, C. (1990). Defense expenditures, economic growth, and peace dividend. *American Political Science Review, 84*(4), 1283–1293.
Mintz, A., & Huang, C. (1991). Guns versus butter: The indirect link. *American Journal of Political Science, 35*, 3.
Mintz, A., & Stevenson, R. T. (1995). Defense expenditures, economic growth, and the peace dividend: A longitudinal analysis of 103 countries. *Journal of Conflict Resolution, 39*(2), 283–305.
Mintz, A., & Ward, M. D. (1989). The political economy of military spending in Israel. *The American Political Science Review, 83*(2), 521–533.
Modelski, G. (1972). *Principles of world politics*. New York: Free Press.
Morrow, J. (1994). *Game theory for political scientists*. Princeton, NJ: Princeton University Press.
Mosley, H. (1985). *The arms race: Econometric and social consequences*. Lexington, MA: Lexington Books.
Muller, A. L. (1978). Quesnay's theory of growth: A comment. *Oxford Economic Papers, 30*, 150–156.
Mueller, M., & Atesoglu, S. (1993a). Defense spending, technological change and economic growth in the United States. *Defence Economics, 4*(3), 259–269.
Mueller, M., & Atesoglu, S. (1993b). A theory of defense spending and economic growth. In: J. Payne & A. Sahu (Eds), *Defense spending and economic growth*. Boulder, CO: Westview Press.
Ogawa, G. (1926). *The effect of the world war upon the commerce and industry in Japan*. New Haven, CT: Yale University Press.
Organski, A. F. (1997). Theoretical link of political capacity to development. In: M. Arbetman & J. Kugler (Eds), *Political capacity and economic behavior* (pp. 47–66). Boulder, CO: Westview.
Organski, A. F. K., & Kugler, J. (1980). *The war ledger*. Chicago: University of Chicago Press.
Osborne, M. J. (2004). *An introduction to game theory*. New York: Oxford University Press.
Ostrom, C., & Job, B. (1986). The president and the political use of force. *American Political Science Review, 80*(2), 541–566.
Owen, R. (1992). *State, power and politics in the making of the modern middle east* (2nd ed.). London: Routledge.
Pagan, A. (1974). A generalized approach to the treatment of autocorrelation. *Australian Economic Papers, 13*, 260–280.
Palestine Facts. (2009). Where did the name Palestine come from? Available at http://www.palestinefacts.org/pf_early.php. Retrieved on May 20, 2009.
Peled, Y. (1992). Ethnic democracy and the legal construction of citizenship: Arab citizens of the Jewish state [Electronic version]. *The American Political Science Review, 86*, 432–443.
Perroff, K., & Podolak-Warren, M. (1979). Does defense cut spending on health? *British Journal of Political Science, 9*, 21–39.
Persky, J. (1989). Retrospectives: Adam Smith's invisible hands. *The Journal of Economic Perspectives, 3*, 195–201.

Pipes, D. (December 1994). Understanding Asad. Available at http://www.meforum.org/196/understanding-asad. Retrieved on August 15, 2009.

Przeworski, A., & Teune, H. (1970). *The logic of contemporary social inquiry*. New York: Wiley.

Ra, S., & SIngh, B. (June 2005). Measuring the economic costs of conflicts: The effect of declining development expenditures on Nepal's economic growth. [Electronic version]. Asian Development Bank, pp. 1–12.

Ram, R. (1986). Government size and economic growth: A new framework and some evidence from cross-section and time-series data. *American Economic Review*, *76*(1), 191–203.

Rapoport, A. (Ed.) (1968). *Clausewitz: On war*. England: Penguin Books.

Rasler, K., & Thompson, R. W. (1988). Defense burden, capital formation, and economic growth. *Journal of Conflict Resolution*, *322*, 61–86.

Rasler, K., & Thompson, W. (1985). War and the economic growth of major powers. *American Journal of Political Science*, *29*(3), 513–538.

Richardson, L. F. (1960). Arms and insecurity. In: N. Rashevsky & E. Trucco (Eds), Pittsburgh: Boxwood Press.

Romer, D. (1996). *Advanced macroeconomics*. New York: The McGraw-Hill Companies, Inc.

Roskin, M. G., & Coyle, J. J. (2008). *Politics of the Middle East: Culture and conflicts* (2nd ed.). Upper Saddle River, NJ: Pearson Prentice Hall.

Rostow, W. W. (1960). *The stages of economic growth: A non communist manifesto*. Cambridge: Cambridge University Press.

Rowthwell, C. E. (1941). War and economic institutions. In: J. Clarkson & T. Cochran (Eds), *War as social institution*. New York: Columbia University Press.

Russett, B. (1970). *What price vigilance? The burden of national defense*. New Haven, CT: Yale University Press.

Russett, B., Starr, H., & Kinsella, D. (2006). *World politics: The menu for choice*. Belmont, CA: Thomson Wadsworth.

Sadat, A. (1977). Sadat Knesset speech 1977. Available at http://www.zionism-israel.com/hdoc/Sadat_Knesset_speech_1977.htm. Retrieved on November 7, 2009.

Samuels, W. J. (1977). The political economy of Adam Smith. *Ethics*, *87*, 189–207.

Sandler, T., & Hartley, K. (1995). *The economics of defense*. Cambridge: Cambridge University Press.

Sartori, G. (1970). Concept misformation in comparative research. *American Political Science Review*, *64*, 1033–1053.

Schneider, F. (2005). The size of shadow economies in 145 countries from 1999 to 2003. *World Affairs*, *XI*(II), 113–129.

Schrodt, P. A. (1978). Richardson's N-nation model and the balance of power. *American Journal of Political Science*, *22*(2), 364–390.

Schumpeter, J. H. (1939). *Business cycles: A theoretical, historical, and statistical analysis of the capitalist process*. London: McGraw-Hill.

Sen, A. (1999). *Development as freedom*. New York: Anchor Books.

Sharara, W. (1981). *Kin and the booty: The foundation of politics in Saudi Arabia*. Beirut: Dar al-Tali'a.

Simowitz, R. (1976). *Bibliography on arms race models*. Bloomington, IN: Center for International Policy Studies, Indiana University.

Singer, D., Bremmer, S., & Stuckey, J. (1972). Capability, distribution, uncertainty and major power war, 1820–1965. In: B. Russett (Ed.), *Peace, war and numbers* (pp. 19–48). Beverly Hills, CA: Sage Publications.

Singer, D., & Small, M. (1992). *Correlates of war project: International and civil war data, 1816–1992, ICPSR 9905*. Ann Arbor, MI: Inter-University Consortium for Political and Social Research.

Small, M., & Singer, D. (1982). *Resort to arms: International and civil wars, 1816–1980*. Beverly Hills, CA: Sage Publications.

Smith, A. (2000). *The wealth of nations*. New York: The Modern Library.

Smith, R. (1980). Military expenditure and investment in OECD countries, 1953–1973. *Journal of Comparative Economics, 4*, 19–32.

Smith, R., & Georgiou, G. (1983). Assessing the effect of military expenditures on OECD economies: A survey. *Arms Control, 4*, 19–32.

Solow, R. (1957). Technical change and the aggregate production function. *The Review of Economics and Statistics, 39*(2), 312–320.

Solow, R. (1988). *Growth theory: An exposition*. New York: Oxford University Press.

Sombart, W. (1913). *Krieg und kapitalism*. Leipzig: Duncher and Humbot.

Stockholm International Peace Research Institute (SIPRI). (1969). *World armaments and disarmament*. New York: Oxford University Press.

Stockholm International Peace Research Institute. (1974). *World armaments and disarmament*. New York: Oxford University Press.

Stockholm International Peace Research Institute. (1976). *World armaments and disarmament*. Stockholm: Almqvist & Wiksell.

Stockholm International Peace Research Institute. (1980). *World armaments and disarmament*. Stockholm: Almqvist & Wiksell.

Stockholm International Peace Research Institute. (1983). *World armaments and disarmament*. New York: Oxford University Press.

Stockholm International Peace Research Institute. (1984). *World armaments and disarmament*. New York: International Publications Service.

Stockholm International Peace Research Institute. (1990). *World armaments and disarmament*. New York: Oxford University Press.

Stockholm International Peace Research Institute. (1991). *World armaments and disarmament*. New York: Oxford University Press.

Stockholm International Peace Research Institute. (1992). *World armaments and disarmament*. New York: Oxford University Press.

Stockholm International Peace Research Institute. (1996). *World armaments and disarmament*. New York: Oxford University Press.

Stockholm International Peace Research Institute. (1997). *World armaments and disarmament*. New York: Oxford University Press.

Stockholm International Peace Research Institute. (2001). *World armaments and disarmament*. New York: Oxford University Press.

Stockholm International Peace Research Institute. (2002). *World armaments and disarmament*. New York: Oxford University Press.

Stockholm International Peace Research Institute. (2007). *World armaments and disarmament*. Stockholm: Almqvist & Wiksell.

Stockholm International Peace Research Institute. (2008). *World armaments and disarmament*. New York: Oxford University Press.

Stoll, R. (1992). "Too little" but not for too long: Public attitude in defense spending. In: A. Mintz (Ed.), *The political economy of military spending in the United States* (pp. 52–64). London: Routledge.

Strategy Page. (2007). Israeli weapons conquer the world [online]. Available at http://www.strategypage.com/htmw/htproc/articles/20071214.aspx. Retrieved on June 7, 2009.

Thorp, W. (1941). Postwar depression. *American Economic Review, 305*(supplement), 352–361.

Tilly, C. (1975). Reflection on the history of European state-making. In: C. Tilly (Ed.), *The formation of national states in Western Europe* (pp. 3–83). Princeton, NJ: Princeton University Press.

United Nations Department for Disarmament Affairs. (2005). Peace and security through disarmament. Available at http://disarmament.un.org/cab/

United Nations Development Program (UNDP). (2003). Human development: Millennium development goals: A compact among nations to end human poverty. New York: Oxford University Press.

UNSC. (1973). United Nations security coucil resolution 338. Available at http://middleeast.about.com/od/documents/qt/me081115d.htm

Vanhanen, T. (2000). A new dataset for measuring democracy, 1810–1998. *Journal of Peace Research, 3*(2), 251–261.

Vanhanen, T. (2003). Democratization and power resources 1850–2000. Available at http://www.fsd.uta.fi/english/data/catalogue/FSD1216/meF1216e.html. Retrieved on October 23, 2009.

Van Raemdonck, D., & Diehl, P. (1989). After shooting stops: Insights on postwar economic growth. *Journal of Peace Research, 26*(3), 249–264.

Vasquez, A. J. (1996). Classics of International Relations. Englewood Cliffs: Prentice Hall.

Veseth, M. (2007). What is International Political Economy? Available at http://www.pugetsound.edu/x12490.xml. Accessed on August 15, 2009.

Waltz, K. (1959). *Man, the state, and war: A theoretical analysis*. New York: Columbia.

Waltz, N. K. (1979). *Theory of International Politics*. New York: Columbia University Press.

Wanat, J. (1974). Bases of budgetary incrementalism [electronic version]. *The American Political Science Review, 68*, 1221–1228.

Ward, M., & Davis, D. (1992). Sizing up the peace dividend: Economic growth and military spending in the United States, 1948–1996. *American Political Science Review, 86*, 748–755.

Ward, M. D. (1984). Differential paths to parity: A study of the contemporary arms race. *American Political Science Review, 78*, 297–317.

Weatherby, J. N. (2001). *The Middle East and North Africa: A political Primer*. New York: Longman.

Weatherby, J. N. (2002). *The Middle East and North Africa: A political primer*. New York: Longman.

Weatherby, J. N., Emmit, B., Evans, J., Gooden, R., Long, D., Reed, I., & Novikova-Carter, O. D. (2009). *The other world: Issues and politics of the developing word* (6th ed). New York: Pearson Longman.

Weatherby, N. J. (2009). *The other world: Issues and politics of the developing countries* (8th ed.). New York: Pearson Longman.

Weed, E. (1983). Military participation ratios, human capital formation, and economic growth: A cross-national analysis. *Journal of Political and Military Sociology, 11*, 11–20.

Wendt, A. (1999). *Social theory of international politics*. New York: Cambridge University Press.

Wheeler, H. (1975). *The effect of war on industrial growth, 1816–1970*. Ph.D. Ann Arbor: University of Michigan.

White, K. (1992). The Durbin-Watson test for autocorrelation in nonlinear models. *The Review of Economics and Statistics*, *74*(2), 370–373.

Wikisource. (2009). United Nations security council resolution 242. Available at http://en.wikisource.org/wiki/United_Nations_Security_Council_Resolution_242.

Wildavsky, A. (1964). *The politics of the budgetary process*. Boston: Little Brown.

Wildavsky, A. (1988). *The new politics of the budgetary process*. Glenview, IL: Scott, Foresman.

Wimberley, L. (2003). *The mouse that roared*. New York: Four Walls Eight Windows.

World Desk reference. Available at http://dev.penhall.com/divisions/has/worlddefense/. Retrieved on February 12, 2008.

Zubaida, S. (1990). The politics of the Islamic investment companies in Egypt. *The British Journal of the Middle Eastern Studies*, *17*, 152–161.

Zubaida, S. (1992). Islam, the state and democracy: Contrasting conceptions of society in Egypt. *Middle East Report*, November–December, pp. 2–10.

APPENDIX A

RESULTS OF THE NON-LINEAR LEAST SQUARES METHODS

Parameter	Kenya	Jamaica	Iran	Paraguay	Panama
$_\lambda$ est. t-statistic	0.187	−1.228	−34E−16	0.008	0.004
	1.634	−23.943**	−1.90	0.599	0.518
Ψ_l	−0.808	1.606	84E−15	0.530	1.382
	−3.582**	1.578	11.46**	0.103	2.047*
Ψ_k	−0.0570	−44.108	74E−16	−0.018	−0.082
	−0.7335	−3.976**	4.44**	−0.136	−2.472*
Π_m	0.240	−0.112	0.878	−0.206	−0.573E−7
	1.783*	−0.981	25**	−0.272	0.271
Ψ_m	−0.573	1.289	−0.12	0.198	−0.70E−8
	−1.223	0.0753	34E+9**	1.161	0.106
Π_n	0.148	−0.677	−0.878	2.781	−1.429
	0.160	−59.080**	−25E+8**	2.296*	−2.181*
Ψ_n	0.559	−0.039	−22E−16	0.552	0.275
	3.111**	−25.371**	−3.432**	1.896*	3.679**
LR1	1.000	33.820	−22E−16	1.000	1.000
	1.000	56.482**	−3.431**	1.000	1.000
	$N = 39$	$N = 37$	$N = 39$	$N = 41$	$N = 38$
	$R^2 = 0.90$	$R^2 = 0.81$	$R^2 = 0.98$	$R^2 = 0.73$	$R^2 = 0.61$
	DW = 2.08	DW = 2.11	DW = 1.96	DW = 1.39	DW = 1.41
$_\lambda$ est. t-statistic	0.018	−1020	0.98E−3	0.008	0.004
	1.634	−14.696**	0.58	0.599	0.518
Ψ_l	−0.808	1.560	−0.053	0.530	1.382
	−3.582**	1.560	−0.975	0.103	2.047*
Ψ_k	−0.057	−39.788	0.002	−0.189	−0.082
	0.735	−23.319**	0.86	−0.136	−2.472*

APPENDIX A. (*Continued*)

Parameter	Kenya	Jamaica	Iran	Paraguay	Panama
Ψ_m	0.240	0.002	0.125E−6	−0.206	−0.573E−7
	1.783*	0.025	1.826*	−0.277	−0.271
Ψ_m	−0.057	0.831	−0.378E−9	0.198	−0870E−8
	−1.223	0.427	−0.041	1.161	−0106
Π_n	0.148	−0.770	0.018	2.781	−0.1429
	0.161	−44.002**	1.782*	2.296*	−2.185*
Ψ_n	0.559	0.036	0.026	0.552	0.275
	3.111**	−21.239**	8.063**	1.896*	3.679**
LR2	1.000	38.342	0.003	1.000	1.000
	1.000	43.796**	2.142*	1.000	1.000
	$N = 39$	$N = 37$	$N = 39$	$N = 41$	$N = 38$
	$R^2 = 0.90$	$R^2 = 0.83$	$R^2 = 0.97$	$R^2 = 1.39$	$R^2 = 0.61$
	DW = 2.08	DW = 2.11	DW = 1.99	DW = 1.39	DW = 1.41
$_\lambda$ est. t-statistic	0.018	−1020	0.002	0.008	0.004
	1.634	−14.696**	0.935	0.599	0.518
Ψ_l	−0.808	1.560	−0.099	0.530	1.382
	−3.582**	1.560	−1.212	0.103	2.047*
Ψ_k	−0.057	−39.788	0.001	−0.189	−0.082
	0.735	−23.319**	0.569	−0.136	−2.472*
Π_m	0.240	0.002	0.464E−7	−0.206	−0.573E−7
	1.783*	0.025	0.688	−0.277	−0.271
Ψ_m	−0.057	0.831	−0.405E−8	0.198	−0.870E−8
	−1.223	0.427	−0.449	1.161	−0.106
Π_n	0.148	−0.770	0.014	2.781	−1.429
	0.161	−44.002**	1.086	2.296*	−2.181*
Ψ_n	0.559	0.036	0.027	0.552	0.275
	3.111**	−21.239**	7.8894**	1.896*	3.679**
LR3	1.000	38.342	0.003	1.000	1.000
	1.000	43.796**	1.516	1.000	1.000
	$N = 39$	$N = 37$	$N = 39$	$N = 41$	$N = 38$
	$R^2 = 0.90$	$R^2 = 0.83$	$R^2 = 0.96$	$R^2 = 0.73$	$R^2 = 0.61$
	DW = 2.08	DW = 2.11	DW = 1.90	DW = 1.39	DW = 1.413
$_\lambda$ est. t-statistic	0.019	−4.449	0.028	0.009	0.832E−3
	1.773*	−36.233**	3.266**	0.667	0.100
Ψ_l	−0.706	1.514	−0.343	−1.572	1.262
	−2.976**	1.514	−0.957	−0.297	1.871*
Ψ_k	−0.649	−55.671	0.042	0.024	−0.773
	−34.816**	1.009	−0.296	0.179	−2.275*

APPENDIX A. (*Continued*)

Parameter	Kenya	Jamaica	Iran	Paraguay	Panama
Π_m	0.246	−0.074	0.508E−6	−0.220	−0.202E−7
	1.903*	−1.339	0.287	−0.296	−0.097
Ψ_m	0.060	90.481	0.100E−6	0.191	−0.129E−7
	−1.536	40.932**	0.762	1.171	−0.149
Π_n	0.1609	−0.860	−0.151	2.490	−1.377
	0.174	−22.41**	−0.341	1.938*	−2.099*
Ψ_n	0.558	−0.108	0.471	0.514	0.308
	3.311**	−6.363**	4.147**	1.747*	3.789**
LR4	−0.169	4.483	0.046	0.030	0.015
	−1.068	24.009**	1.521	0.819	1.365
	$N = 39$	$N = 37$	$N = 39$	$N = 41$	$N = 38$
	$R^2 = 0.90$	$R^2 = 0.92$	$R^2 = 0.97$	$R^2 = 0.74$	$R^2 = 0.63$
	DW = 2.22	DW = 2.09	DW = 2.17	DW = 1.38	DW = 1.37
λ est. t-statistic	0.009	−0.971	0.028	0.009	0.071
	1.177	−14.999**	3.554**	0.703	3.106**
Ψ_l	0.962	1.554	0.710	−2.072	−0.195
	0.662	1.554	0.838	−0.422	−2.322*
Ψ_k	−0.090	−39.090	0.026	0.022	−0.110
	−1.085	−24.794**	0.638	0.168	−1.095
Π_m	0.237	0.066	0.756E−6	−0.323	0.804
	1.768*	0.679	0.410	−0.438	0.003
Ψ_m	−0.628	0.266	0.110E−6	0.153	−0.195E−7
	−1.2660	0.276	0.839	1.013	−1.344
Π_n	0.108	−0.783	−0.179	2.466	−0.543
	0.106	−48.060**	−0.407	2.040*	−1.095
Ψ_n	0.718	−.0356	0.455	0.527	0.739
	4.521**	−22.347**	4.194**	1.947*	1.806*
LR5	−0.068	38.719	−0.038	0.055	−0.018
	−1.391	47.461**	−0.901	1.519	−0.911
	$N = 39$	$N = 37$	$N = 39$	$N = 41$	$N = 38$
	$R^2 = 0.91$	$R^2 = 0.82$	$R^2 = 0.97$	$R^2 = 0.74$	$R^2 = 0.57$
	DW = 2.18	DW = 2.11	DW = 2.20	DW = 1.44	DW = 1.60
λ est. t-statistic	0.022	−4.835	0.034	−0.006	0.832E−3
	1.836*	−27.674**	4.252**	0.459	0.100
Ψ_l	−0.855	1.550	0.087	−1.982	1.262
	−3.889**	1.550	0.418	−0.361	1.871*

APPENDIX A. *(Continued)*

Parameter	Kenya	Jamaica	Iran	Paraguay	Panama
Ψ_k	−0.041	−59.834	0.025	0.068	−0.077
	−0.645	−28.683**	0.746	0.442	−2.275*
Π_m	0.324	−0.090	0.547E−6	−0.266	−0.202E−7
	2.211*	−1.189*	0.304	−0.366	−0.097
Ψ_m	−0.553	97.061	0.115E−6	0.172	−0.129E−7
	−1.428	31.707**	1.068	1.135	−0.149
Π_n	0.066	−0.094	−0.290	2.473	−1.377
	0.069	−20.786**	−0.688	2.155*	−2.099*
Ψ_n	.497	−0.186	0.392	0.567	0.308
	2.878**	−4.33**	4.203**	1.830*	3.789**
LR6	−0.094	4.857	−0.146	−0.610	0.015
	−1.65	21.545**	−2.075*	−1.388	1.365
	$N = 39$	$N = 37$	$N = 39$	$N = 41$	$N = 38$
	$R^2 = 0.91$	$R^2 = 0.91$	$R^2 = 0.97$	$R^2 = 0.74$	$R^2 = 0.63$
	DW = 1.86	DW = 2.01	DW = 2.13	DW = 1.43	DW = 1.37
λ est. t-statistic	0.017	−4.574	0.027	0.017	0.007
	1.628	−53.711**	3.420**	1.940*	1.348
Ψ_l	−0.579	1.526	0.564	−0.777	2.151
	−0.817	1.526	1.095	−0.193	2.516*
Ψ_k	−0.536	−57.017	0.023	−0.071	−0.750
	−0.722	−44.468**	0.595	−0.542	−2.901*
Π_m	0.242	−0.085	0.149E−5	−0.717	−0.703E−7
	1.80*	−1.256	0.791	−0.963	0.336
Ψ_m	−0.056	92.609	0.109E−6	0.135	−0.509
	−1.16	57.364**	0.782	1.092	−0.661
Π_n	0.121	−0.089	−0.2590	2.374	−1.399
	0.127	−33.072**	−0.603	1.915*	−2.343*
Ψ_n	0.570	−0.136	0.486	0.360	0.283
	3.303**	−11.018**	4.365**	2.299*	4.404**
LR7	−0.112	4.608	−0.035	0.137	−0.030
	−0.348	38.089**	−1.280	1.988*	−1.245
	$N = 39$	$N = 37$	$N = 39$	$N = 41$	$N = 38$
	$R^2 = 0.90$	$R^2 = 0.91$	$R^2 = 0.97$	$R^2 = 0.75$	$R^2 = 0.62$
	DW = 2.09	DW = 2.09	DW = 2.13	DW = 1.42	DW = 1.53
λ est. t-statistic	0.017	−4.527	0.034	0.006	0.004
	1.536	−36.986**	4.252**	0.459	0.492

APPENDIX A. *(Continued)*

Parameter	Kenya	Jamaica	Iran	Paraguay	Panama
Ψ_l	−0.825	1.522	0.087	−1.985	1.327
	−3.621**	1.521	0.418	−0.361	1.732*
Ψ_k	−0.063	−56.509	0.0257	0.068	−0.812
	−0823	−35.422**	0.746	0.442	−2.370*
Π_m	0.238	−0.089	0.547E−6	−0.266	−0.584E−7
	1.788*	−1.683	0.304	−0.366	0.261
Ψ_m	−.059	91.806	0.115E−6	0.172	−0.895E−8
	−1.283	41.658**	1.086	1.135	−0.107
Π_n	0.089	0.088	−0.290	2.473	−1.427
	0.912	−22.155**	−0.688	2.155*	−2.106*
Ψ_n	0.572	−0.129	0.392	0.567	0.276
	3.078**	−6.732**	4.203**	1.830*	3.370**
LR8	0.012	4.549	−0.146	−0.061	0.0019
	0.508	23.308*	−2.075*	−1.38	0.167
	$N = 39$	$N = 37$	$N = 39$	$N = 41$	$N = 38$
	$R^2 = 0.90$	$R^2 = 0.92$	$R^2 = 0.97$	$R^2 = 0.75$	$R^2 = 0.61$
	DW = 2.06	DW = 2.09	DW = 2.13	DW = 1.42	DW = 1.40

* Significant at 0.05 level.
** Significant at 0.01 level.

Parameter	Sri Lanka	Singapore	Sierra Leon	Senegal	Rwanda
λ est. *t*-statistic	−0.025	0.088	0.034	−0.359	−.002
	−1.563	11.746**	3.633**	−0.399	−0.134
Ψ_l	3.228	−0.308	−6.277	0.486	1.656
	2.354*	0.917	−4.393**	0.387	1.834**
Ψ_k	−0.074	0.004	0.039	0.304	−0.426
	−0.340	0.162	0.814	0.094	−0.254
Π_m	−0.397	0.268	1.219	−0.883	−0.243
	−3.864**	0.398	3.610**	−2.741**	−1.351
Ψ_m	0.102	0.027	0.276	0.462	0.146
	1.357	1.278	3.584**	2.837**	1.069
Π_n	1.955	−0.616	0.119E−4	−0.334	−0.267
	3.368**	−3.390**	3.379**	−3.99	−1.661
Ψ_n	0.825	0.431	0.270E−6	0.406	0.258
	2.340**	2.184*	0.879	4.184	2.258*

APPENDIX A. (*Continued*)

Parameter	Sri Lanka	Singapore	Sierra Leon	Senegal	Rwanda
LR1	1.00	1.00	1.00	1.00	−0.130
	1.00	1.00	1.00	1.00	−1.884*
	$N = 43$	$N = 36$	$N = 36$	$N = 40$	$N = 32$
	$R^2 = 0.72$	$R^2 = 0.99$	$R^2 = 0.76$	$R^2 = 0.87$	$R^2 = 0.71$
	DW = 2.44	DW = 1.40	DW = 1.63	DW = 2.02	DW = 2.12
λ est. t-statistic	−0.025	0.088	0.034	−0.003	0.055
	−1.515	11.746**	4.038**	−0.399	2.032*
Ψ_l	3.192	−0.308	−6.359	0.486	−0.085
	2.094*	−0.917	−4.948**	0.387	0.860
Ψ_k	−0.068	0.004	0.419	0.304	−0.602
	−0.285	0.162	0.946	0.936	−0.982
Π_m	−0.396	0.268	1.218	−0.884	0.167
	−3.799**	0.398	3.647**	−2.741**	0.810
Ψ_m	0.103	0.027	0.254	0.462	−0.002
	1.388	1.278	3.891**	2.83**	0.034
Π_n	1.952	−0.616	0.127E−4	−0.334	−0.177
	3.56**	−3.390**	3.687**	−3.99**	−1.510
Ψ_n	0.825	0.043	0.249E−6	0.406	0.152
	2.366*	2.184*	0.817	4.184**	2.300*
LR2	−0.001	1.00	−0.157	1.00	−0.195
	−0.053	1.00	−2.068*	1.00	−2.892**
	$N = 43$	$N = 36$	$N = 36$	$N = 40$	$N = 32$
	$R^2 = 0.73$	$R^2 = 0.99$	$R^2 = 0.80$	$R^2 = 0.87$	$R^2 = 0.72$
	DW = 2.44	DW = 1.40	DW = 1.74	DW = 2.02	DW = 2.04
λ est. t-statistic	0.025	0.088	0.034	−0.359	0.018
	−1.515	11.746**	4.037**	0.399	0.542
Ψ_l	3.192	−0.308	−6.359	0.486	0.561
	2.093*	−0.917	−4.948**	0.387	0.754
Ψ_k	0.089	0.004	0.042	0.030	−0.033
	−0.285	0.162	0.946	0.0934	−0.266
Π_m	−0.396	0.026	1.218	−0.883	−0.003
	−3.799**	0.398	3.647**	−2.741**	−0.011
Ψ_m	0.103	0.027	0.254	0.462	0.063
	1.388	1.278	3.89**	2.83**	0.455
Π_n	1.952	−0.616	0.127E−4	−0.334	−0.222
	3.557**	−3.390**	3.687**	−3.99**	−1.593

APPENDIX A. (*Continued*)

Parameter	Sri Lanka	Singapore	Sierra Leon	Senegal	Rwanda
Ψ_n	0.825	0.043	0.2499	0.406	0.210
	2.367*	2.184*	0.817	4.184**	2.379*
LR3	−0.001	1.00	−0.157	1.00	−0.110
	0.053	1.00	−2.069*	1.00	−2.265*
	$N = 43$	$N = 36$	$N = 36$	$N = 40$	$N = 32$
	$R^2 = 0.73$	$R^2 = 0.99$	$R^2 = 0.98$	$R^2 = 0.87$	$R^2 = 0.73$
	DW = 2.44	DW = 1.40	DW = 1.74	DW = 2.02	DW = 1.97
λ est. t-statistic	−.028	−0.630	−0.442	0.006	−0.009
	−2.089*	−19.301**	−6.406**	0.580	−0.585
Ψ_l	1.242	45.127	288.18	−0.136	1.248
	0.594	1.304	1.650	−0.131	1.402
Ψ_k	0.255	14.704	15.081	0.241	−0.097
	0.721	1.300	1.139	0.752	−0.472
Π_m	−0.383	0.382	0.449	−0.635	−0.328
	−3.823**	3.477**	1.748*	−2.172*	−1.78*
Ψ_m	0.774	−0.053	69.584	0.332	0.272
	0.931	−0.045	0.891	2.278*	1.697*
Π_n	2.116	0.837	0.100E−4	−0.328	−0.196
	3.648**	4.255**	−0.120E−4	−4.283**	−1.062
Ψ_n	0.959	−26.440**	−1.120E−4	0.370	0.261
	2.760**	−0.997	−0.198	4.252**	1.937*
LR4	−0.030	0.706	0.212	−0.025	0.078
	−1.437*	20.873**	1.695*	−0.774	0.973
	$N = 43$	$N = 36$	$N = 36$	$N = 40$	$N = 32$
	$R^2 = 0.74$	$R^2 = 0.99$	$R^2 = 0.39$	$R^2 = 0.88$	$R^2 = 0.69$
	DW = 2.48	DW = 1.34	DW = 1.79	DW = 2.13	DW = 1.97
λ est. t-statistic	−0.028	−0.630	−0.613	−0.913E−3	−0.003
	−2.089*	−19.301**	−3.785**	0.980E−1	1.196
Ψ_l	1.242	45.727	824.78	1.946	1.435
	0.594	1.304	0.908	1.378	1.196
Ψ_k	0.255	14.704	54.273	−0.148	−0.083
	0.721	1.130	0.782	−0.531	−0.471
Π_m	−0.383	0.382	0.473	−0.761	−0.220
	−3.823**	3.477**	2.146**	−2.583**	−1.129
Ψ_m	0.077	−0.053	440.15	0.449	0.196
	0.931	−0.045	0.706	2.889**	1.345

APPENDIX A. (*Continued*)

Parameter	Sri Lanka	Singapore	Sierra Leon	Senegal	Rwanda
Π_n	2.116	0.837	0.121	−0.317	−0.167
	3.648**	4.255**	2.204*	−4.169**	−0.948
Ψ_n	0.959	−26.440	−0.249E−3	0.400	0.251
	2.760**	−0.997	−0.602	4.494**	2.002*
LR5	−0.030	0.706	0.254	−0.048	−0.030
	−1.437	20.873**	1.445	−2.046*	−1.125
	$N = 43$	$N = 36$	$N = 36$	$N = 40$	$N = 32$
	$R^2 = 0.74$	$R^2 = 0.99$	$R^2 = 0.37$	$R^2 = 0.89$	$R^2 = 0.68$
	DW = 2.48	DW = 1.34	DW = 1.21	DW = 2.28	DW = 2.06
λ est. t-statistic	−0.022	0.088	0.011	−0.0013	−0.009
	−1.191	11.746**	1.102	0.142	−0.508
Ψ_l	3.030	−0.308	−3.642**	0.281	1.353
	1.848*	−0.917	−3.283**	0.239	1.284
Ψ_k	−0.252	0.004	0.052	0.072	−0.118
	−0.651	0.162	0.879	0.247	−0.599
Π_m	−0.416	0.026	1.322	−0.804	−0.297
	−3.739**	0.398	6.87**	−2.636	−1.538
Ψ_m	0.101	0.276	0.696	0.416	0.233
	1.430	1.278	3.922**	2.633**	1.529
Π_n	1.853	−0.616	−0.155	−0.340	−0.214
	3.226**	−3.390**	−0.493	−4.051**	−1.174
Ψ_n	0.771	0.431	0.602E−4	0.408	0.294
	2.251*	2.184*	0.214	4.281**	2.174*
LR6	0.227	1.00	0.791	−0.040	1.00
	0.433	1.00	1.506	0.837	1.00
	$N = 43$	$N = 36$	$N = 36$	$N = 40$	$N = 32$
	$R^2 = 0.7$	$R^2 = 0.99$	$R^2 = 0.92$	$R^2 = 0.87$	$R^2 = 0.67$
	DW = 2.47	DW = 1.40	DW = 1.62	DW = 2.09	DW = 2.06
λ est. t-statistic	−0.022	0.630	0.051	−0.002	−0.225
	−1.191	−19.301**	5.968**	−0.261	−25.795**
Ψ_l	3.030	45.727	−4.432	0.721	−15.969
	1.85*	1.304	−4.577**	0.530	−5.102**
Ψ_k	−0.252	14.704	0.630	0.641	−5.592
	−0.651	1.130	0.229	0.195	−7.042**
Π_m	−0.416	0.382	1.428	−0.888	−0.077
	−3.739**	3.477**	4.318**	−2.893**	−0.196

APPENDIX A. (*Continued*)

Parameter	Sri Lanka	Singapore	Sierra Leon	Senegal	Rwanda
Ψ_m	0.101	−0.055	0.187	0.452	−0.217
	1.430	−0.450	4.219**	2.883**	−0.348
Π_n	1.853	0.837	−0.190	−0.322	0.564E−4
	3.226**	4.255**	−0.401	−3.614**	222.880**
Ψ_n	0.771	−26.44	0.155	0.390	7.080**
	2.251**	−0.997	0.739	3.65**	234.900**
LR7	0.0227	0.706	0.924	−0.122E−1	0.237
	0.433	20.873**	0.591	−0.348	5.268**
	$N = 43$	$N = 36$	$N = 36$	$N = 40$	$N = 32$
	$R^2 = 0.73$	$R^2 = 0.99$	$R^2 = 0.84$	$R^2 = 0.87$	$R^2 = 0.99$
	DW = 2.47	DW = 1.34	DW = 1.30	DW = 1.99	DW = 1.72
λ est. t-statistic	−0.217	−0.630	−0.398	−0.327E−3	0.052
	−1.192	−19.301**	−5.923**	−0.035	1.855*
Ψ_l	3.030	45.727	294.68	0.495	−0.073
	1.848*	1.304	1.313	0.438	−0.602
Ψ_k	−0.252	14.704	17.046	0.034	−0.040
	−0.651	1.130	0.958	0.123	−0.608
Π_m	−0.416	0.382	0.508	−0.667	0.074
	−3.739**	3.477**	1.784*	−1.989**	0.367
Ψ_m	0.101	−0.053	70.762	0.377	0.016
	1.430	−0.045	1.032	2.368*	0.233
Π_n	1.853	0.837	0.161E−4	−0.374	0.224
	3.226**	4.255**	1.715*	−4.307**	−1.641
Ψ_n	0.771	−26.440	−0.122E−4	0.442	0.167
	2.251*	−0.997	−0.239	4.427**	2.412*
LR8	0.022	0.706	−0.208	−0.389	−0.176
	0.433	20.873**	−0.470	−1.105	−2.629**
	$N = 43$	$N = 36$	$N = 36$	$N = 40$	$N = 32$
	$R^2 = 0.73$	$R^2 = 0.99$	$R^2 = 0.33$	$R^2 = 0.87$	$R^2 = 0.71$
	DW = 2.47	DW = 1.34	DW = 1.23	DW = 2.15	DW = 2.10

* Significant at 0.05 level.

** Significant at 0.01 level.

APPENDIX A. (*Continued*)

Parameter	Morocco	Mexico	Ethiopia	El-Salvador	Egypt
λ est. *t*-statistic	0.040	0.005	0.003	−0.303	0.01
	3.068**	0.919	1.565	−7.685**	4.458**
	−0.614E−7	−1.429	−0.135	1.000	−0.326
	−0.394	−2.768**	−1.797*	1.000	−5.369**
Ψ_l	0.045	−0.277	0.003	1.000	0.506
	0.844	−2.02*	1.251	1.000	0.476
Π_m	0.110E−7	−0.602E−7	−0.018	−0.775E−6	0.618
	0.080	−0.477	−3.136**	−0.775E−6	1.256
Ψ_m	−0.204E−6	−0.356E−6	−0.007	0.984	0.001
	−2.313*	−2.050*	−3.343**	0.984	0.545
Π_n	0.399E−6	−0.229	0.410	1.00	−0.402
	0.112	−0.676	5.109**	1.00	−2.651**
Ψ_n	0.171E−6	0.866	0.035	0.985	0.021
	1.680	6.830**	10.694**	0.985	7.770**
LR1	1.000	1.000	0.921E−3	1.000	−0.003
	1.000	1.000	0.811	1.000	−1.945*
	$N = 43$	$N = 43$	$N = 33$	$N = 43$	$N = 43$
	$R^2 = 0.80$	$R^2 = 0.99$	$R^2 = 0.94$	$R^2 = 0.001$	$R^2 = 0.92$
	DW = 1.49	DW = 1.766	DW = 2.14	DW = 1.77	DW = 1.89
λ est. *t*-statistic	0.052	0.005	0.314	0.022	0.009
	3.380**	0.919	1.285	2.081*	3.441**
Ψ_l	−0.581	−1.429	−0.124	0.389E−7	−0.313
	−0.547	−2.768**	−1.596	0.286	−4.152**
Ψ_k	0.024	−0.277	0.314	0.185	0.007
	0.592	−2.02*	1.200	0.391	0.765
Π_m	−0.127E−7	−0.602E−7	−0.017	−0.139E−6	0.763E−3
	−0.096	−0.477	−3.049**	−0.129	0.178
Ψ_m	−0.135E−6	−0.356E−6	−0.722	0.966E−7	−0.001
	−1.924*	−2.050*	−3.060**	0.982	−0.801
Π_n	0.893E−6	−0.229	0.403	0.446E−5	−0.412
	0.281	−0.676	5.278*	0.101	−2.564**
Ψ_n	0.116E−6	0.866	0.036	0.213E−7	0.023
	1.525	6.830**	10.604**	0.275	8.233**
LR2	−0.057	1.000	0.988	−0.152	1.000
	−1.705*	1.000	1.095	−3.496**	1.000
	$N = 43$	$N = 43$	$N = 33$	$N = 43$	$N = 43$
	$R^2 = 0.28$	$R^2 = 0.99$	$R^2 = 0.94$	$R^2 = 0.27$	$R^2 = 0.92$
	DW = 1.62	DW = 1.76	DW = 2.09	DW = 2.64	DW = 1.72

APPENDIX A. (*Continued*)

Parameter	Morocco	Mexico	Ethiopia	El-Salvador	Egypt
λ est. *t*-statistic	0.520	0.005	0.003	0.026	0.009
	3.380**	0.919	1.565	2.081*	4.458*
Ψ_l	−0.581E−7	−1.429	−0.134	0.389	−0.326
	−0.547	−2.768**	−1.797*	0.285	−5.369**
Ψ_k	0.238E−1	−0.277	0.003	0.185	0.005
	0.591	−2.022**	1.251	0.391	0.476
Π_m	−0.127E−7	−0.602	−0.180	−0.139E−6	0.006
	−0.096	−0.477	−3.136**	−0.128	1.256
Ψ_m	−0.134E−6	−0.356	−0.007	0.966E−7	0.112
	−1.924*	−2.050*	−3.343**	0.982	0.545
Π_n	0.893E−6	−0.229	0.410	0.446	−0.402
	0.281	−0.676	5.109**	0.102	−2.651**
Ψ_n	0.445E−6	0.866	0.036	0.213E−7	0.021
	1.525	6.830**	10.694*	0.275	7.770
LR3	−0.579	1.00	0.921	−0.152	−0.003
	−1.705*	1.00	0.811	−3.495**	−1.945
	$N = 43$	$N = 43$	$N = 33$	$N = 43$	$N = 43$
	$R^2 = 0.28$	$R^2 = 0.99$	$R^2 = 0.94$	$R^2 = 0.28$	$R^2 = 0.92$
	DW = 1.62	DW = 1.76	DW = 2.14	DW = 2.64	DW = 1.89
λ est. *t*-statistic	0.008	0.005	0.003	−0.144	0.009
	0.311	0.906	1.374	−2.946**	3.612**
Ψ_l	−0.120	−1.309	−0.111	0.80E−6	−0.302
	−0.326	−1.464	−1.489	0.218	−4.079**
Ψ_k	0.089	−0.275	0.003	−0.414	0.006
	0.825	−1.996*	1.259	−0.393	0.656
Π_m	0.501E−7	−0.571E−7	−0.017	0.146E−6	0.103
	0.353	−0.431	−3.019**	0.001	0.249
Ψ_m	−0.594E−6	−0.355E−6	−0.007	0.499E−6	−0.002
	−1.117	−2.0537*	−3.034**	0.230	−0.947
Π_n	0.480	−0.227	0.412	−0.189E−4	−0.413
	0.857	−0.678	5.667**	−0.400	−2.759**
Ψ_n	0.463E−6	0.863	0.363	0.304	0.023
	1.062	6.558**	10.391**	0.126	8.544**
LR4	0.041	−0.004	1.000	0.175	−0.307
	1.356	−0.163	1.000	3.160	−0.417
	$N = 43$	$N = 43$	$N = 33$	$N = 43$	$N = 43$
	$R^2 = 0.25$	$R^2 = 0.99$	$R^2 = 0.94$	$R^2 = 0.25$	$R^2 = 0.92$
	DW = 1.56	DW = 1.75	DW = 2.23	DW = 2.45	DW = 1.77

APPENDIX A. (*Continued*)

Parameter	Morocco	Mexico	Ethiopia	El-Salvador	Egypt
λ est. t-statistic	0.009	0.005	0.009	−0.272	0.021
	0.396	0.905	3.137**	−6.975**	3.049**
Ψ_l	−0.160E−7	−2.236	−0.096	1.000	−1.331
	−0.052	−2.472**	−1.918*	1.000	−1.076
Ψ_k	0.098	−0.271	0.64E−3	1.000	0.013
	1.048	−1.967*	0.315	1.000	0.082
Π_m	−0.137E−7	−0.1002E−6	−0.228	−0.612E−5	0.028
	−0.103	−0.747	−3.878**	−0.612E−5	0.384
Ψ_m	−0.693E−6	−0.403E−3	−0.006	0.985	−0.016
	−1.441	−2.331*	−3.513**	0.985	−0.589
Π_n	0.46E−5	−0.259	0.411	1.000	−10.084
	0.933	−0.768	6.000**	1.000	−3.099**
Ψ_n	0.429E−6	0.872	0.033	0.986	0.411
	1.260	7.013**	10.465**	0.986	4.521**
LR5	0.044	0.029	−0.006	1.000	0.485
	1.610	1.103	−2.705**	1.000	1.067
	$N = 43$	$N = 43$	$N = 33$	$N = 43$	$N = 43$
	$R^2 = 0.25$	$R^2 = 0.99$	$R^2 = 0.94$	$R^2 = 0.00$	$R^2 = 0.94$
	DW = 1.61	DW = 1.85	DW = 2.21	DW = 1.46	DW = 1.73
λ est. t-statistic	0.046	0.005	0.003	−0.303	0.009
	3.303**	0.929	1.374	−7.685**	3.441**
Ψ_l	−0.235-6	−1.416	−0.111	1.000	−0.313
	−1.0762	−2.682**	−1.489	1.000	−4.152**
Ψ_k	0.052	−0.276	0.312	1.000	0.773
	0.998	−1.993*	1.259	1.000	0.765
Π_m	0.101E−5	−0.640E−7	−0.178	−0.775E−6	0.763
	0.577	−0.506	−3.019**	−0.775E−6	0.178
Ψ_m	−0.174E−6	−0.366E−6	−0.007	0.984	−0.134
	−1.760*	−2.025*	−3.034**	0.984	−0.801
Π_n	−0.825E−6	−0.229	0.412	1.000	−0.412
	−0.213	−0.689	5.668**	1.000	−2.564**
Ψ_n	0.119E−6	0.867	0.363	0.985	0.023
	1.285	7.014	10.391**	0.985	8.233**
LR6	1.000	−0.005	1.000	1.000	1.000
	1.000	−0.230	1.000	1.000	1.000
	$N = 43$	$N = 43$	$N = 33$	$N = 43$	$N = 43$
	$R^2 = 0.24$	$R^2 = 0.99$	$R^2 = 0.94$	$R^2 = 0.001$	$R^2 = 0.92$
	DW = 1.53	DW = = 1.78	DW = 2.23	DW = 1.77	DW = 1.72

APPENDIX A. (*Continued*)

Parameter	Morocco	Mexico	Ethiopia	El-Salvador	Egypt
λ est. t-statistic	0.021	0.006	0.005	−0.303	0.011
	0.757	1.450	1.518	−7.685**	2.879**
Ψ_l	−0.122E−7	0.494	−0.119	1.000	2.638
	−0.044	0.572	−1.773*	1.000	3.024**
Ψ_k	0.802	−0.267	0.003	1.000	0.104
	0.925	−2.192*	1.413	1.000	0.417
Π_m	−0.854	−0.18E−7	−0.020	−0.775E−6	0.055
	−0.061	−0.153	−2.886**	−0.775E−6	0.582
Ψ_m	−0.446E−6	−0.32E−6	−0.006	0.984	−0.263
	−0.945	−2.028*	−2.793**	0.984	−0.062
Π_n	0.299E−5	−0.223	0.428	1.000	−7.449
	0.761	−0.682	5.595**	1.000	−2.341*
Ψ_n	0.297E−6	0.828	0.003	0.985	0.552
	1.147	8.149**	8.953**	0.985	6.426**
LR7	0.028	−0.060	−0.001	1.000	−0.070
	0.787	2.653**	−0.676	1.000	−2.607**
	$N = 43$	$N = 43$	$N = 33$	$N = 43$	$N = 43$
	$R^2 = 0.24$	$R^2 = 0.99$	$R^2 = 0.94$	$R^2 = 0.001$	$R^2 = 0.99$
	DW = 1.61	DW = 1.88	DW = 2.23	DW = 1.77	DW = 1.63
λ est. t-statistic	0.046	0.005	0.336	−0.303	0.009
	3.302**	0.929	1.374	−7.685**	3.441**
Ψ_l	−0.235E−6	−1.416	−0.111	1.000	−0.313
	−1.076	−2.682**	−1.489	1.000	−4.151**
Ψ_k	0.051	−0.276	0.003	1.000	0.007
	0.998	−1.993*	1.259	1.000	0.765
Π_m	0.101E−5	−0.640E−7	−0.178	−0.775E−6	0.763
	0.577	−0.506	−3.019**	−0.775E−6	0.178
Ψ_m	−0.175E−6	−0.366	−0.688	0.985	−0.001
	−1.760*	−2.025*	−3.034**	0.985	−0.801
Π_n	−0.825E−6	−0.229	0.412	1.000	−0.412
	−0.213	−0.689	5.667**	1.000	−2.564
Ψ_n	0.119E−6	0.867	0.036	0.985	0.232
	1.285	7.014**	1.03391**	0.985	8.233
LR8	1.00	−0.005	1.000	1.000	1.000
	1.00	−0.230	1.000	1.000	1.000
	$N = 43$	$N = 43$	$N = 33$	$N = 43$	$N = 43$
	$R^2 = 0.24$	$R^2 = 0.99$	$R^2 = 0.94$	$R^2 = 0.001$	$R^2 = 0.92$
	DW = 1.60	DW = 1.78	DW = 2.23	DW = 1.77	DW = 1.72

* Significant at 0.05 level.

** Significant at 0.01 level.

APPENDIX A. (*Continued*)

Parameter	Honduras	Gabon	Zimbabwe	Zaïr	Uruguay
λ est. t-statistic	0.060	−0.083	−0.040	−0.006	0.436
	5.237**	−2.443*	−2.290*	−0.192	0.241
Ψ_l	−0.196	19.076	8.157	5.603	−2.855
	−2.812**	2.511*	1.551	2.134*	−0.579
Ψ_k	0.107E−3	−0.411	−1.627	−0.679	0.285
	0.008	−1.211	−1.740*	−2.932**	0.010
Π_m	−0.022	−0.801	−0.739	0.152	0.301
	0.543	−3.651**	−0.934	2.162*	3.53**
Ψ_m	−0.642	0.101	−0.125	−0.034	0.23
	−0.921	0.331	−0.812	−0.388	3.445**
Π_n	−2.366	0.267	5.857	0.35	0.257
	−3.325**	0.841	4.032**	1.288	1.595
Ψ_n	0.096	0.296	1.633	0.158	0.755
	2.374*	0.551	3.623**	1.466	12.677**
LR1	1.00	1.00	−0.903	1.00	1.00
	1.00	1.00	−1.195	1.00	1.00
	$N = 37$	$N = 22$	$N = 31$	$N = 26$	$N = 41$
	$R^2 = 0.92$	$R^2 = 0.82$	$R^2 = 0.85$	$R^2 = 0.9$	$R^2 = 0.99$
	DW = 2.54	DW = 2.05	DW = 2.01	DW = 1.76	DW = 1.91
λ est. t-statistic	0.060	−0.830	−0.029	−0.007	0.043
	5.237**	−2.443*	−1.675	−0.259	0.241
Ψ_l	−0.196	19.076	6.412	5.73	−2.85
	−2.812**	2.511*	1.345	2.410*	−0.58
Ψ_k	0.107E−3	−0.411	−1.387	−0.700	0.286
	0.008	−1.211	−1.602	−3.078**	0.010
Π_m	−0.022	−0.801	−0.806	0.157	0.301
	0.543	−3.651**	−0.919	2.146*	3.535**
Ψ_m	−0.006	0.101	−0.123	−0.458	0.235
	−0.921	0.331	−0.787	−0.483	3.445**
Π_n	−2.366	0.267	6.631	0.012	0.257
	−3.325**	0.841	4.790**	0.317	1.595
Ψ_n	0.962	0.296	1.386	0.162	0.755
	2.374*	0.551	3.214**	1.599	12.677
LR2	1.00	1.00	0.204	0.012	1.00
	1.00	1.00	0.423	0.317	1.00
	$N = 37$	$N = 22$	$N = 31$	$N = 26$	$N = 41$
	$R^2 = 0.92$	$R^2 = 22$	$R^2 = 0.85$	$R^2 = 0.69$	$R^2 = 0.99$
	DW = 2.54	DW = 2.05	DW = 1.94	DW = 1.79	DW = 1.91

APPENDIX A. (*Continued*)

Parameter	Honduras	Gabon	Zimbabwe	Zaïr	Uruguay
λ est. t-statistic	0.609	−0.083	−0.317	−0.705	0.436E−3
	5.237**	−2.443*	−1.701*	−0.259	0.242
Ψ_l	−0.196	19.076	6.756	5.731	−2.854
	−2.812**	2.511*	1.352	2.41*	−0.579
Ψ_k	0.107E−3	−0.411	−1.390	−0.700	0.003
	0.872	−1.211	−1.599	−3.078**	0.010
Π_m	−0.022	−0.801	−0.090	0.157	0.030
	−0.543	−3.651**	−1.069	2.146*	3.535**
Ψ_m	−0.642	0.101	−0.082	−0.458	0.236
	0.921	0.330	−0.525	−0.483	3.445
Π_n	−2.366*	0.267	6.552	0.377	0.257
	−3.325**	0.841	4.539**	1.373	1.595
Ψ_n	0.962	0.296	1.479	0.162	0.755
	2.374*	0.551	3.120**	1.559	12.677**
LR3	1.00	1.00	−0.011	0.012	1.00
	1.00	1.00	−0.257	0.317	1.00
	$N = 37$	$N = 22$	$N = 31$	$N = 26$	$N = 41$
	$R^2 = 0.92$	$R^2 = 0.82$	$R^2 = 0.85$	$R^2 = 0.69$	$R^2 = 0.99$
	DW = 2.54	DW = 2.05	DW = 2.03	DW = 1.80	DW = 1.96
λ est. t-statistic	0.055	−0.122	−0.345	−0.005	−0.11E−3
	4.374**	−4.238**	−2.173*	−0.192	0.062
Ψ_l	−0.280	33.384	6.620	5.603	−6.874
	−2.279**	3.146**	1.441	2.134*	−1.156
Ψ_k	−0.001	−1.074	−1.121	−0.6790	0.014
	−0.088	−1.869*	−1.269	−2.932**	0.050
Π_m	−0.027	−0.624	−0.082	0.152	0.029
	0.742	−3.06**	−1.021	2.162*	3.652**
Ψ_m	−0.009	−0.424	−0.133	−0.034	0.240
	−1.030	−0.811	−0.857	0.388	3.615**
Π_n	−2.359	0.534	6.784	0.347	0.220
	−3.386**	2.08*	5.043**	1.289	1.375
Ψ_n	0.119	0.968	1.563	0.158	0.755
	2.268*	1.170	3.818**	1.466	13.179**
LR4	0.015	0.217	−0.037	1.00	0.036
	1.021	1.717*	−0.808	1.00	1.113
	$N = 37$	$N = 22$	$N = 31$	$N = 26$	$N = 41$
	$R^2 = 0.92$	$R^2 = 0.86$	$R^2 = 0.85$	$R^2 = 0.69$	$R^2 = 0.99$
	DW = 2.60	DW = 2.62	DW = 2.02	DW = 1.77	DW = 2.04

APPENDIX A. (*Continued*)

Parameter	Honduras	Gabon	Zimbabwe	Zaïr	Uruguay
λ est. t-statistic	0.055	−547.07	−1.999	0.010	−0.473E−3
	3.547**	−0.435	−20.390**	0.392	−0.247
Ψ_l	−0.224	135.29	50.123	4.768	−3.993
	−2.146*	0.435	2.317*	2.472**	−0.805
Ψ_k	0.735	1017.7	3305	−0.510	−0.620
	0.512	0.432	2.974**	−2.444*	−0.872
Π_m	−0.025	0.145E−3	0.370	0.122	0.032
	−0.647	0.308	8.364**	1.732*	3.971
Ψ_m	−0.856	3.2.52	2116	−0.041	0.261
	−0.965	0.433	3.208**	−0.553	3.748**
Π_n	−2.341	0.001	0.432	0.366	0.175
	−3.077**	0.409	0.201	1.316	1.015
Ψ_n	0.114	748.770	−5254.1	0.136	0.737
	1.87	0.433	−2.924**	1.580	12.510
LR5	0.090	547.15	2.050	−0.044	0.087
	0.541	0.435	21.232**	−1.065	0.978
	$N = 37$	$N = 22$	$N = 31$	$N = 26$	$N = 41$
	$R^2 = 0.92$	$R^2 = 0.51$	$R^2 = 0.864$	$R^2 = 0.70$	$R^2 = 0.99$
	DW = 2.60	DW = 1.70	DW = 1.95	DW = 1.78	DW = 2.03
λ est. t-statistic	0.065	−0.083	−0.026	−0.006	−0.11E−3
	4.197**	−2.443*	−1.588	−0.197	−0.062
Ψ_l	−0.441	19.076	2.384	5.603	−6.874
	−0.302	2.511**	0.567	2.134*	−1.156
Ψ_k	0.9E−3	−0.411	−1.013	−0.679	0.014
	0.067	−1.211	−1.422	−2.932**	0.050
Π_m	−0.023	−0.801	−0.072	0.152	0.029
	−0.636	−3.651**	−0.858	2.162*	3.652**
Ψ_m	−0.009	0.101	−0.110	−0.345	0.240
	−1.214	0.330	−0.765	−0.388	3.615
Π_n	−2.316	0.267	7.185	0.347	0.220
	−3.317**	0.841	5.834**	1.288	1.375
Ψ_n	0.111	0.296	1.329	0.158	0.755
	2.210*	0.551	3.224**	1.466	13.179
LR6	−0.343	1.00	0.734	1.00	0.362
	−1.512	1.00	1.398	1.00	1.113
	$N = 37$	$N = 22$	$N = 31$	$N = 26$	$N = 41$
	$R^2 = 0.92$	$R^2 = 0.82$	$R^2 = 0.86$	NA	$R^2 = 0.99$
	DW = 2.67	DW = 2.05	DW = 1.95	DW = 1.76	DW = 2.04

APPENDIX A. (*Continued*)

Parameter	Honduras	Gabon	Zimbabwe	Zaïr	Uruguay
λ est. t-statistic	0.568	−0.061	0.033	0.009	0.056
	3.993**	−2.143*	−1.936*	0.403	3.993**
Ψ_l	−0.253	17.281	6.977	4.920	−0.253
	−1.623	3.147**	1.435	2.687**	−1.623
Ψ_k	−0.680	−0.158	−1.303	−0.537	−0.680
	−0.492	−0.452	−1.507	−2.823**	−0.049
Π_m	−0.024	−0.774	−0.980	0.137	−0.024
	−0.673	−3.861**	−1.207	2.054*	−0.673
Ψ_m	−0.007	0.089	−0.092	−0.058	−0.007
	0.945	0.367	−0.629	0.759	−0.945
Π_n	−2.346	0.285	6.485	0.432	−2.346
	−3.351**	0.94	4.691**	1.518	−3.351
Ψ_n	0.108	0.206	1.487	0.136	0.108
	2.093*	0.519	3.686**	1.686*	2.093
LR7	0.009	−0.963	−0.022	−0.045	0.008
	0.462	−1.029	−0.543	−1.180	0.462
	$N = 37$	$N = 22$	$N = 31$	$N = 26$	$N = 41$
	$R^2 = 0.92$	$R^2 = 0.82$	$R^2 = 0.85$	$R^2 = 0.71$	$R^2 = 0.92$
	DW = 2.57	DW = 1.96	DW = 1.99	DW = 1.80	DW = 2.57
λ est. t-statistic	0.058	−0.083	0.026	0.011	−0.11E−3
	4.572**	−2.44*	−1.588	0.392	−0.062
Ψ_l	−0.880	19.076	2.384	4.768	−6.874
	0.757	2.511*	0.567	2.47*	−1.156
Ψ_k	0.7E−6	−0.411	−1.013	−0.510	0.013
	0.5E−4	−1.211	−1.422	−2.444*	0.050
Π_m	−0.015	−0.801	−0.727	0.122	0.029
	−0.419	−3.651**	−0.852	1.732	3.652**
Ψ_m	−0.0070	0.101	−0.110	−0.412	0.240
	−1.035	0.331	−0.765	−0.553	3.615**
Π_n	−2.397	0.267	7.185	0.366	0.220
	−3.348**	0.841*	5.834**	1.316	1.375
Ψ_n	0.101	0.296	1.329	0.136	0.755
	2.273*	0.551	3.224**	1.580	13.179**
LR8	−0.025	1.00	0.734	−0.044	0.036
	−1.236	1.00	1.398	−1.065	1.11
	$N = 37$	$N = 22$	$N = 31$	$N = 26$	$N = 41$
	$R^2 = 0.92$	$R^2 = 0.82$	$R^2 = 0.86$	$R^2 = 0.70$	$R^2 = 0.99$
	DW = 2.60	DW = 2.05	DW = 1.96	DW = 1.77	DW = 2.04

* Significant at 0.05 level.

** Significant at 0.01 level.

APPENDIX A. (*Continued*)

Parameter	Ecuador	Dominican	Cost Rica	India	Haiti
λ est. *t*-statistic	−0.022	−0.004	0.001	−0.855E−3	−0.499
	−6.658**	−2.572**	0.382	−0.539	−50.181**
Ψ_l	0.995	−0.873	0.017	0.044	10.675
	4.813**	−0.815	0.308	0.543	6.765**
Ψ_k	0.022	0.968	−0.118	0.009	6.925
	1.333	0.827	−1.425	2.112*	5.256**
Π_m	0.672E−8	−50.471	0.517	−0.007	0.423E−10
	0.039	−52.383**	2.194*	−0.572	1.912*
Ψ_m	−0.172E−8	−0.004	0.228E−7	0.002	−0.311E−4
	−0.528	−31.327**	2.472**	0.616	−0.866
Π_n	0.254E−5	7.948	0.256	−0.911	−0.742E−7
	2.841**	1.900*	4.003**	−1.228	−30.221**
Ψ_n	0.080	0.641	0.030	0.206	0.403
	14.696**	6.132**	12.580**	4.362**	21.317**
LR1	1.000	1.000	1.000	1.000	1.000
	1.000	1.000	1.000	1.000	1.000
	$N = 39$	$N = 43$	$N = 43$	$N = 43$	$N = 43$
	$R^2 = 0.90$	$R^2 = 0.62$	$R^2 = 0.96$	$R^2 = 0.80$	$R^2 = 0.01$
	DW = 1.39	DW = 1.90	DW = 1.71	DW = 2.10	DW = 0.28
λ est. *t*-statistic	0.022	−0.004	0.001	0.020	−0.499
	−6.658**	−2.572**	0.382	2.852**	−50.181**
Ψ_l	0.995	−0.873	0.017	−0.166	10.675
	4.813**	−0.814	0.308	−0.547	6.765**
Ψ_k	0.022	0.968	−0.012	0.108	6.925
	1.333	0.827	−1.425	1.267	5.256**
Π_m	0.675E−8	−50.471	0.517	0.598	0.423E−10
	0.039	−52.383**	2.194*	1.644	1.912*
Ψ_m	−0.172	−0.004	0.228E−7	−0.433	−0.311E−4
	−0.528	−31.327**	2.472**	−0.006	−0.866
Π_n	0.254E−5	7.948	0.256	−77.519	−0.742E−7
	2.841**	1.900*	4.003**	−3.471**	−30.221**
Ψ_n	0.80	0.641	0.305	0.509	0.403
	14.696**	6.132**	12.580**	4.626**	21.317**
LR2	1.000	1.000	1.000	−0.013	1.000
	1.000	1.000	1.000	−1.026	1000
	$N = 39$	$N = 43$	$N = 43$	$N = 43$	$N = 43$
	$R^2 = 0.90$	$R^2 = 0.62$	$R^2 = 0.96$	$R^2 = 0.83$	$R^2 = 0.01$
	DW = 1.38	DW = 1.90	DW = 1.71	DW = 2.09	DW = 0.28

APPENDIX A. (*Continued*)

Parameter	Ecuador	Dominican	Cost Rica	India	Haiti
λ est. *t*-statistic	−0.022	−0.004	0.001	0.020	−0.499
	−6.658**	−2.572**	0.382	2.849**	−50.181**
Ψ_l	0.995	−0.873	0.018	−0.220	10.675
	4.813**	−0.814	0.308	−0.711	6.765**
Ψ_k	0.022	0.968	−0.012	0.107	6.925
	1.333	0.827	−1.425	1.221	5.256**
Π_m	0.675E−8	−50.471	0.517	0.635	0.423E−10
	0.039	−52.383**	2.194*	1.664	1.912*
Ψ_m	−0.172E−8	−0.004	0.228E−7	−0.295	−0.311E−4
	−0.053	−31.327**	2.472**	−0.363	−0.866
Π_n	0.254E−5	7.948	0.256	−75.69	−0.742E−7
	2.841**	1.900*	4.003**	−3.190**	−30.221**
Ψ_n	0.080	0.641	0.030	0.537	0.403
	14.696**	6.131**	12.580**	4.328**	21.317**
LR3	1.000	1.000	1.000	−0.015	1.000
	1.000	1.000	1.000	−1.097	1.000
	$N = 39$	$N = 43$	$N = 43$	$N = 43$	$N = 43$
	$R^2 = 0.90$	$R^2 = 0.62$	$R^2 = 0.96$	$R^2 = 0.83$	$R^2 = 0.01$
	DW = 1.38	DW = 1.90	DW = 1.71	DW = 1.99	DW = 0.28
λ est. *t*-statistic	−0.45E−3	0.162E−7	−1.049	0.020	−0.499
	−0.695	0.517	−6.057**	2.849**	−50.181**
Ψ_l	−0.247	0.073	−0.641	−0.436	10.675
	−0.164	2.845**	−0.650	−1.654	6.765**
Ψ_k	0.163	0.057	−0.016	0.102	6.953
	1.105	2.91**	−0.035	1.162	5.265**
Π_m	0.129E−5	473.59	0.166	0.633	0.423E−10
	0.452	10.285**	0.242	1.693*	1.912*
ψ_m	0.321E−6	0.030	0.233	−0.003	−0.311E−4
	0.898	10.285**	0.150	−0.036	−0.866
Π_n	0.193	−0.051	−0.230	−80.600	−0.742
	0.800	−0.456	−7.745**	−3.377**	−30.221**
Ψ_n	0.891	0.203E−3	0.101	0.519	0.403
	18.700**	0.067	0.066	4.459**	21.317**
LR4	−0.002	−0.61E−3	1.047	0.546	1.000
	−0.499	0.679	6.050**	0.460	1.000
	$N = 39$	$N = 43$	$N = 43$	$N = 43$	$N = 43$
	$R^2 = 0.94$	$R^2 = 0.90$	$R^2 = 0.42$	$R^2 = 0.82$	$R^2 = 0.01$
	DW = 1.71	DW = 2.26	DW = 1.31	DW = 2.11	DW = 0.28

APPENDIX A. *(Continued)*

Parameter	Ecuador	Dominican	Cost Rica	India	Haiti
λ est. t-statistic	−0.506	−0.004	−1.049	0.020	−0.499
	−7.956**	−2.572**	−6.057**	2.875**	−50.181**
Ψ_l	−12.026	−0.873	−0.641	−0.372	10.675
	−0.223	−0.814	−0.650	−1.662	6.765**
Ψ_k	−4.022	0.968	−0.016	0.107	6.952
	−0.113	0.827	−0.035	1.232	5.256**
Π_m	−0.550E−6	−50.471	0.166	0.615	0.423
	−0.317	−52.383**	0.242	1.657	1.912*
Ψ_m	0.537E−5	−0.004	0.233	0.248	−0.311E−4
	0.187	−31.33**	0.150	0.035	−0.866
Π_n	−0.732E−6	7.948	−0.230	−77.826	−0.742E−7
	−0.440	1.900*	−7.745**	−3.387**	−30.221**
Ψ_n	−2.185	0.641	0.101	0.512	0.403
	−0.089	6.132**	0.066	4.446**	21.317**
LR5	0.540	1.000	1.047	1.000	1.000
	5.137**	1.000	6.050**	1.000	1.000
	$N = 39$	$N = 43$	$N = 43$	$N = 43$	$N = 43$
	$R^2 = 0.46$	$R^2 = 0.62$	$R^2 = 0.42$	$R^2 = 0.822$	$R^2 = 0.01$
	DW = 1.07	DW = 1.90	DW = 1.31	DW = 2.05	DW = 2.22
λ est. t-statistic	0.004	−0.492E−3	−1.049	0.018	−0.013
	0.489	−0.186	−6.057**	2.955**	−2.178*
Ψ_l	0.007	1.215	−0.641	−1.824	1.188
	0.086	1.013	−0.650	−0.980	2.839**
Ψ_k	0.164	0.918	−0.016	0.119	−0.077
	1.235	1.114	−0.035	1.381	−2.498**
Π_m	0.114E−5	−28.949	0.166	0.580	−0.135E−6
	0.453	−29.798**	0.242	1.608	−1.402
Ψ_m	0.380E−6	−0.002	0.233	0.014	0.160E−7
	1.413	−18.452**	0.150	0.206	1.226
Π_n	−0.192E−3	7.776	−0.230	−81.992	0.037
	−0.465	1.918*	−7.745**	−3.595**	2.417*
Ψ_n	0.753	0.584	0.101	0.525	0.018
	4.93**	7.789**	0.066	−3.595**	3.925**
LR6	−0.075	−0.098	1.047	0.048	−0.017
	−1.889*	−2.882**	6.050**	0.856	−4.203**
	$N = 39$	$N = 43$	$N = 43$	$N = 43$	$N = 43$
	$R^2 = 0.95$	$R^2 = 0.71$	$R^2 = 0.42$	$R^2 = 0.83$	$R^2 = 0.84$
	DW = 1.87	DW = 2.20	DW = 1.31	DW = 2.12	DW = 2.22

APPENDIX A. (*Continued*)

Parameter	Ecuador	Dominican	Cost Rica	India	Haiti
λ est. t-statistic	−0.623E−3	−0.008	−1.049	−0.676E−4	−0.027
	−0.752	−1.789*	−6.057**	0.058	−6.61**
Ψ_l	0.195	0.294	−0.641	6.435	2.51
	0.202	2.118*	−0.650	1.611	6.44**
Ψ_k	0.165	0.007	−0.016	0.312	−0.099
	1.010	2.814**	−0.035	2.121*	−0.784
Π_m	0.209E−5	0.999	0.166	−0.075	−0.123
	0.751	0.999	0.242	−0.178	−1.140
Ψ_m	0.337E−6	0.034	0.233	0.019	0.262
	0.887	7.402**	0.150	0.139	1.444
Π_n	0.001	0.013	−0.230	−40.226	0.042
	0.842	0.094	−7.745**	−1.524	2.368*
Ψ_n	0.893	0.002	0.101	0.735	0.246
	17.564**	0.349	0.066	3.976**	3.468**
LR7	−0.037	0.281	1.047	−0.133	−0.007
	−1.197	1.366	6.050**	−1.634	−2.909**
	$N = 39$	$N = 43$	$N = 43$	$N = 43$	$N = 43$
	$R^2 = 0.94$	$R^2 = 0.91$	$R^2 = 0.42$	$R^2 = 0.80$	$R^2 = 0.78$
	DW = 1.82	DW = 2.20	DW = 1.31	DW = 2.09	DW = 1.96
λ est. t-statistic	−0.507E−3	−0.342E−3	−1.049	0.186	−0.772
	−0.690	−0.124	−6.057**	2.955**	−50.757**
Ψ_l	0.696	0.996	−0.641	−1.824	3.399
	0.745	0.866	−0.650	−0.980	3.101**
Ψ_k	0.143	0.821	−0.016	0.119	1.561
	1.047	0.946	−0.035	1.380	1.547
Π_m	−0.175E−6	−20.799	0.166	0.580	0.439E−10
	0.066	−3.797**	0.242	1.608	0.955
Ψ_m	0.279	−0.001	0.233	0.144E−3	−0.149E−3
	0.779	−3.424**	0.150	0.206	−0.668
Π_n	0.001	8.119	−0.230	−81.992	−0.477E−7
	0.800	1.891*	−7.745**	−3.595**	−21.543**
Ψ_n	0.839	0.581	0.101	0.525	2.045
	18.097**	7.448**	0.066	4.757**	13.036**
LR8	−0.090	−0.009	1.047	0.048	0.646
	−2.523**	−2.961**	6.050**	0.857	1.742*
	$N = 39$	$N = 43$	$N = 43$	$N = 43$	$N = 43$
	$R^2 = 0.95$	$R^2 = 0.71$	$R^2 = 0.42$	$R^2 = 0.82$	$R^2 = 0.02$
	DW = 1.81	DW = 2.20	DW = 1.31	DW = 2.12	DW = 1.31

* Significant at 0.05 level.
** Significant at 0.01 level.

APPENDIX A. (*Continued*)

Parameter	Nigeria	Niger	Nepal	Mauritius	Malaysia
λ est. t-statistic	0.114	0.046	0.055	0.035	0.004
	7.125**	27.685**	3.238**	2.689**	0.380
Ψ_l	0.253	0.123E−4	−0.839	3.858	0.115
	2.513*	0.318	−3.962**	2.549**	0.104
Ψ_k	−0.113	−1.007	−0.060	−0.196	0.078
	−2.676*	−0.743	−1.118	3.045**	0.620
Π_m	−0.107	−0.065	−2.109	−0.196	0.063
	−1.226	−0.221	−2.651**	−3.045**	2.590**
Ψ_m	0.002	−0.225E−5	0.155	−.009	−0.022
	1.012	−0.169*	3.397**	0.024	−1.015
Π_n	−0.744	−0.904E−4	−1.020	−2.680	−3.468
	−3.890**	−260.410**	−1.590	−2.308*	−5.012**
Ψ_n	0.011	8.3462	0.070	0.372	0.582
	1.614	310.880**	1.656	3.576**	3.064**
LR1	1.000	1.000	1.00	1.00	1.00
	1.000	1.000	1.00	1.00	1.00
	$N = 43$	$N = 28$	$N = 28$	$N = 33$	$N = 43$
	$R^2 = 0.72$	$R^2 = 1.000$	$R^2 = 0.57$	$R^2 = 0.81$	$R^2 = 0.725$
	DW = 1.48	DW = 1.46	DW = 1.96	DW = 1.80	DW = 2.11
λ est. t-statistic	0.112	0.0461	0.055	0.035	0.004
	6.771**	27.685**	3.238**	2.689**	0.380
Ψ_l	0.288	0.123E−4	−0.839	3.858	0.115
	2.466**	0.318	−3.962**	2.549**	0.104
Ψ_k	−0.129	−1.007	−0.060	−0.196	0.077
	−2.578**	−0.747	−1.118	−3.045**	0.620
Π_m	−0.161	−0.654	−2.109	−0.354	0.063
	−1.797*	−0.221	−2.651**	−3.932**	2.590*
Ψ_m	0.003	−0.225E−5	0.155	−0.009	−0.022
	1.095	−0.169	3.397**	−0.350	−1.015
Π_n	−0.685	−0.904	−1.020	−2.680	−3.468
	−3.120**	−260.410**	−1.590	−2.308**	−5.012**
Ψ_n	0.012	8.346	0.070	0.372	0.582
	1.570	310.880**	1.656	3.576**	3.064**
LR2	0.101	1.000	1.000	1.00	1.00
	1.413	1.000	1.000	1.00	1.00
	$N = 43$	$N = 28$	$N = 28$	$N = 33$	$N = 43$
	$R^2 = 0.73$	$R^2 = 1.00$	$R^2 = 1.00$	$R^2 = 0.81$	$R^2 = 0.72$
	DW = 1.50	DW = 1.46	DW = 1.96	DW = 1.81	DW = 2.11

APPENDIX A. (*Continued*)

Parameter	Nigeria	Niger	Nepal	Mauritius	Malaysia
λ est. t-statistic	0.112	0.046	0.055	0.035	0.004
	6.771**	27.685**	3.238**	2.689**	0.380
Ψ_l	0.288	0.123E−4	−0.839	3.858	0.115
	2.466**	0.319	−3.962**	2.549**	0.104
Ψ_k	−0.129	−1.006	−0.060	−0.196	0.077
	−2.578**	−0.743	−1.118	−3.045**	0.620
Π_m	−0.161	−0.654E−10	−2.109	−0.354	0.063
	−1.797**	−0.221	−2.651**	−3.932**	2.590**
Ψ_m	0.003	−0.224	0.155	−0.009	−0.022
	1.095	−0.169	3.975**	−0.350	−1.015
Π_n	−0.685	−0.904E−4	−1.020	−2.680	−3.468
	−3.120**	−260.41**	−1.590	−2.308*	−5.012**
Ψ_n	0.012	8.346	0.070	0.372	0.582
	1.570	310.880**	1.656	3.576**	3.064**
LR3	0.101	1.000	1.000	1.00	1.00
	1.413	1.000	1.000	1.00	1.00
	$N = 43$	$N = 28$	$N = 28$	$N = 33$	$N = 43$
	$R^2 = 0.73$	$R^2 = 1.00$	$R^2 = 1.00$	$R^2 = 0.81$	$R^2 = 0.72$
	DW = 1.50	DW = 1.46	DW = 1.96	DW = 1.81	DW = 2.11
λ est. t-statistic	0.117	0.053	0.086	3.59	−1.230
	5.972**	9.211**	5.538**	2.543**	−1.012
Ψ_l	0.241	−0.366E−6	−0.449	3.599	6710.6
	2.089*	−0.178	−3.623**	2.265*	0.170
Ψ_k	−0.107	0.009	−0.035	−0.211	−1552.9
	−2.071*	0.159	−1.212	−2.582**	0.170
Π_m	−0.111	−0.598E−11	−2.968	−0.366	0.042
	−1.188	−0.335	−4.134**	−3.856**	0.962
Ψ_m	0.248	−0.237E−6	0.109	−0.001	−37.22
	0.908	−0.325	3.665**	−0.383	−0.164
Π_n	−0.752	0.121E−4	−1.343	−2.888	0.220
	−3.213**	468.86**	−2.623**	−2.345*	0.887
Ψ_n	0.010	−0.171	0.060	0.382	490.40
	1.434	−90.139**	2.394*	3.476**	0.173
LR4	−0.016	1.000	−0.045	0.016	1.276
	−0.256	1.000	−2.433*	0.343	1.045
	$N = 43$	$N = 28$	$N = 28$	$N = 33$	$N = 43$
	$R^2 = 1.00$	$R^2 = 0.66$	$R^2 = 0.81$	$R^2 = 0.14$	$R^2 = 0.14$
	DW = 1.48	DW = 1.20	DW = 2.34	DW = 1.87	DW = 0.92

APPENDIX A. *(Continued)*

Parameter	Nigeria	Niger	Nepal	Mauritius	Malaysia
λ est. t-statistic	0.108	0.357	0.085	0.030	−1.230
	4.464**	906.950**	5.157**	2.435*	−1.012
Ψ_l	0.305	−0.283E−3	−0.508	4.809	6710.6
	1.558	−0.581	−3.717**	2.841**	0.170
Ψ_k	−0.139	−0.169E−3	−0.038	−0.285	−1552.9
	−1.509	−3.847**	−1.295	−2.660**	−0.170
Π_m	−0.112	−0.539E−11	−2.682	−0.340	0.042
	−1.159	−0.603	−3.780**	−3.686**	0.962
Ψ_m	0.003	−0.343E−8	0.107	0.002	−37.228
	0.832	−0.551	3.104**	0.066	−0.164
Π_n	−0.753	0.999E−5	−1.036	−2.252	0.220
	−3.518**	10490**	−1.915*	−1.944*	0.173
Ψ_n	0.141	0.129E−3	0.058	0.402	490.400
	1.077	5.684**	2.381*	3.715**	0173
LR5	0.021	−0.024	−0.036	0.309	1.276
	0.394	−12.195**	−2.094*	1.183	1.045
	$N = 43$	$N = 28$	$N = 28$	$N = 33$	$N = 43$
	$R^2 = 0.72$	$R^2 = 1.000$	$R^2 = 0.62$	$R^2 = 0.81$	$R^2 = 0.72$
	DW = 1.52	DW = 1.88	DW = 2.13	DW = 1.86	DW = 2.11
λ est. t-statistic	0.113	−0.897	0.060	0.034	−1.230
	6.580**	−30.889**	3.044**	2.543**	−1.012
Ψ_l	0.260	−0.104E−3	−0.874	3.56	6710
	2.39*	−1.368	−2.633**	2.265*	0.170
Ψ_k	−0.118	15.887	−0.050	−0.211	−1552.9
	−2.425*	3.526**	−0.909	−2.582**	−0.170
Π_m	−0.106	0.952E−10	−2.433	−0.366	0.042
	−1.150	1.964*	−2.582**	−3.856**	0.962
Ψ_m	0.002	0.436E−5	0.516	−0.007	−37.228
	0.999	0.077	3.524**	−0.383	−0.164
Π_n	−0.734	0.986E−5	−1.079	−2.888	0.220
	−3.162**	1594.500**	−1.573	−2.345*	0.887
Ψ_n	0.011	0.447	0.068	0.382	490.400
	1.511	0.771	1.542	3.476**	0.173
LR6	0.012	0.945	0.010	0.164	1.276
	1.251	0.950	0.361	0.434	1.0455
	$N = 43$	$N = 28$	$N = 28$	$N = 33$	$N = 43$
	$R^2 = 0.72$	$R^2 = 1.00$	$R^2 = 0.57$	$R^2 = 0.80$	$R^2 = 0.14$
	DW = 1.47	DW = 0.49	DW = 1.78	DW = 1.87	DW = 2.02

APPENDIX A. (*Continued*)

Parameter	Nigeria	Niger	Nepal	Mauritius	Malaysia
λ est. t-statistic	0.098	0.345	0.076	0.034	0.004
	4.535**	509.560**	4.762**	2.543**	0.475
Ψ_l	0.369	0.161E−6	−0.35	3.599	0.955
	2.225*	0.247	−2.018*	2.265*	0.607
Ψ_k	−0.185	−0.475E−4	−0.025	−0.211	0.090
	−1.990*	−0.951	−0.756	−2.583**	0.702
Π_m	−0.132	−0.365E−11	−2.735	−0.366	0.067
	−1.492	0.306	−3.846**	−3.856**	2.664**
Ψ_m	0.005	−0.716E−8	0.103	−0.001	−0.023
	0.889	−0.445	2.662**	−0.383	−1.145
Π_n	−0.742	0.999E−5	−0.908	−2.888	−3.373
	−3.164**	5374.400**	−1.593*	−2.345*	−5.149**
Ψ_n	0.019	0.713E−4	0.062	0.382	0.583
	1.241	1.355	2.16*	3.476**	3.640**
LR7	0.069	−0.324	−0.041	0.016	−0.305
	1.310	−5.065**	−2.070*	0.434	−0.713
	$N = 43$	$N = 28$	$N = 28$	$N = 33$	$N = 43$
	$R^2 = 0.73$	$R^2 = 1.00$	$R^2 = 0.61$	$R^2 = 0.80$	$R^2 = 0.73$
	DW = 1.57	DW = 1.40	DW = 2.00	DW = 1.87	DW = 2.14
λ est. t-statistic	0.113	0.366	0.092	0.034	−1.230
	6.580**	146.610**	6.885**	2.543**	−1.012
Ψ_l	0.260	−0.182E−5	−0.045	−0.211	6710.60
	2.393*	−1.186	−0.406	2.265*	0.1706
Ψ_k	−0.118	−0.779E−4	−0.012	−0.211	−1552.9
	−2.425*	−1.973*	−0.63	−2.582**	−0.170
Π_m	−0.106	−0.310E−10	−3.506	−0.366	0.043
	−1.150	0.876	−6.123**	−3.856**	0.962
Ψ_m	0.002	−0.938E−8	0.073	−0.001	−37.229
	0.999	−0.388	3.184**	−0.383	−0.162
Π_n	−0.734	0.998E−5	−0.97	−2.888	0.220
	−3.162**	6546**	−2.21*	−2.345*	0.173
Ψ_n	0.011	0.498E−4	0.044	0.382	490.40
	1.511	1.435	2.348*	3.476**	0.173
LR8	0.012	−0.373	−0.863	0.016	1.276
	1.251	−1.863*	−4.409**	0.434	1.045
	$N = 43$	$N = 28$	$N = 28$	$N = 33$	$N = 43$
	$R^2 = 0.72$	$R^2 = 1.00$	$R^2 = 0.74$	$R^2 = 0.80$	$R^2 = 0.14$
	DW = 1.49	DW = 0.72	DW = 1.99	DW = 1.87	DW = 0.92

* Significant at 0.05 level.

** Significant at 0.01 level.

APPENDIX A. (*Continued*)

Parameter	Jordan	Chile	Cameron	Burundi	Pakistan
λ est. t-statistic	−63E−4	−0.096	−1.832	−0.115	−0.001
	−8.34**	−7.344**	−29.887**	−6.897**	−0.073
Ψ_l	0.166	11.763	1.010	16.648	−0.698
	80.19**	1.717*	1.010	2.678**	−1.484
Ψ_k	0.065	−20.684	1.004	−0.098	1.881
	2.889**	−1.487	1.004	−0.252	1.492
Π_m	22EE−4	0.116	0.998	−0.57E−3	1.00
	0.601	9.409**	0.998	−0.103	1.00
Ψ_m	0.999	3.371	0.966	0.332E−5	0.259
	79E+3**	4.884**	0.967	1.505	1.978*
Π_n	218.65	−0.141	1.179	−1.598	13.890
	0.592	−2.235*	1.269	−0.802	1.693*
Ψ_n	−3.656	0.894E−5	0.469	0.039	0.275
	−71.43**	2.254*	1.212	−0.108	1.783*
LR1	−82E−4	2.254	1.00	1.00	−0.031
	−2.30**	1.499	1.00	1.00	−0.424
	$N = 43$	$N = 43$	$N = 30$	$N = 30$	$N = 43$
	$R^2 = 1.00$	$R^2 = 0.99$	$R^2 = 0.48$	$R^2 = 0.31$	$R^2 = 0.68$
	DW = 1.97	DW = 1.38	DW = 2.08	DW = 1.76	DW = 2.02
λ est. t-statistic	−63E−4	−0.082	−1.832	−0.099	−0.715E−3
	−8.34**	−6.575**	−29.887**	−4.938**	−0.063
Ψ_l	0.166	−0.476	1.010	1.3.007	−0.944
	80.19**	−0.406	1.010	2.130*	−2.145*
Ψ_k	0.065	−2.666	1.004	−0.090	1.458
	2.889**	−0.217	1.004	−0.281	1.328
Π_m	22EE−4	0.094	0.998	−0.88E−3	1.00
	0.601	6.535**	0.998	−0.166	1.00
Ψ_m	0.999	2.272	0.966	0.255E−51	0.256
	79E+3**	4.525**	0.967	1.293	2.207*
Π_n	218.65	−0.123E−3	1.179	−1.301	10.558
	0.592	−1.927*	1.269	−0.743	1.343
Ψ_n	−82E−4	0.519E−5	0.469	0.042	0.326
	−71.43**	1.572	1.212	0.171	2.300*
LR2	−82E−4	−0.572	1.001	−0.079	0.041
	−2.30**	−1.763*	1.001	−1.790*	1.508
	$N = 43$	$N = 43$	$N = 30$	$N = 30$	$N = 43$
	$R^2 = 1.00$	$R^2 = 0.99$	$R^2 = 0.47$	$R^2 = 0.36$	$R^2 = 0.70$
	DW = 1.97	DW = 1.50	DW = 2.08	DW = 1.89	DW = 1.80

APPENDIX A. (*Continued*)

Parameter	Jordan	Chile	Cameron	Burundi	Pakistan
λ est. t-statistic	−62E−4	−0.080	−1.832	0.099	−0.002
	−7.955**	−6.446**	−29.887**	−4.938**	−0.186
Ψ_l	0.167	−0.472	1.007	13.007	−0.950
	76.54**	−0.407	1.010	2.130*	−1.912*
Ψ_k	0.063	−2.662	1.004	−0.090	1.671
	2.73**	−0.221	1.004	0.281	1.391
Π_m	0.98E−3	0.941	0.998	−0.88E−3	1.00
	0.256	6.544**	0.998	−0.166	1.00
Ψ_m	0.999	2.273	0.966	0.255E−5	0.232
	0.76E+5**	4.420**	0.967	1.294	1.916*
Π_n	94.489	−0.124E−3	1.179	−1.301	12.818
	0.247	−1.921*	1.269	−0.743	1.648
Ψ_n	−3.66	0.519E−5	0.469	0.042	0.331
	−70.01**	1.544	1.212	0.171	2.151
LR3	−55E−4	−0.575	1.00	−0.079	0.305
	−2.04*	−1.782*	1.00	−1.790*	1.177
	$N = 43$	$N = 43$	$N = 30$	$N = 30$	$N = 43$
	$R^2 = 1.00$	$R^2 = 1.00$	$R^2 = 0.47$	$R^2 = 0.37$	$R^2 = 0.70$
	DW = 1.96	DW = 1.50	DW = 2.08	DW = 1.90	DW = 1.78
λ est. t-statistic	−55E−4	−0.021	−1.832	−0.087	−0.002
	−3.24**	−5.193**	−29.685**	−4.215**	−0.116
Ψ_l	0.165	1.007	1.010	9.991	−0.686
	77.98	3.134**	1.010	1.703*	−1.298
Ψ_k	0.07	−0.147	1.004	−0.159	1.942
	2.78**	−1.309	1.004	−0.626	1.479
Π_m	25E−4	0.002	0.998	−0.002	1.00
	0.658	4.522**	0.998	−0.478	1.00
Ψ_m	0.999	0.018	0.966	0.252E−5	0.241
	74E+3	6.319**	0.967	1.663	2.052*
Π_n	255.40	−0.948	1.179	−2.653	15.086
	−66.22**	−0.367	1.270	−1.796*	1.975*
Ψ_n	−3.653	−0.47E−7	0.469	0.172	0.287
	−66.22**	−1.028	1.217	0.771	1.977*
LR4	14E−4	0.118	1.001	−0.174	−0.005
	−0.72	3.282**	1.001	−3.467**	−0.207
	$N = 43$	$N = 43$	$N = 30$	$N = 30$	$N = 43$
	$R^2 = 1.00$	$R^2 = 0.68$	$R^2 = 0.07$	$R^2 = 0.49$	$R^2 = 0.68$
	DW = 1.97	DW = 1.51	DW = 2.01	DW = 2.02	DW = 1.95

APPENDIX A. (*Continued*)

Parameter	Jordan	Chile	Cameron	Burundi	Pakistan
λ est. t-statistic	−55E−4	−0.084	−0.636	−0.235	−0.055
	−3.24**	−7.634**	−1.842*	−3.265**	−2.180*
Ψ_l	0.165	0.958	−20.952	−46.721	−2.195
	77.98	3.765**	−0.325	−0.945	−1.117
Ψ_k	0.07	−11.840	65.576	−3.341	4.797
	2.78**	−1.143	0.451	−0.789	2.715**
Π_m	25E−4	0.103	1.129	1.001	1.00
	0.658	9.353**	1.632	0.972	1.00
Ψ_m	0.999	2.473	7.168	0.419	−0.854
	74E+3	0.512	1.446	−0.292	−0.292
Π_n	255.40	−0.121	−11.561	4.648	31.668
	−66.22**	−2.087*	−3.636**	0.947	4.080**
Ψ_n	−3.653	0.603E−5	−1.381	7.003	0.567
	−66.22**	1.895*	−0.131	0.732	1.750*
LR5	14E−4	−0.184	0.663	0.225	0.071
	−0.72	−3.223**	1.909*	2.801*	2.721**
	$N = 43$	$N = 43$	$N = 30$	$N = 38$	$N = 43$
	$R^2 = 1.00$	$R^2 = 0.99$	$R^2 = 0.71$	$R^2 = 0.65$	$R^2 = 0.71$
	DW = 1.97	DW = 1.50	DW = 1.40	DW = 2.23	DW = 2.13
λ est. t-statistic	−55E−4	−0.012	−0.002	−0.115	−0.047
	−3.24**	−3.099**	−0.119	−6.897**	−3.581**
Ψ_l	0.165	0.144	0.866	16.648	3.252
	77.98	0.476	0.941	2.678*	1.605
Ψ_k	0.07	−0.017	0.949	−0.098	4.329
	2.78**	−0.186	1.794*	−0.252	2.707**
Π_m	25E−4	0.02	−1.050	−0.57E−3	1.00
	0.658	4.334**	−1.125	−0.104	1.00
Ψ_m	0.999	0.015	0.262	0.332E−5	−0.157
	74E+3	5.593**	1.543	1.505	−0.582
Π_n	255.40	0.263E−3	1.978	−1.598	37.814
	−66.22**	0.102	0.641	−0.802	4.054**
Ψ_n	−3.653	−0.434E−7	0.474	−0.295	0.630
	−66.22**	0.982	2.083	−0.108	2.389*
LR6	14E−4	0.088	1.00	1.00	−0.506
	−0.72	2.698**	1.00	1.00	−2.178*
	$N = 43$	$N = 43$	$N = 30$	$N = 30$	$N = 43$
	$R^2 = 1.00$	$R^2 = 0.65$	$R^2 = 0.91$	$R^2 = 0.31$	$R^2 = 0.70$
	DW = 1.97	DW = 1.73	DW = 1.56	DW = 1.76	DW = 2.04

APPENDIX A. (*Continued*)

Parameter	Jordan	Chile	Cameron	Burundi	Pakistan
λ est. *t*-statistic	31E−4	−0.001	−0.010	−0.171	−0.259E−3
	0.482	−0.243	−1.291	−4.318**	−0.018
Ψ_l	0.16	0649	5.231	13.94	−1.050
	71.39**	2.002*	2.071*	1.824*	−1.195
Ψ_k	0.069	−0.083	1.591	−0.163	1.753
	2.75**	−1.078	2.582**	−0.281	1.363
Π_m	39E−4	0.001	−1.048	−0.001	1.00
	0.89	2.408*	−1.140	−0.273	1.00
Ψ_m	0.99	0.013	0.276	0.548E−5	0.235
	69E+7**	4.592**	1.470	1.448	2.129*
Π_n	391.54	−0.917E−7	1.132	−0.278	13.830
	0.883	−0.338	0.489	−0.156	1.674
Ψ_n	−3.654	−0.372E−7	0.555	0.285	0.287
	−66.61**	−1.029	3.057**	0.095	2.199*
LR7	35E−4	−0.014	−0.096	0.104	0.011
	−0.529	−1.662	−1.698*	1.88*	0.380
	$N = 43$	$N = 43$	$N = 30$	$N = 30$	$N = 43$
	$R^2 = 1.00$	$R^2 = 0.60$	$R^2 = 0.91$	$R^2 = 0.37$	$R^2 = 0.68$
	DW = 1.97	DW = 1.52	DW = 1.60	2.04	DW = 1.995
λ est. *t*-statistic	31E−4	−0.016	−0.002	−0.120	−0.035
	0.482	−5.642**	−0.119	−6.650**	−2.391*
Ψ_l	0.482	0.104	0.865	17.434	3.092
	71.39**	9.839**	0.941	2.696**	1.568
Ψ_k	0.069	−0.036	0.949	−0.776	3.944
	2.75**	−0.392	1.795*	−0.196	2.705**
Π_m	39E−4	0.002	−1.050	−0.258E−3	1.00
	0.89	4.711**	−1.125	−0.046	1.00
Ψ_m	0.99	0.015	0.262	0.349E−5	0.002
	69E+7**	6.871**	1.543	1.519	0.011
Π_n	391.54	−0.128E−5	1.978	−1.480	31.282
	0.883	−0.577	0.641	−0.819	3.655**
Ψ_n	−3.654	−0.356E−7	0.474	−0.516	0.454
	−66.61**	0.860	2.083*	−0.184	2.246*
LR8	35E−4	0.013	1.00	0.355	−0.057
	−0.529	4.243**	1.00	0.616	−2.557**
	$N = 43$	$N = 43$	$N = 30$	$N = 30$	$N = 43$
	$R^2 = 1.00$	$R^2 = 0.99$	$R^2 = 0.91$	$R^2 = 0.32$	$R^2 = 0.72$
	DW = 1.97	DW = 1.52	DW = 1.60	DW = 1.786	DW = 2.09

* Significant at 0.05 level.

** Significant at 0.01 level.

APPENDIX A. (*Continued*)

Parameter	Guyana	Guatemala	Kuwait	Korea	Colombia
λ est. t-statistic	0.021	0.020	−0.018	0.002	−0.005
	1.255	1.31	−0.877	1.313	−3.729**
Ψ_l	−6.218	−0.449	0.713	−0.213	0.149
	−1.356	−1.427	1.011	−0.294	2.355*
Ψ_k	0.004	0.091	0.439	0.047	0.037
	0.050	1.581	2.460**	0.409	1.553
Π_m	0.327	0.131	0.076	−0.299	1.000
	1.358	1.041	0.696	−1.650	1.000
Ψ_m	0.154	−0.016	−0.132	0.305	0.16E−3
	1.69*	0.423	−1.244	2.183*	1.003
Π_n	−0.396	0.496	−0.315	0.803	0.201
	−0.301	1.276	−1.294	1.453	1.022
Ψ_n	0.497	0.496	0.431	0.493	0.177
	2.778**	2.328*	2.377*	2.915**	5.166**
LR1	1.000	1.000	1.000	1.000	1.000
	1.000	1.000	1.000	1.000	1.000
	$N = 23$	$N = 39$	$N = 31$	$N = 43$	$N = 43$
	$R^2 = 0.96$	$R^2 = 0.81$	$R^2 = 0.99$	$R^2 = 0.99$	$R^2 = 0.77$
	DW = 2.00	DW = 1.88	DW = 1.64	DW = 2.08	DW = 1.88
λ est. t-statistic	0.021	0.021	−0.018	0.008	0.016
	1.255	1.353	−0.877	1.313	2.201*
Ψ_l	−6.218	−0.338	0.713	−0.213	−1.933
	−1.356	−0.990	1.011	−0.294	−4.700**
Ψ_k	0.004	0.106	0.439	0.047	0.381
	0.050	1.718*	2.460**	0.409	0.894
Π_m	0.327	0.147	0.076	−0.299	1.000
	1.358	1.138	0.696	−1.651	1.000
Ψ_m	0.154	−0.107	−0.132	0.304	0.030
	1.69*	−0.284	−1.244	2.194*	1.048
Π_n	−0.396	12.865	−0.315	0.803	3.279
	−0.301	1.345	−1.294	1.145	0.536
Ψ_n	0.497	0.478	0.431	0.492	0.325
	2.778**	2.205*	2.377*	2.915**	2.766**
LR2	1.000	−0.014	1.000	1.000	−0.325
	1.000	−0.596	1.000	1.000	2.766**
	$N = 23$	$N = 39$	$N = 31$	$N = 43$	$N = 43$
	$R^2 = 0.96$	$R^2 = 0.80$	$R^2 = 0.99$	$R^2 = 0.99$	$R^2 = 0.77$
	DW = 2.00	DW = 1.91	DW = 1.64	DW = 2.08	DW = 2.22

APPENDIX A. (*Continued*)

Parameter	Guyana	Guatemala	Kuwait	Korea	Colombia
λ est. t-statistic	0.021	0.021	−0.018	0.008	0.016
	1.255	1.353	−0.877	1.313	2.201*
Ψ_l	−6.218	−0.338	0.713	−0.213	−1.932
	−1.356	−0.990	1.011	−0.294	−4.700**
Ψ_k	0.004	0.106	0.439	0.047	0.381
	0.050	1.718*	2.460**	0.409	0.894
Π_m	0.327	0.147	0.076	−0.299	1.000
	1.358	1.138	0.696	−1.651	1.000
Ψ_m	0.154	−0.012	−0.132	0.304	0.030
	1.69*	−0.284	−1.244	2.184*	1.047
Π_n	−0.396	12.865	−0.315	0.803	3.279
	−0.301	1.345	−1.294	1.145	0.536
Ψ_n	0.497	0.478	0.431	0.492	0.325
	2.778**	2.205*	2.377*	2.915**	2.766**
LR3	1.000	−0.014	1.000	1.000	−0.039
	1.000	−0.596	1.000	1.000	−2.214*
	$N = 23$	$N = 39$	$N = 31$	$N = 43$	$N = 43$
	$R^2 = 0.96$	$R^2 = 0.81$	$R^2 = 0.99$	$R^2 = 0.99$	$R^2 = 0.76$
	DW = 2.00	DW = 1.91	DW = 1.64	DW = 2.08	DW = 2.22
λ est. t-statistic	0.076	0.021	−0.024	0.008	−0.014
	2.886**	1.416	−1.244	1.484	−1.070
Ψ_l	−0.792	−0.659	0.741	1.368	4.059
	−0.494	−2.037*	1.176	1.076	1.829*
Ψ_k	0.023	0.092	0.463	0.551	1.396
	0.782	1.758*	2.786**	0.506	0.962
Π_m	0.375	0.052	0.064	−0.143	1.000
	1.915*	0.366	0.591	−0.699	1.000
Ψ_m	0.029	−0.018	−0.123	0.256	0.001
	0.850	−0.505	−1.056	1.843*	0.027
Π_n	−1.017	12.361	−0.275	0.702	7.971
	−1.017	1.342	−1.081	1.030	0.912
Ψ_n	0.192	0.472	0.431	0.550	0.653
	1.949*	2.367*	2.280*	3.180**	5.305**
LR4	−0.167	0.306	0.032	−0.038	−0.128
	−4.824**	1.260	0.887	−1.491	−3.355**
	$N = 23$	$N = 39$	$N = 31$	$N = 43$	$N = 43$
	$R^2 = 0.967$	$R^2 = 0.81$	$R^2 = 0.99$	$R^2 = 0.99$	$R^2 = 0.76$
	DW = 2.00	DW = 1.91	DW = 1.64	DW = 2.10	DW = 1.77

APPENDIX A. (*Continued*)

Parameter	Guyana	Guatemala	Kuwait	Korea	Colombia
λ est. t-statistic	0.076	0.016	−2.293	0.008	−0.014
	2.886**	1.159	−4.299**	1.470	−1.070
Ψ_l	−0.792	−0.616	−281.62	0.284	4.059
	−0.494	−1.554	−0.547	0.303	1.829*
Ψ_k	0.023	0.806	178.27	0.056	1.396
	0.782	1.315	0.602	0.515	0.962
Π_m	0.375	0.087	0.088	0.224	1.000
	1.915*	0.598	1.934*	−1.051	1.000
Ψ_m	0.029	−0.029	561.62	0.282	0.001
	0.850	−0.645	0.558	1.753*	0.027
Π_n	−1.017	11.487	0.010	0.673	7.971
	−1.017	1.227	0.208	0.896	0.912
Ψ_n	0.192	0.539	3.736	0.512	0.653
	1.949*	2.524**	1.068	2.894	5.305**
LR5	−0.167	0.016	2.293	−0.163	0.323
	−4.824**	0.731	4.276**	−0.809	2.761**
	$N = 23$	$N = 39$	$N = 31$	$N = 43$	$N = 43$
	$R^2 = 0.967$	$R^2 = 0.81$	$R^2 = 0.99$	$R^2 = 0.99$	$R^2 = 0.74$
	DW = 2.00	DW = 1.88	DW = 1.82	DW = 2.06	DW = 2.16
λ est. t-statistic	0.076	−0.006	−0.018	0.005	−0.004
	2.886**	−2.829**	−0.877	0.889	−0.429
Ψ_l	−0.792	0.274	0.713	−1.185	4.971
	−0.494	2.590**	1.011	−1.365	2.407
Ψ_k	0.023	0.004	0.439	0.006	0.796
	0.782	1.047	2.460**	0.059	0.786
Π_m	0.375	−0.007	0.076	1.576	1.000
	1.915*	1.321	0.695	2.013*	1.000
Ψ_m	0.029	−0.003	−0.315	0.246	0.007
	0.850	−0.861	−1.243	1.540	0.156
Π_n	−1.017	0.362	−0.315	0.112	4.866
	−1.017	0.896	−1.295	0.157	0.710
Ψ_n	0.192	0.041	0.431	0.609	0.566
	1.949*	8.006**	2.377*	3.086**	3.751**
LR6	−0.167	−0.565	1.000	0.142	−0.167
	−4.824**	−0.605	1.000	0.723	−2.799**
	$N = 23$	$N = 33$	$N = 31$	$N = 43$	$N = 43$
	$R^2 = 0.967$	$R^2 = 0.79$	$R^2 = 0.99$	$R^2 = 0.86$	$R^2 = 0.76$
	DW = 2.00	DW = 1.96	DW = 1.64	DW = 1.96	DW = 2.03

APPENDIX A. (*Continued*)

Parameter	Guyana	Guatemala	Kuwait	Korea	Colombia
λ est. t-statistic	0.076	0.019	−0.449	0.006	−0.004
	2.886**	1.518	−7.024**	1.109	−0.429
Ψ_l	−0.792	−0.897	−0.404	1.344	4.971
	−0.494	−1.381	−0.134	1.024	2.407*
Ψ_k	0.023	0.095	0.434	0.806	0.796
	0.782	1.641	0.522	0.729	0.786
Π_m	0.375	0.136	0.194	−0.177	1.000
	1.915*	1.084	1.867*	−0.870	1.000
Ψ_m	0.029	−0.029	−0.137	0.277	0.008
	0.850	−0.635	−0.219	1.876*	0.156
Π_n	−1.017	10.017	0.308	0.842	4.866
	−1.017	1.043	1.134	1.222	0.711
Ψ_n	0.192	0.495	4.376	0.581	−0.566
	1.949*	2.679	2.132*	3.102**	3.754**
LR7	−0.167	0.022	0.433	−0.032	0.167
	−4.824**	0.789	6.393**	−1.382	−2.799**
	$N = 23$	$N = 39$	$N = 31$	$N = 43$	$N = 43$
	$R^2 = 0.967$	$R^2 = 0.80$	$R^2 = 0.99$	$R^2 = 0.99$	$R^2 = 0.76$
	DW = 2.00	DW = 1.84	DW = 1.88	DW = 2.08	DW = 2.04
λ est. t-statistic	0.076	−0.006	0.018	0.005	−0.004
	2.886**	−2.422*	−0.877	0.889	−0.429
Ψ_l	−0.792	0.272	0.713	−1.185	4.971
	−0.494	2.217*	1.011	−1.365	2.407*
Ψ_k	0.023	0.472	0.439	0.006	0.796
	0.782	1.053	2.460*	0.059	0.786
Π_m	0.375	0.007	0.076	1.576	1.000
	1.915*	1.296	0.696	2.013	1.000
Ψ_m	0.029	−0.002	−0.132	0.246	0.007
	0.850	−0.803	−1.243	1.540	0.156
Π_n	−1.017	0.357	−0.315	0.112	4.866
	−1.017	0.892	−1.294	0.157	0.710
Ψ_n	0.192	0.041	0.431	0.609	0.566
	1.949*	7.132	2.377**	3.086**	3.754
LR8	−0.167	−0.240	1.000	0.014	−0.167
	−4.824**	0.218	1.000	0.723	−2.799
	$N = 23$	$N = 39$	$N = 31$	$N = 43$	$N = 43$
	$R^2 = 0.967$	$R^2 = 0.79$	$R^2 = 0.99$	$R^2 = 0.86$	$R^2 = 0.76$
	DW = 2.00	DW = 1.95	DW = 1.89	DW = 1.95	DW = 2.05

* Significant at 0.05 level.

** Significant at 0.01 level.

APPENDIX A. (*Continued*)

Parameter	Malawi	Tunisia	Trinidad	Togo	Thailand
λ est. *t*-statistic	0.611	0.033	18E−11	−0.882	0.323
	4.332**	3.653**	−1.69*	−0.504	2.616**
Ψ_l	0.263	0.260	31E−10	−2.128	0.142
	0.835	0.347	28.55**	−1.383	0.517
Ψ_k	−0.228	−0.430	−11E−10	0.293	0.109
	−2.590**	−0.865	−2.27*	1.600	1.790*
Π_m	0.052	−0.291	1.000	0.001	−0.357
	0.376	−2.991**	15E+12	0.395	−1.180
Ψ_m	0.094	0.010	25E−10	0.015	0788
	2.233*	0.484	4.1**	0.98	2.640**
Π_n	2.308	−2.598	−1.000	−0.912	−1.837
	1.567	−2.535**	−16E+12	−2.773**	−2.118*
Ψ_n	−0.106	0.408	−14E+10	0.744	0.175
	−0.361	3.656**	−29.15**	2.962**	1.594
LR1	1.00	1.00	14E+16	1.00	1.00
	1.00	1.00	−1.69	1.00	1.00
	$N = 36$	$N = 41$	$N = 21$	$N = 25$	$N = 43$
	$R^2 = 0.84$	$R^2 = 0.76$	$R^2 = 1.00$	$R^2 = 0.74$	$R^2 = 0.90$
	DW = 1.83	DW = 1.93	DW = 1.60	DW = 2.40	DW = 1.25
λ est. *t*-statistic	0.061	0.033	18E−11	−0.008	0.029
	4.33**	3.653**	−1.69	0.504	3.067**
Ψ_l	0.263	0.260	31E+10	−2.882	0.098
	0.835	0.347	28.55**	−1.383	0.426
Ψ_k	−0.228	−0.430	−11E−10	0.293	0.125
	−2.590*	−0.65	−2.27*	1.600	2.265*
Π_m	0.051	0.291	1.000	0.001	−0.390
	0.376	−2.991**	15E+8**	0.395	−1.408
Ψ_m	0.094	0.010	25E−10	0.015	0.727
	2.233*	0.484	4.106**	0.798	2.725**
Π_n	2.308	−2.598	−1.000	−0.912	−1.81
	1.567	−2.535**	−16E11**	−2.773**	−2.27*
Ψ_n	−0.011	0.408	−14E−10	0.744	0.207
	−0.361	3.656**	−29.15**	2.962**	2.047*
LR2	1.00	1.00	14E−16	1.00	0.029
	1.00	1.00	−0.596	1.00	1.845*
	$N = 36$	$N = 41$	$N = 21$	$N = 25$	$N = 43$
	$R^2 = 0.83$	$R^2 = 0.76$	$R^2 = 1.00$	$R^2 = 0.74$	$R^2 = 0.83$
	DW = 1.83	DW = 1.93	DW = 1.60	DW = 2.40	DW = 1.27

APPENDIX A. (*Continued*)

Parameter	Malawi	Tunisia	Trinidad	Togo	Thailand
λ est. t-statistic	0.061	0.0339	0.18E−9	−0.008	0.029
	4.332**	3.653**	−1.69	0.504	3.067**
Ψ_l	0.263	0.260	31E−10	−2.128	0.098
	0.835	0.347	28.55**	−1.383	0.426
Ψ_k	−0.228	−0.043	−11E−10	0.293	0.125
	−2.590**	−0.865	−2.27*	1.60	2.265*
Π_m	0.517	−0.291	1.000	0.137	−0.390
	−2.991**	15E+8**	0.395	−1.408	
Ψ_m	0.094	0.010	25E10	0.014	0.727
	2.233*	0.484	4.10**	0.798	2.725**
Π_n	2.308	−2.598	−0.354	−0.912	−1.817
	1.567	−2.535**	−2.059*	−2.773**	−2.277*
Ψ_n	−0.011	0.408	−1.000	0.744	0.207
	−0.361	3.656**	−16EE+10	2.962**	2.047*
LR3	1.00	1.00	0.416E−16	1.00	0.298
	1.00	1.00	0.596	1.00	1.845*
	$N = 36$	$N = 41$	$N = 21$	$N = 25$	$N = 43$
	$R^2 = 0.84$	$R^2 = 0.76$	$R^2 = 1.00$	$R^2 = 0.74$	$R^2 = 0.83$
	DW = 1.82	DW = 1.93	DW = 1.60	DW = 2.40	DW = 1.27
λ est. t-statistic	0.052	0.034	−17E−11	−0.163	0.033
	3.220**	3.584**	−1.26	−0986	3.432**
Ψ_l	0.168	−0.061	47E−10	−1.478	0.254
	0.471	−0.081	4.085**	−0.955	0.994
Ψ_k	−0.199	−0.002	−12E−10	0.273	0.957
	−2.263*	−0.038	−3.81**	1.473	2.114*
Π_m	−0.046	−0.257	1.000	0.120	−0.405
	−0.262	−2.486**	68E+11**	0.397	−1 441*
Ψ_m	−0.142	0.007	68E+11**	0.127	0.068
	1.861*	0.358	4.10**	0807	2.573**
Π_n	2.286	−2.665	−0.354	−0.782	−1.887
	1.576	−2.583**	−2.059*	−2.522*	−2.253*
Ψ_n	−0.056	0.387	−1.000	0.713	0.189
	−0.960	3.503**	−16EE+10	3.313**	2.101*
LR4	−0.099	−0.026	0.416E−16	−0.162	−0.016
	−1.222	−1.129	0.596	−2.324*	−1.509
	$N = 36$	$N = 41$	$N = 21$	$N = 25$	$N = 43$
	$R^2 = 0.84$	$R^2 = 0.77$	$R^2 = 1.00$	$R^2 = 0.78$	$R^2 = 0.90$
	DW = 2.01	DW = 1.86	DW = 1.60	DW = 1.90	DW = 1.31

APPENDIX A. (*Continued*)

Parameter	Malawi	Tunisia	Trinidad	Togo	Thailand
λ est. t-statistic	−0.344	0.028	−17E−11	0.001	0.046
	−6.465**	3.290**	−1.26	0.055	4.084**
Ψ_l	23.325	−0.594	47E−10	−0.626	−0.283
	0.414	−0.712	4.085**	−0.325	−2.426*
Ψ_k	−3.880	−0.802	−12E−10	0.390	0.058
	−0.399	−1.050	−3.81**	2.046*	1.919*
Π_m	−0.948	−0.290	1.000	0.002	−0.411
	−3.918**	−3.202**	−1.478	0.651	−1.632
Ψ_m	11.182	0.001	0.167E−4	0.011	0.036
	2.086*	0.426	0.244	0.750	1.945*
Π_n	5.313	−2.936	0.354E−4	0.709	−1.537
	4.226**	−2.998**	−2.059*	−1.722*	−2.271**
Ψ_n	−11.567	0.447	−0.808	0.606	0.115
	−1.533	4.258**	−1.446	2.367*	1.958*
LR5	0.344	0.057	0.416E−5	−0.827	0.330
	5.144**	1.850*	1.372	−0.870	3.452**
	$N = 36$	$N = 41$	$N = 21$	$N = 25$	$N = 43$
	$R^2 = 0.64$	$R^2 = 0.79$	$R^2 = 1.00$	$R^2 = 0.74$	$R^2 = 0.92$
	DW = 1.36	DW = 2.12	DW = 1.46	DW = 2.35	DW = 1.44
λ est. t-statistic	0.046	0.339	16E−11	0.008	0.034
	3.171**	3.653**	1.20	0.504	4.426**
Ψ_l	0.302	0.260	33E−10	−2.128	0.545
	0.761	0.347	−3.36**	−1.383	1.944*
Ψ_k	−0.228	−0.431	0.9E−9	0.293	0.095
	−2.466**	−0.866	31.81**	1.600	2.839**
Π_m	−0.060	−0.291	1.000	0.001	−0.483
	−0.359	−2.991**	91E+7	0.395	−1.795*
Ψ_m	0.163	0.010	3E−9	0.014	0.053
	2.175*	0.484	−4.68**	0.798	2.416*
Π_n	2.571	−2.598	−1.000	−0.912	−1.754
	1.806*	−2.535**	−9E+8**	−2.773**	−2.386*
Ψ_n	−0.057	0.408	15E−10	0.744	0.182
	−1.047	3.656**	3.61**	2.962**	2.450**
LR6	−0.125	1.00	11E−16	1.00	−0.027
	−1.883*	1.00	0.41	1.00	−2.446**
	$N = 36$	$N = 41$	$N = 21$	$N = 25$	$N = 43$
	$R^2 = 0.82$	$R^2 = 0.76$	$R^2 = 1.00$	$R^2 = 0.74$	$R^2 = 0.91$
	DW = 1.77	DW = 1.93	DW = 1.80	DW = 2.40	DW = 1.35

APPENDIX A. (*Continued*)

Parameter	Malawi	Tunisia	Trinidad	Togo	Thailand
λ est. t-statistic	−0.390	0.032	16E−11	−0.011	0.026
	−3.114**	3.637**	1.20	−0.558	4.171**
Ψ_l	48.512	−0.063	−3E−10	−2.411	0.771
	0.452	−0.081	−3.36**	−1.399	1.816*
Ψ_k	−6.397	−0.063	9E−9	0.231	0.145
	−0.348	−1.027	31.81**	0.943	3.052**
Π_m	−0.886	−0.290	−1.000	0.001	−0.607
	−3.212**	−3.095**	91E+7**	0.293	−2.093*
Ψ_m	16.129	0.007	−30E−10	0.015	0.059
	1.309	0.332	−4.684**	0.903	1.834*
Π_n	3.553	−2.785	−1.000	0.977	−2.0811
	2.478**	−2.772**	−9E8**	−2.424*	−2.580**
Ψ_n	−18.616	0.421	15E−10	0.786	0.244
	−1.085	3.949**	3.61**	2.681**	2.736**
LR7	0.345	0.028	11E−16	0.026	−0.216
	2.450**	1.244	0.413	0.395	−1.735*
	$N = 36$	$N = 41$	$N = 21$	$N = 25$	$N = 43$
	$R^2 = 0.48$	$R^2 = 0.77$	$R^2 = 1.00$	$R^2 = 0.74$	$R^2 = 0.90$
	DW = 1.56	DW = 2.07	DW = 1.79	DW = 2.38	DW = 1.36
λ est. t-statistic	0.046	0.033	0.417	−0.015	0.034
	3.17**	3.653**	229.29**	0.6999	4.426**
Ψ_l	0.302	0.260	0.005	−2.715	0.545
	0.761	0.347	67.78**	−1.295	1.944*
Ψ_k	−0.228	−0.430	−0.451E−3	0.305	0.951
	−2.466**	0.865	−9.504**	1.487	2.839**
Π_m	−0.599	−0.291	−0.251	0.002	−0.483
	−0.359	−2.991**	−4.286**	0.591	−1.795*
Ψ_m	0.163	0.010	0.475E−4	0.018	0.530
	2.175*	0.484	0.770	1.021	2.416*
Π_n	2.571	−2.598	−0.584E−4	−1.008	−1.754
	1.806*	−2.535**	−5.171**	−2.487*	−2.386*
Ψ_n	−0.573	0.107	−0.109E−3	0.852	0.182
	−1.048	3.656**	−1.860*	2.348*	2.450**
LR8	−0.124	1.00	1.00	0.024	−0.274
	−1.884*	1.00	1.00	0.480	−2.446**
	$N = 36$	$N = 41$	$N = 21$	$N = 25$	$N = 43$
	$R^2 = 0.85$	$R^2 = 0.76$	$R^2 = 1.00$	$R^2 = 0.74$	$R^2 = 0.91$
	DW = 1.77	DW = 1.93	DW = 1.79	DW = 1.90	DW = 1.35

* Significant at 0.05 level.

** Significant at 0.01 level.

APPENDIX A. (*Continued*)

Parameter	UAE	Venezuela	Uganda	Benin	Bangladesh
λ est. *t*-statistic	0.007	0.002	−0.235	0.095	−0.035
	1.065	0.287	−3.259**	5.356**	−1.728*
Ψ_l	1.165	−0.226	−0.180	−0.379E−8	0.514
	2.045*	−0556	−2.197*	−0.634	0.379
Ψ_k	−0.324	−0.203	0.286	0.092	0.005
	−1.735*	−2.652**	2.196*	0.482	0.538
Π_m	0.167	−0.364	1.649	−4.094	−0.484
	0.021	−1.854*	2.388*	−0.709	−1.575
Ψ_m	−0.147	−0.041	−0.811	−0.972E−9	0.212
	−1.535	−0.671	−2.440*	−0.1002E−1	0.971
Π_n	−4.952	0.803	−0.131E−7	−0.509	0.166
	−4.773**	2.598**	−3.021**	−3.192**	2.987**
Ψ_n	0.998	0.868	0456	0.089	0.219
	11.875**	5.681**	14.859**	2.321*	1.142
LR1	2.105	1.00	0.275	1.00	1.00
	0.412	1.00	1.913*	1.00	100
	$N = 26$	$N = 43$	$N = 20$	$N = 33$	$N = 30$
	$R^2 = 0.99$	$R^2 = 0.93$	$R^2 = 0.97$	$R^2 = 0.69$	$R^2 = 0.46$
	DW = 1.52	DW = 1.89	DW = 2.37	DW = 2.52	DW = 1.96
λ est. *t*-statistic	0.007	0.002	0.001	0.095	−0.035
	1.065	0.287	0.117	5.356**	−1.728*
Ψ_l	1.165	−0.226	−22.856**	−0.379E−8	0.514
	2.045*	−0.556	−3.964	−0.634	0.379
Ψ_k	−03.24	−0.202	3.637**	0.091	0.056
	−1.735*	−2.652**	3.964**	0.482	0.538
Π_m	0.167	−0.364	2.401	−4.095	−0.484
	0.021	−1.854*	2.769**	−0.709	−1.575*
Ψ_m	−0.147	−0.041	−0.093	−0.971E−9	0.166
	−1.535	−0.671	−3.975	−0.010	0.971
Π_n	−4.952	0.803	−0.175E−3	−0.509	0.166
	−4.773**	2.598**	−3.345**	−3.192**	2.987**
Ψ_n	0.998	0.868	0.222E−3	0.088	0.219
	11.875**	5.681**	8.674**	2.322*	1.142
LR2	2.105	1.00	−0.086	1.00	1.00
	0.412	1.00	−1.116	1.00	1.00
	$N = 26$	$N = 43$	$N = 20$	$N = 33$	$N = 30$
	$R^2 = 0.99$	$R^2 = 0.93$	$R^2 = 0.98$	$R^2 = 0.69$	$R^2 = 0.46$
	DW = 1.53	DW = 1.89	DW = 2.37	DW = 2.52	DW = 1.96

APPENDIX A. (*Continued*)

Parameter	UAE	Venezuela	Uganda	Benin	Bangladesh
λ est. t-statistic	0.007	0.002	0.001	0.095	−0.035
	1.065	0.287	0.117	5.356**	−1.728*
Ψ_l	1.165	−0.226	−22.856	−0.379	0.515
	2.045*	−0.556	−3.964**	−0.633	0.379
Ψ_k	−0.324	−0.202	3.637	0.092	0.056
	−1.735*	−2.652**	3.964**	0.482	0.538
Π_m	0.167	−0.364	−0.092	−4.094	−0.484
	0.021	−1.854*	−3.975**	−0.709	−1.575
Ψ_m	−0.147	−0.041	−0.175E−7	−0.971	0.212
	−1.535	−0.671	−3.345**	−0.010	0.971
Π_n	−4.952	0.803	−0.175E−7	−0.509	0.166
	−4.773**	2.598**	−3.345**	−3.192**	2.987**
Ψ_n	0.998	0.868	0.222E−3	0.088	0.219
	11.875**	5.681**	8.674**	2.324*	1.141
LR3	2.105	1.00	−0.085	1.00	1.00
	0.412	1.00	−1.116	1.00	1.00
	$N = 26$	$N = 43$	$N = 20$	$N = 33$	$N = 30$
	$R^2 = 0.99$	$R^2 = 0.93$	$R^2 = 0.98$	$R^2 = 0.69$	$R^2 = 1.96$
	DW = 1.53	DW = 1.89	DW = 1.47	DW = 2.52	DW = 1.96
λ est. t-statistic	0.007	0.57E−3	−0.393	0.053	−0.035
	1.08	0.103	−3.876**	1.536	−1.758*
Ψ_l	1.165	0.787	−0.003	−0.37E−8	0.683
	2.079*	0.506	−0.004	−0.562	0.486
Ψ_k	−0324	−0.208	0.642E−3	0.160	0.065
	−1.745*	−2.671	0.005	1.14	0.600
Π_m	0.167	−0.370	2.090	−17E−7	−0.500
	0.022	−1.996*	4.032**	−1.82*	−1.581
Ψ_m	−0.147	−0.044	−0.287E−3	0.877	0.218
	−1.553	−0.697	0.090	29.74**	1.012
Π_n	−4.925	0.808	−0.143E−7	0.19E+7	0.186
	−4.741	2.643**	−4.423**	1.894*	2.504**
Ψ_n	0.998	0.891	0.186E−3	−0.87	0.233
	12.113**	5.581**	11.322**	−24.74**	1.207
LR4	2.379	−0.031	0.388	69E−2	−0.016
	0.425	−0.687	2.859**	0.42	−0.419
	$N = 26$	$N = 43$	$N = 20$	$N = 33$	$N = 30$
	$R^2 = 0.99$	$R^2 = 0.93$	$R^2 = 0.98$	$R^2 = 0.97$	$R^2 = 0.46$
	DW = 1.53	DW = 1.94	DW = 1.41	DW = 2.04	DW = 2.03

APPENDIX A. (*Continued*)

Parameter	UAE	Venezuela	Uganda	Benin	Bangladesh
λ est. t-statistic	−9.448	0.003	0.515	0.069	−0.455
	−5.486**	0.444	4.806**	1.570	−3.013**
Ψ_l	−17.921	−0.844	0.022	−0.37E−8	4.649
	−5.319**	−0.642	0.702	0.714	1.482
Ψ_k	5.310	−0.196	−0.003	−0.162	0.033
	3.641**	−2.571**	−0.700	−1.169	0.305
Π_m	6.145	−0.264	0.290	−18E−7	−0.354
	14.030**	−0.927	0.279	−1.95	−1.188
Ψ_m	8.210	−0.032	0.773E−4	0.876	0.055
	2.846*	−0.535	0.609	30.28**	0.229
Π_n	−1.547	0.709	−0.236E−8	0.20E+7	0.197
	−1.664	1.912*	−0.382	−2.037**	3.648**
Ψ_n	0.192	0.824	−0.312E−5	0.877	0.375
	0.112	4.532**	−0.708	−24.76**	1.731*
LR5	9.504	0.203	−0.759	0.007	−0.074
	5.477**	0.482	−5.705**	−0.584	1.825*
	$N = 26$	$N = 43$	$N = 20$	$N = 33$	$N = 30$
	$R^2 = 0.90$	$R^2 = 0.93$	$R^2 = 0.96$	$R^2 = 0.97$	$R^2 = 0.5$
	DW = 2.27	DW = 1.87	DW = 1.33	DW = 2.05	DW = 2.36
λ est. t-statistic	0.704	0.003	−0.048	0.053	−0.106
	1.100	0.714	−0.603	1.531	−6.573**
Ψ_l	1.165	7.097	−0.159	−0.37E−8	4.907
	2.040*	2.922**	−0.965	−0.562	2.016*
Ψ_k	−0.324	−0.196	0.025	0.16	0.054
	−1.776*	−3.102**	0.954	−1.14	0.485
Π_m	0.167	0.011	−2.512	−0.17E−5	0.182
	0.021	0.059	−1.082	−1.87	0.642
Ψ_m	−0.147	0.045	−0.489E−3	0.877	−0.582
	−1.514	−0.916	−0.720	29.74**	−1.918*
Π_n	−4.952	0.330	0.133E−7	0.19E+7	0.123
	−4.735**	1.125	0.949	1.894	2.879**
Ψ_n	0.998	0.764	0.134E−3	0.905	1.077
	11.646**	7.005**	5.307**	2.391*	3.609**
LR6	2.062	−0.241	−1.635	0.69E−2	0.100
	0.408	−2.696**	−2.492*	0.422	4.682**
	$N = 26$	$N = 43$	$N = 20$	$N = 33$	$N = 30$
	$R^2 = 0.99$	$R^2 = 0.94$	$R^2 = 0.97$	$R^2 = 0.97$	$R^2 = 0.67$
	DW = 1.53	DW = 2.17	DW = 1.57	DW = 2.04	DW = 1.97

APPENDIX A. (*Continued*)

Parameter	UAE	Venezuela	Uganda	Benin	Bangladesh
λ est. *t*-statistic	−10.172	0.557E−3	0.353	0.043	−0.110
	−5.3664**	0.125	−1.929*	1.55	−3.764**
Ψ_l	−30.293	2.686	1.046	−12E−10	−0.198
	−4.652**	2.416*	3.173**	−0.369	−0.093
Ψ_k	6.097	−0.226	−0.166	0.141	0.318
	3.796**	−3.215**	−3.165**	−0.938	1.964*
Π_m	5.709	−0.181	1.363	−16E−7	0.279
	14.655**	−0.991	2.049*	−1.657	0.750
Ψ_m	3.359	−0.035	0.006	0.875	−0.373
	1.939*	−0.607	3.145**	29.77**	−1.040
Π_n	−1.440	0.578	−0.925E−8	18E+5	0.342
	−1.701*	1.944*	−2.264*	−24.23**	0.542
Ψ_n	−10.378	0.850	0.176E−4	25E−4	0.733
	−6.308**	6.748**	6.127**	−0.165	2.297*
LR7	10.226	−0.097	0.223	−0.439	0.094
	5.350**	−2.724**	1.116	1.555	3.193**
	$N = 26$	$N = 43$	$N = 20$	$N = 33$	$N = 30$
	$R^2 = 0.90$	$R^2 = 0.94$	$R^2 = 0.97$	$R^2 = 0.97$	$R^2 = 0.60$
	DW = 2.27	DW = 2.02	DW = 1.36	DW = 2.02	DW = 1.97
λ est. *t*-statistic	0.070	0.557E−3	0.245	0.043	0.117
	1.087	0.125	−2.975**	1.566	−5.387**
Ψ_l	1.165	2.68	1.340	−069E−11	1.501
	2.070*	2.417*	3.267**	−0.148	0.711
Ψ_k	−0.324	−0.226	−0.214	−0.155	−0.073
	−1.793*	−3.216**	−3.263**	−1.080	−0.578
Π_m	0.167	−0.182	2.000	−17E−7	0.111
	0.022	−0.991	2.795**	−1.812	0.397
Ψ_m	−0.147	−0.035	0.007	0.875	−0.333
	−1.540	−0.607	3.183**	29.47**	−1.189
Π_n	−4.952	0.578	−0.141E−3	−0.442	0.314
	−4.785**	1.943*	−3.189**	−2.789**	0.700
Ψ_n	0.998	0.851	0.227E−3	0.876	0.75
	12.027**	6.748**	11.737**	23.82	2.894**
LR8	2.30	−0.097	0.192	−20E−4	0.107
	0.421	−2.724**	1.276	−0.165	4.791**
	$N = 26$	$N = 43$	$N = 20$	$N = 33$	$N = 30$
	$R^2 = 0.99$	$R^2 = 0.94$	$R^2 = 0.97$	$R^2 = 0.97$	$R^2 = 0.71$
	DW = 1.53	DW = 2.02	DW = 1.45	DW = 2.02	DW = 1.97

* Significant at 0.05 level.

** Significant at 0.01 level.

APPENDIX A. (*Continued*)

Parameter	Bahrain	Argentina	Algeria	Brazil	Bolivia
λ est. t-statistic	−0.729	−0.686	0.34E−13	−0.174	−1.30
	−16.189**	−12.595**	3.41**	−4.726**	−22.207**
Ψ_l	0.997	1.000	−0.21E−20	0.999	1.001
	0.997	1.000	−4.417**	0.999	1.001
Ψ_k	0.990	1.000	0.14E−13	0.990	1.010
	0.990	1.000	1.499	0.990	1.010
Π_m	1.000	1.000	−0.15E−12	0.999	0.998
	1.000	1.000	−7.478**	0.999	1.150
Ψ_m	0.988	0.999	1.00	1.000	0.969
	0.988	0.999	0.29E+15	1.000	0.969
Π_n	0.404E−5	−0.604E−5	0.2E−18	−0.235E−3	−0.923E−3
	0.404E−5	−0.605E−5	2.99	−0.235E−3	−0.177E−3
Ψ_n	0.984	0.950	−1.000	0.983	0.928
	0.984	0.950	−0.15E+14	0.983	0.929
LR1	1.000	1.000	0.25	1.000	1.000
	1.000	1.000	3.357	1.000	1.000
	$N = 32$	$N = 41$	$N = 41$	$N = 43$	$N = 37$
	$R^2 = 0.99$	$R^2 = 0.00$	$R^2 = 1.00$	$R^2 = 0.05$	$R^2 = 0.30$
	DW = 1.88	DW = 1.73	DW = 1.89	DW = 2.04	DW = 1.36
λ est. t-statistic	−0.729	−0.686	0.34E−13	−0.174	−1.30
	−16.189**	−12.595**	3.471**	−4.726**	−22.207**
Ψ_l	0.997	1.000	−0.21E−20	0.999	1.001
	0.997	1.000	−4.417**	0.999	1.001
Ψ_k	0.990	1.000	0.14E−13	0.990	1.010
	0.990	1.000	1.499	0.990	1.010
Π_m	1.000	1.000	−0.15E−12	0.999	1.001
	1.000	1.000	−0.17E−6	0.999	1.001
Ψ_m	0.988	0.999	1.00	1.001	0.998
	0.988	0.999	0.29E15	1.001	1.150
Π_n	0.404E−5	−0.604E−5	2E−17	−0.235E−3	−0.923E−3
	0.404E−5	−0.605E−5	2.99**	−0.232E−3	−0.002
Ψ_n	0.984	0.950	−1.000	0.982	0.928
	0.984	0.950	1.000	0.982	0.928
LR2	1.000	1.000	0.25E−13	1.000	1.000
	1.000	1.000	3.471**	1.000	1.000
	$N = 32$	$N = 41$	$N = 41$	$N = 2.42$	$N = 37$
	$R^2 = 0.99$	$R^2 = 0.00$	$R^2 = 1.00$	$R^2 = 0.05$	$R^2 = 0.02$
	DW = 1.44	DW = 1.73	DW = 1.89	DW = 2.04	DW = 1.36

APPENDIX A. (*Continued*)

Parameter	Bahrain	Argentina	Algeria	Brazil	Bolivia
λ est. *t*-statistic	−0.729	−0.686	−0.485E−4	−0.174	−1.30
	−16.189**	−12.595**	−0.838	−5.726**	−22.207**
Ψ_l	0.997	1.000	0.821E−11	0.999	1.001
	0.997	1.000	0.352	1.019	1.001
Ψ_k	0.990	1.000	0.003	0.990	1.001
	0.990	1.000	1.087	0.990	1.001
Π_m	1.000	1.000	0.317	0.999	0.998
	1.000	1.000	0.955	1.008	1.150
Ψ_m	0.988	0.999	0.002	1.000	0.969
	0.988	0.999	2.575**	1.032	0.969
Π_n	0.404E−5	−0.604E−5	0.029	−0.32E−3	0.923
	0.404E−5	−0.605E−5	1.610	−0.629E−3	−0.002
Ψ_n	0.984	0.950	0.017	0.982	−0.928
	0.984	0.950	4.447**	0.984	−0.928
LR3	1.000	1.000	−0.003	1.000	1.000
	1.000	1.000	−2.293*	1.000	1.000
	$N = 32$	$N = 41$	$N = 41$	$N = 43$	$N = 37$
	$R^2 = 0.99$	$R^2 = 0.00$	$R^2 = 0.82$	$R^2 = 0.07$	$R^2 = 0.30$
	DW = 1.44	DW = 1.73	DW = 1.23	DW = 2.04	DW = 1.36
λ est. *t*-statistic	−0.729	−0.686	−0.035	−0.174	−1.398
	−16.189**	−12.595**	−28.752**	−5.726**	−21.841**
Ψ_l	0.997	1.000	0.366	0.999	1.001
	0.997	1.000	17.416**	1.019	1.001
Ψ_k	0.990	1.000	0.670	0.990	1.010
	0.990	1.000	1.136	0.990	1.010
Π_m	1.000	1.000	0.329E−6	0.999	0.998
	1.000	1.000	1.534	1.008	1.212
Ψ_m	0.988	0.999	0.181	1.000	0.969
	0.988	0.999	2.681**	1.000	0.969
Π_n	0.404E−5	−0.604E−5	0.021	−0.232	−0.923E−3
	0.404E−5	−0.605E−5	1.035	−0.629	−0.001
Ψ_n	0.984	0.950	0.036	0.982	0.928
	0.984	0.950	4.054**	0.984	0.928
LR4	1.000	1.000	0.413	1.000	1.000
	1.000	1.000	3.007**	1.000	1.000
	$N = 32$	$N = 41$	$N = 41$	$N = 43$	$N = 37$
	$R^2 = 0.99$	$R^2 = 0.00$	$R^2 = 0.80$	$R^2 = 0.07$	$R^2 = 0.02$
	DW = 1.44	DW = 1.72	DW = 1.53	DW = 1.39	DW = 1.02

APPENDIX A. (*Continued*)

Parameter	Bahrain	Argentina	Algeria	Brazil	Bolivia
λ est. t-statistic	−0.729	−0.686	−0.033	−0.174	−1.398
	−16.189**	−12.595**	−25.767**	−5.726**	−21.266**
Ψ_l	0.997	1.000	0.326E−8	0.999	1.001
	0.997	1.000	11.723**	1.019	1.001
Ψ_k	0.990	1.000	0.006	0.990	1.010
	0.990	1.000	0.992	0.990	1.010
Π_m	1.000	1.000	0.472E−6	0.999	0.998
	1.000	1.000	2.014*	1.008	1.371
Ψ_m	0.988	0.999	0.186	1.000	0.969
	0.988	0.999	2.492**	1.031	0.969
Π_n	0.404E−5	−0.604E−5	0.243	−0.232E−3	−0.92E−3
	0.404E−5	−0.605E−5	0.972	−0.629E−3	−0.13E−2
Ψ_n	0.984	0.950	0.353	0.982	0.928
	0.984	0.950	4.158**	0.984	0.929
LR5	1.000	1.000	0.4E−3	1.000	1.000
	1.000	1.000	0.230	1.000	1.002
	$N = 32$	$N = 41$	$N = 41$	$N = 43$	$N = 37$
	$R^2 = 0.99$	$R^2 = .00$	$R^2 = 0.75$	$R^2 = 0.07$	$R^2 = 0.02$
	DW = 1.44	DW = 1.78	DW = 1.27	DW = 1.44	DW = 1.94
λ est. t-statistic	−0.729	−0.686	0.004	−0.174	−1.398
	−16.189**	−12.595**	4.286**	−4.726**	−22.049**
Ψ_l	0.997	1.000	−0.196E−9	0.999	1.001
	0.997	1.000	−5.185**	0.999	1.001
Ψ_k	0.990	1.000	0.005	0.990	1.010
	0.990	1.000	2.043*	0.990	1.010
Π_m	1.000	1.000	−0.301E−5	0.999	0.998
	1.000	1.000	−2.126*	0.999	1.169
Ψ_m	0.988	0.999	0.483	1.000	0.962
	0.988	0.999	2.153*	1.000	0.969
Π_n	0.404E−5	−0.604E−5	0.270	−0.234E−3	−0.001
	0.404E−5	−0.605E−5	1.519	−0.232E−3	−0.19
Ψ_n	0.984	0.950	0.017	0.982	0.928
	0.984	0.950	5.371**	0.982	0.929
LR6	1.000	1.000	1.000	1.000	0.999
	1.000	1.000	1.000	1.000	1.005
	$N = 32$	$N = 41$	$N = 41$	$N = 43$	$N = 37$
	$R^2 = 0.99$	$R^2 = 0.00$	$R^2 = 0.85$	$R^2 = 0.00$	$R^2 = 0.03$
	DW = 1.44	DW = 1.73	DW = 1.36	DW = 2.16	DW = 1.47

APPENDIX A. (*Continued*)

Parameter	Bahrain	Argentina	Algeria	Brazil	Bolivia
λ est. t-statistic	−0.729	−0.686	−0.033	−0.174	−1.398
	−16.189**	−12.595**	−24.890**	−5.755**	−21.423**
Ψ_l	0.997	1.000	0.308E−8	0.999	1.001
	0.997	1.000	11.322**	1.016	1.001
Ψ_k	0.990	1.000	0.006	0.990	1.001
	0.990	1.000	0.976	0.990	1.001
Π_m	1.000	1.000	0.524E−6	0.999	0.998
	1.000	1.000	2.084*	0.990	0.998
Ψ_m	0.988	0.999	0.019	1.008	0.969
	0.988	0.999	2.938**	1.026	0.969
Π_n	0.404E−5	−0.604E−5	0.021	−0.23E−3	−0.001
	0.404E−5	−0.605E−5	0.980	−0.67E−3	−0.155
Ψ_n	0.984	0.950	0.333	0.982	0.928
	0.984	0.950	3.834**	0.984	0.928
LR7	1.000	1.000	0.002	1.000	0.999
	1.000	1.000	1.301	1.000	1.002
	$N = 32$	$N = 41$	$N = 41$	$N = 43$	$N = 37$
	$R^2 = 0.99$	$R^2 = 0.00$	$R^2 = 0.76$	$R^2 = 0.00$	$R^2 = 0.02$
	DW = 1.44	DW = 1.79	DW = 1.36	DW = 1.48	DW = 1.42
λ est. t-statistic	−0.729	−0.686	−0.032	−0.174	−0.139
	−16.189**	−12.595**	−25.216**	−5.674**	−21.897**
Ψ_l	0.997	1.000	0.317E−8	0.999	1.001
	0.997	1.000	15.571**	1.025	1.001
Ψ_k	0.990	1.000	0.001	0.990	1.010
	0.990	1.000	0.284	0.990	1.010
Π_m	1.000	1.000	0.493E−6	0.999	0.998
	1.000	1.000	2.126*	1.014	1.198
Ψ_m	0.988	0.999	0.025	1.001	0.969
	0.988	0.999	3.745**	1.040	0.969
Π_n	0.404E−5	−0.604E−5	0.0.02	−0.23E−3	−0.104
	0.404E−5	−0.605E−5	0.097	−0.55E−3	−0.002
Ψ_n	0.984	0.950	0.022	0.982	0.928
	0.984	0.950	2.770**	0.984	0.929
LR8	1.000	1.000	−0.006	1.000	0.999
	1.000	1.000	−3.589**	1.000	1.001
	$N = 32$	$N = 41$	$N = 43$	$N = 43$	$N = 37$
	$R^2 = 0.99$	$R^2 = 0.00$	$R^2 = 0.82$	$R^2 = 0.00$	$R^2 = 0.32$
	DW = 1.44	DW = 1.72	DW = 1.68	DW = 1.82	DW = 1.17

* Significant at 0.05 level.

** Significant at 0.01 level.

APPENDIX A. (*Continued*)

Parameter	Ghana	Mali	Nicaragua	Saudi Arabia	Turkey
λ est. *t*-statistic	−0.930	0.103	−2.561	−0.458	25E−6
	−16.033**	0.933	−26.862**	−9.429**	0.72
Ψ_l	1.000	1.000	1.000	1.000	49E−5
	1.000	1.000	1.000	1.000	−2.32
Ψ_k	1.000	1.000	1.000	1.000	27E−5
	1.000	1.000	1.000	1.000	1.366
Π_m	0.229E−6	1.000	1.000	1.000	86E−6
	0.229E−6	1.000	1.000	1.000	2.742
Ψ_m	0.943	0.965	1.000	0.960	1.000
	0.943	0.965	1.000	0.961	1.000
Π_n	1.000	0.56E−5	0.502E−6	0.5E−5	−0.1-3
	1.000	0.56E−5	0.505E−6	0.5E−5	−2.47**
Ψ_n	1.000	0.965	0.851	0.999	1.000
	1.000	0.965	0.851	0.999	−1.23
LR1	1.000	1.000	1.000	1.000	25E−6
	1.000	1.000	1.000	1.000	−1.235
	$N = 36$	$N = 22$	$N = 27$	$N = 43$	$N = 43$
	$R^2 = 0.00$	$R^2 = 0.99$	$R^2 = 0.01$	$R^2 = 0.33$	$R^2 = 1.00$
	DW = 1.91	DW = 1.99	DW = 2.00	DW = 1.70	DW = 1.67
λ est. *t*-statistic	−0.930	0.103	−2.561	−0.458	−0.269
	−16.033**	0.933	−26.862**	−9.429**	−7.047**
Ψ_l	1.000	1.000	1.000	1.000	1.001
	1.000	1.000	1.000	1.000	1.001
Ψ_k	1.000	1.000	1.000	1.000	1.001
	1.000	1.000	1.000	1.000	1.001
Π_m	0.229E−6	1.000	1.000	1.000	1.119
	0.229E−6	1.000	1.000	1.000	1.119
Ψ_m	0.943	0.965	1.000	0.960	0.974
	0.943	0.965	1.000	0.961	0.974
Π_n	1.000	0.56E−5	0.502E−6	0.5E−5	−0.300
	1.000	0.56E−5	0.505E−6	0.5E−5	−0.300
Ψ_n	1.000	0.965	0.851	0.999	0.974
	1.000	0.965	0.851	0.999	0.974
LR2	1.000	1.000	1.000	1.000	1.000
	1.000	1.000	1.000	1.000	1.000
	$N = 36$	$N = 22$	$N = 27$	$N = 43$	$N = 43$
	$R^2 = 0.00$	$R^2 = 0.99$	$R^2 = 0.01$	$R^2 = 0.33$	$R^2 = 1.00$
	DW = 2.00	DW = 1.99	DW = 2.00	DW = 1.70	DW = 1.80

APPENDIX A. (*Continued*)

Parameter	Ghana	Mali	Nicaragua	Saudi Arabia	Turkey
λ est. t-statistic	−0.930	0.103	−2.561	−0.458	−0.269
	−16.033**	0.933	−26.862**	−9.429**	−7.047**
Ψ_l	1.000	1.000	1.000	1.000	1.001
	1.000	1.000	1.000	1.000	1.001
Ψ_k	1.000	1.000	1.000	1.000	1.008
	1.000	1.000	1.000	1.000	1.008
Π_m	0.229E−6	1.000	1.000	1.000	1.119
	0.229E−6	1.000	1.000	1.000	1.119
Ψ_m	0.943	0.965	1.000	0.960	0.974
	0.943	0.965	1.000	0.961	0.974
Π_n	1.000	0.56E−5	0.502E−6	0.5E−5	−0.3000
	1.000	0.56E−5	0.505E−6	0.5E−5	−0.3000
Ψ_n	1.000	0.965	0.851	0.999	0.974
	1.000	0.965	0.851	0.999	0.974
LR3	1.000	1.000	1.000	1.000	1.000
	1.000	1.000	1.000	1.000	1.000
	$N = 36$	$N = 22$	$N = 27$	$N = 43$	$N = 43$
	$R^2 = 0.00$	$R^2 = 0.99$	$R^2 = 0.01$	$R^2 = 0.33$	$R^2 = 1.00$
	DW = 1.85	DW = 1.99	DW = 2.23	DW = 1.70	DW = 1.69
λ est. t-statistic	−0.930	0.103	−2.561	−0.458	−0.269
	−16.033**	0.933	−26.862**	−9.429**	−7.047**
Ψ_l	1.000	1.000	1.000	1.000	1.001
	1.000	1.000	1.000	1.000	1.001
Ψ_k	1.000	1.000	1.000	1.000	1.001
	1.000	1.000	1.000	1.000	1.001
Π_m	0.229E−6	1.000	1.000	1.000	1.119
	0.229E−6	1.000	1.000	1.000	1.119
Ψ_m	0.943	0.965	1.000	0.960	0.974
	0.943	0.965	1.000	0.961	0.974
Π_n	1.000	0.56E−5	0.502E−6	0.5E−5	−0.300
	1.000	0.56E−5	0.505E−6	0.5E−5	−0.300
Ψ_n	1.000	0.965	0.851	0.999	0.974
	1.000	0.965	0.851	0.999	0.974
LR4	1.000	1.000	1.000	1.000	1.000
	1.000	1.000	1.000	1.000	1.000
	$N = 36$	$N = 22$	$N = 27$	$N = 43$	$N = 43$
	$R^2 = 0.00$	$R^2 = 0.99$	$R^2 = 0.01$	$R^2 = 0.33$	$R^2 = 1.00$
	DW = 2.00	DW = 1.20	DW = 1.72	DW = 1.70	DW = 1.80

APPENDIX A. (*Continued*)

Parameter	Ghana	Mali	Nicaragua	Saudi Arabia	Turkey
λ est. *t*-statistic	−0.930	0.103	−2.561	−0.458	−0.269
	−16.033**	0.933	−26.862**	−9.429**	−7.047**
Ψ_l	1.000	1.000	1.000	1.000	1.001
	1.000	1.000	1.000	1.000	1.001
Ψ_k	1.000	1.000	1.000	1.000	1.008
	1.000	1.000	1.000	1.000	1.008
Π_m	0.229E−6	1.000	1.000	1.000	1.119
	0.229E−6	1.000	1.000	1.000	1.119
Ψ_m	0.943	0.965	1.000	0.960	0.974
	0.943	0.965	1.000	0.961	0.974
Π_n	1.000	0.56E−5	0.502E−6	0.5E−5	−0.300
	1.000	0.56E−5	0.505E−6	0.5E−5	−0.300
Ψ_n	1.000	0.965	0.851	0.999	0.974
	1.000	0.965	0.851	0.999	0.974
LR5	1.000	1.000	1.000	1.000	1.000
	1.000	1.000	1.000	1.000	1.000
	$N = 36$	$N = 22$	$N = 27$	$N = 43$	$N = 43$
	$R^2 = 0.00$	$R^2 = 0.99$	$R^2 = 0.01$	$R^2 = 0.33$	$R^2 = 1.00$
	DW = 2.15	DW = 1.95	DW = 1.72	DW = 1.70	DW = 1.80
λ est. *t*-statistic	−0.930	0.103	−2.561	−0.458	−0.269
	−16.033**	0.933	−26.862**	−9.429**	−7.047**
Ψ_l	1.000	1.000	1.000	1.000	1.001
	1.000	1.000	1.000	1.000	1.001
Ψ_k	1.000	1.000	1.000	1.000	1.008
	1.000	1.000	1.000	1.000	1.008
Π_m	0.229E−6	1.000	1.000	1.000	1.119
	0.229E−6	1.000	1.000	1.000	1.119
Ψ_m	0.943	0.965	1.000	0.960	0.974
	0.943	0.965	1.000	0.961	0.974
Π_n	1.000	0.56E−5	0.502E−6	0.5E−5	−0.300
	1.000	0.56E−5	0.505E−6	0.5E−5	−0.300
Ψ_n	1.000	0.965	0.851	0.999	0.974
	1.000	0.965	0.851	0.999	0.974
LR6	1.000	1.000	1.000	1.000	1.000
	1.000	1.000	1.000	1.000	1.000
	$N = 36$	$N = 22$	$N = 27$	$N = 43$	$N = 43$
	$R^2 = 0.00$	$R^2 = 0.99$	$R^2 = 0.01$	$R^2 = 0.33$	$R^2 = 1.00$
	DW = 1.97	DW = 1.33	DW = 2.00	DW = 1.70	DW = 1.80

APPENDIX A. (*Continued*)

Parameter	Ghana	Mali	Nicaragua	Saudi Arabia	Turkey
λ est. *t*-statistic	−0.930	0.103	−2.561	−0.458	−0.269
	−16.033**	0.933	−26.862**	−9.429**	−7.047**
Ψ_l	1.000	1.000	1.000	1.000	1.001
	1.000	1.000	1.000	1.000	1.001
Ψ_k	1.000	1.000	1.000	1.000	1.008
	1.000	1.000	1.000	1.000	1.008
Π_m	0.229E−6	1.000	1.000	1.000	1.119
	0.229E−6	1.000	1.000	1.000	1.119
Ψ_m	0.943	0.965	1.000	0.960	0.974
	0.943	0.965	1.000	0.961	.0974
Π_n	1.000	0.56E−5	0.502E−6	0.5E−5	−0.300
	1.000	0.56E−5	0.505E−6	0.5E−5	−0.300
Ψ_n	1.000	0.965	0.851	0.999	0.974
	1.000	0.965	0.851	0.999	0.974
LR7	1.000	1.000	1.000	1.000	1.000
	1.000	1.000	1.000	1.000	1.000
	$N = 36$	$N = 22$	$N = 27$	$N = 43$	$N = 43$
	$R^2 = 0.00$	$R^2 = 0.99$	$R^2 = 0.01$	$R^2 = 0.33$	$R^2 = 1.00$
	DW = 2.05	DW = 2.14	DW = 1.72	DW = 1.70	DW = 1.85
λ est. *t*-statistic	−0.930	0.103	−2.561	−0.458	−0.269
	−16.033**	0.933	−26.862**	−9.429**	−7.047**
Ψ_l	1.000	1.000	1.000	1.000	1.001
	1.000	1.000	1.000	1.000	1.001
Ψ_k	1.000	1.000	1.000	1.000	1.008
	1.000	1.000	1.000	1.000	1.008
Π_m	0.229E−6	1.000	1.000	1.000	1.119
	0.229E−6	1.000	1.000	1.000	1.119
Ψ_m	0.943	0.965	1.000	0.960	0.974
	0.943	0.965	1.000	0.961	0.974
Π_n	1.000	0.56E−5	0.502E−6	0.5E−5	−0.300
	1.000	0.56E−5	0.505E−6	0.5E−5	−0.300
Ψ_n	1.000	0.965	0.851	0.999	0.974
	1.000	0.965	0.851	0.999	0.974
LR8	1.000	1.000	1.000	1.000	1.000
	1.000	1.000	1.000	1.000	1.000
	$N = 36$	$N = 22$	$N = 27$	$N = 43$	$N = 43$
	$R^2 = 0.00$	$R^2 = 0.99$	$R^2 = 0.01$	$R^2 = 0.33$	$R^2 = 1.00$
	DW = 2.13	DW = 2.12	DW = 1.85	DW = 1.70	DW = 1.85

* Significant at 0.05 level.

** Significant at 0.01 level.

APPENDIX B

CROSS-NATIONAL TIME SERIES RESULTS WITH A SINGLE POLITICAL OR CONFLICT VARIABLE

Parameter	All States	MENA-N/OI	MENA-OI	Arab World	MENA
Ψ_l est. t-stat	0.403	1.875	0.209	1.278	1.427
	28.08**	25.15**	7.646**	26.42**	24.55**
Ψ_k	0.7E−10	−0.327	−0.365	−1.144	−0.677
	0.217	−0.360	−2.251**	−2.045*	−0.989
Π_m	0.596	−0.759	−0.774	0.370	0.004
	41.48**	−7.873**	−3.334**	5.849**	0.077
Ψ_m	0.93E−4	0.167	0.958	0.529	0.14E−3
	18.90**	27.17**	93.60**	6.721**	20.28**
Π_n	−0.689	−1.764	−3.946	4.677	0.390
	−2.547**	−0.397	−2.744**	1.518	0.096
Ψ_n	−0.2E−9	−0.580	−0.653	−0.577	−1.078
	−0.283	−0.357	−3.215**	−0.757	−1.122
LR1	−0.38E−6	−0.295E−5	0.015	0.572	−0.409
	−0.122	−1.68*	0.280	0.378	−2.091*
	$N = 2{,}349$	$N = 251$	$N = 200$	$N = 350$	$N = 451$
	$R^2 = 1.00$	$R^2 = 0.88$	$R^2 = 0.99$	$R^2 = 0.79$	$R^2 = 0.72$
	DW = 1.23	DW = −1.679	DW = 1.78	DW = 1.13	DW = 1.12
Ψ_l est. t-stat	0.403	1.864	0.210	1.278	1.425
	28.100**	25.09**	7.748**	26.48**	24.55**
Ψ_k	0.78E−10	−0.300	−0.369	−1.165	−0.778
	0.217	−0.332	−2.263**	−2.082*	−1.137
Π_m	0.597	−0.739	−0.784	0.366	0.269
	41.59**	−7.692**	−3.409**	5.790**	0.056
Ψ_m	0.935	0.16E−3	0.958	0.54E−4	0.135
	19.08**	27.48**	94.04**	7.156**	20.24**

APPENDIX B. (*Continued*)

Parameter	All States	MENA-N/OI	MENA-OI	Arab World	MENA
Π_n	−0.685	1.624	−3.945	4.310	3.812
	−2.544**	0.398	−2.743**	1.512	1.010
Ψ_n	−0.192	−0.305	−0.648	−0.487	−0.834
	−0.283	−0.018	−3.176**	−0.636	−0.861
LR2	−0.312	−0.426	0.002	−0.156	−0.396
	−2.462**	−2.216*	0.037	−0.921	−2.337**
	$N = 2{,}349$	$N = 251$	$N = 200$	$N = 350$	$N = 451$
	$R^2 = 1.00$	$R^2 = 0.88$	$R^2 = 0.99$	$R^2 = 0.79$	$R^2 = 0.72$
	DW = 1.24	DW = 1.33	DW = 1.78	DW = 1.13	DW = 1.14
Ψ_l est. t-stat	0.402	1.882	0.210	1.281	1.439
	28.08**	25.16**	7.730	26.33**	24.69**
Ψ_k	0.78E−10	−0.578	−0.368	−1.168	−0.940
	0.217	−0.632	−2.241**	−2.064*	−1.358
Π_m	0.597	−0.747	−0.078	0.004	0.037
	41.63**	−7.745**	−3.410**	5.836**	0.077
Ψ_m	0.94E−4	0.17E−3	0.958	0.54E−4	0.136
	19.12**	27.41**	93.82**	7.142**	20.34**
Π_n	−0.69E−5	1.853	−3.946	4.271	3.836
	−2.568**	0.450	−2.743**	1.496	1.015
Ψ_n	−0.19E−9	0.633	−0.649	−0.522	−0.760
	−0.283	0.039	−3.179**	−0.676	−0.779
LR3	−0.345	−0.263	0.003	−0.048	−0.313
	−2.869**	−1.628*	0.079	−0.353	−2.219*
	$N = 2349$	$N = 251$	$N = 200$	$N = 350$	$N = 451$
	$R^2 = 1.00$	$R^2 = 0.88$	$R^2 = 0.99$	$R^2 = 0.79$	$R^2 = 0.72$
	DW = 1.24	DW = 1.32	DW = 1.78	DW = 1.13	DW = 1.14
Ψ_l est. t-stat	0.404	1.871	0.209	1.279	1.426
	28.11**	25.000**	7.720**	26.44**	24.45**
Ψ_k	0.84E−10	−0.509	−0.355	−1.139	−0.876
	0.232	−0.555	−2.113*	−2.016*	−1.255
Π_m	0.596	−0.755	−0.078	0.368	−0.166
	41.45**	−7.803**	−3.424**	5.827**	−0.035
Ψ_m	0.930	0.165	0.958	0.538	0.136
	18.96**	27.26**	93.65**	7.124**	20.22**
Π_n	−0.675	0.440	−3.955	4.237	3.506
	−2.496**	0.106	−2.749**	1.485	0.925
Ψ_n	−0.205	−1.357	−0.658‘	−0.567	−1.279
	−0.302	−0.161	−3.209**	−0.743	−1.322

APPENDIX B. (*Continued*)

Parameter	All States	MENA-N/OI	MENA-OI	Arab World	MENA
LR4	0.533	−0.129	0.011	−0.002	−0.149
	0.619	−1.013	0.311	−0.020	1.35
	$N = 2349$	$N = 251$	$N = 200$	$N = 350$	$N = 451$
	$R^2 = 1.00$	$R^2 = 0.88$	$R^2 = 0.99$	$R^2 = 0.79$	$R^2 = 0.72$
	DW = 1.23	DW = 1.30	DW = 1.78	DW = 1.13	DW = 1.12
Ψ_l est. t-stat	0.404	1.871	0.210	1.278	1.427
	28.20**	24.94**	7.757**	26.42**	24.42**
Ψ_k	0.78E−10	−0.370	−0.368	−1.13	−0.693
	0.217	−0.403	−2.277*	−2.019*	−1.010
Π_m	0.595	−0.753	−0.078	0.368	0.003
	41.52**	−7.772**	−3.412**	5.834**	0.062
Ψ_m	0.93E−4	0.16E−3	0.958	0.537	0.13E−3
	19.07**	27.05**	94.15**	7.107**	20.03**
Π_n	−0.767	0.971	−3.946	4.188	3.397
	−2.835**	0.234	−2.743**	1.453	0.891
Ψ_n	−0.192E−9	−0.644	−0.647	−0.573	−1.160
	−0.283	−0.394	−3.203**	−0.750	−1.202
LR5	0.274	0.589	−0.016	0.024	0.070
	2.808**	0.326	−0.165	0.125	0.369
	$N = 2349$	$N = 251$	$N = 200$	$N = 350$	$N = 451$
	$R^2 = 1.00$	$R^2 = 0.88$	$R^2 = 0.99$	$R^2 = 0.79$	$R^2 = 0.86$
	DW = 1.23	DW = 1.30	DW = 1.78	DW = 1.13	DW = 1.12
Ψ_l est. t-stat	0.403	1.872	0.210	1.277	1.426
	28.11**	24.99**	7.773**	26.44**	24.47**
Ψ_k	0.78E−10	−0.464	−0.370	−1.203	−0.766
	0.217	−0.507	−2.292**	−2.137*	−1.114
Π_m	0.596	−0.755	−0.078	0.370	0.433
	41.55**	−7.797**	−3.408**	5.868**	0.906
Ψ_m	0.93	0.16E−3	0.958	0.55E−4	0.135
	19.01**	27.12**	94.19**	4.210**	20.10**
Π_n	−0.752	1.886	−3.943	5.572	4.541
	−2.771**	0.445	−2.740**	1.745*	1.179
Ψ_n	−0.19E−9	−0.570	−0.649	−0.594	−1.199
	−0.283	−0.349	−3.197**	−0.779	−1.245
LR6	−0.201	−0.160	−0.007	−0.413	−0.323
	−1.971*	−0.704	0.094	−0.927	−1.452
	$N = 2349$	$N = 251$	$N = 200$	$N = 350$	$N = 451$
	$R^2 = 1.00$	$R^2 = 0.88$	$R^2 = 0.99$	$R^2 = 0.79$	$R^2 = 0.72$
	DW = 1.23	DW = 1.30	DW = 1.78	DW = 1.36	DW = 1.28

APPENDIX B. (*Continued*)

Parameter	All States	MENA-N/OI	MENA-OI	Arab World	MENA
Ψ_l est. *t*-stat	0.403	1.873	0.209	1.277	1.426
	28.11**	25.00**	7.744**	26.42**	24.40**
Ψ_k	0.814E–10	–0.388	–0.367	–1.124	–0.72
	0.225	–0.425	–2.273**	–2.011*	–1.043
Π_m	0.596	–0.755	–0.769	0.363	0.38E–3
	41.49**	–7.797**	–3.330**	5.723**	0.008
Ψ_m	0.929	0.165	0.958	0.53E–4	0.13E–3
	18.95**	27.01**	94.20**	7.071**	20.08**
Π_n	–0.687	0.767	–3.936	3.963	3.344
	–2.551**	0.185	–2.737**	1.383	0.879
Ψ_n	–0.19E–9	–0.678	–0.668	–0.492	–1.082
	–0.293	–0.415	–3.237*	–0.643	–1.116
LR7	–0.331	0.147	–0.026	0.180	0.143
	–0.286	0.704	–0.488	0.926	0.766
	$N = 2349$	$N = 251$	$N = 200$	$N =$ $N = 350$	N = 451
	$R^2 = 1.00$	$R^2 = 0.88$	$R^2 = 0.99$	$R^2 = 0.79$	$R^2 = 0.72$
	DW = 1.23	DW = 1.30	DW = 1.79	DW = 1.13	DW = 1.12
Ψ_l est. *t*-stat	0.403	1.872	0.210	1.278	1.425
	28.10**	25.03**	7.767**	26.45**	24.49**
Ψ_k	0.949	–0.542	–0.375	–1.186	–0.830
	0.262	–0.588	–2.321*	–2.103*	–1.205
Π_m	0.596	–0.758	–0.772	0.369	0.464
	41.53**	–7.829**	–3.366**	5.847**	0.097
Ψ_m	0.930	0.16E–3	0.958	0.543	0.13E–3
	18.98**	27.07**	94.26**	7.174**	20.09**
Π_n	–0.709	1.912	–3.929	4.588	4.265
	–2.627**	0.458	–2.733**	1.581	1.122
Ψ_n	–0.194	–0.495	–0.654	–0.564	–1.158
	–0.286	0.303	–3.233**	–0.740	–1.205
LR8	–0.122	–0.242	–0.345	–0.179	–0.386
	–1.276	–1.054	0.566	–0.655	–1.862**
	$N = 2349$	$N = 251$	$N = 200$	$N = 350$	$N = 451$
	$R^2 = 1.00$	$R^2 = 0.88$	$R^2 = 0.99$	$R^2 = 0.79$	$R^2 = 0.72$
	DW = 1.23	DW = 1.30	DW = 1.78	DW = 1.13	DW = 1.13

*Significant at 0.05 level.

**Significant at 0.01 level.

APPENDIX B. (*Continued*)

Parameter	L. America	Africa	Asia	Caribbean
Ψ_l	0.339	0.157		
	17.45**	2.934**		
Ψ_k	0.57E−6	0.194		
	0.134	0.178		
Π_m	0.661	0.842		
	33.99**	15.65**		
Ψ_m	0.95E−4	0.10E−3		
	13.18**	6.980**		
Π_n	0.007	−1.732		
	0.034	−2.793**		
Ψ_n	0.756	0.119		
	0.034	1.253		
LR1	−1.085	−0.14E−5		
	−0.594	−0.334		
	$N = 649$	$N = 718$		
	$R^2 = 1.00$	$R^2 = 1.00$		
	DW = 1.45	DW = 1.22		
Ψ_l	0.340	0.162	0.183	0.277
	17.52**	3.00**	13.94**	6.263**
Ψ_k	0.50E−6	0.961	−0.173	−0.266
	0.118	0.187	−2.028**	−3.481**
Π_m	0.659	0.837	0.002	0.096
	33.93**	15.53**	0.325	2.748**
Ψ_m	0.95E−4	0.10E−3	0.974	0.875
	1.3.25**	6.985**	118.8**	24.18**
Π_n	0.050	−1.769	−91415	2258.7
	0.228	−2.846**	−0.330	0.3140
Ψ_n	0.050	0.2E−8	−1.401	0.129
	0.229	1.248	−4.399**	1.670
LR2	−0.363	0.218	0.001	−0.746
	−1.346	0.657	0.077	−0.634
	$N = 649$	$N = 718$	$N = 346$	$N = 178$
	$R^2 = 1.00$	$R^2 = 1.00$	$R^2 = 0.99$	$R^2 = 0.97$
	DW = 1.45	DW = 1.22	DW = 1.63	DW = 1.93
Ψ_l	0.340	0.162	0.183	0.277
	17.53**	2.99**	13.94**	6.263**
Ψ_k	0.49E−6	0.96E−10	−0.174	−0.266
	0.117	0.187	−2.028*	−3.481**

APPENDIX B. (*Continued*)

Parameter	L. America	Africa	Asia	Caribbean
Π_m	0.659	0.838	0.003	0.096
	33.94**	15.52**	0.325	2.748**
Ψ_m	0.95E−4	0.10E−3	0.975	0.874
	13.25**	6.95**	118.8**	24.18**
Π_n	0.052	−1.765	−91415	2258.7
	0.235	−2.837**	−0.330	0.314
Ψ_n	0.523	0.12E−8	−1.401	0.129
	0.235	1.248	−4.399**	1.670
LR3	−0.378	0.158	0.001	−0.074
	−1.418	0.505	0.077	−0.634
	$N = 649$	$N = 718$	$N = 346$	$N = 178$
	$R^2 = 1.00$	$R^2 = 1.00$	$R^2 = 0.99$	$R^2 = 0.97$
	DW = 1.45	DW = 1.22	DW = 1.62	DW = 1.93
Ψ_l	0.339	0.159	0.183	0.27596
	17.47**	2.959**	14.02**	6.224**
Ψ_k	0.14E−6	0.88E−10	−0.155	−0.267
	0.032	0.175	−1.857*	−3.481**
Π_m	0.660	0.841	0.003	0.962
	33.95**	15.65**	0.385	2.744**
Ψ_m	0.95E−4	0.10E−3	0.975	0.876
	13.18**	7.022	119.5**	24.21**
Π_n	0.009	−1.736	−25726	2350.2
	0.043	−2.798**	−0.930	0.3253
Ψ_n	0.967	0.12E−8	−1.449	0.12895
	0.044	1.255	−4.559**	1.672
LR4	0.092	−0.021	−0.023	−0.865
	0.548	−0.090	−1.907*	−0.097
	$N = 679$	$N = 718$	$N = 346$	$N = 178$
	$R^2 = 1.00$	$R^2 = 1.000$	$R^2 = 0.99$	$R^2 = 0.97$
	DW = 1.11	DW = 1.21	DW = 1.63	DW = 1.92
Ψ_l	0.340	0.158	0.182	0.257
	17.53**	2.953**	13.93**	6.215**
Ψ_k	0.17E−5	0.920	−0.169	−0.267
	0.403	0.179	−2.019*	−3.789**
Π_m	0.659	0.841	0.003	0.098
	33.89**	15.67**	0.328	2.783**

APPENDIX B. *(Continued)*

Parameter	L. America	Africa	Asia	Caribbean
Ψ_m	0.953	0.10E−3	0.975	0.876
	13.25**	7.042**	119.1**	24.23**
Π_n	0.680	−1.737	−15175	1580
	0.031	−2.803**	0.054	0.2136
Ψ_n	0.007	0.20E−8	−1.551	0.12919
	0.030	1.252	−4.620**	1.676
LR5	0.235	0.132	−0.019	−0.036
	1.377	0.526	−1.378	−0.420
	$N = 649$	$N = 718$	$N = 346$	$N = 178$
	$R^2 = 1.00$	$R^2 = 1.00$	$R^2 = 0.99$	$R^2 = 0.97$
	DW = 1.45	DW = 1.21	DW = 1.62	DW = 1.92
Ψ_l	0.339	0.158	0.183	0.275
	17.46**	2.954**	13.97**	6.236**
Ψ_k	0.64E−6	0.81E−10	−0.166	−0.265
	0.147	0.157	−1.976*	−3.468**
Π_m	0.660	0.841	0.317	0.094
	33.98**	15.68**	0.344	2.665**
Ψ_m	0.95E−4	0.10E−3	0.975	0.876
	13.17**	7.032**	118.9	24.24**
Π_n	0.863	−1.638	−94265	3325.1
	0.039	−2.612**	−0.3419	0.457
Ψ_n	0.008	0.12E−8	−1.374	0.127
	0.039	1.260	−4.282**	1.658
LR6	−0.146	−0.289	−0.010	−0.064
	0.039	−1.038	−0.682	−0.886
	$N = 649$	$N = 718$	$N = 346$	$N = 178$
	$R^2 = 1.00$	$R^2 = 1.00$	$R^2 = 0.99$	$R^2 = 0.97$
	DW = 1.44	DW = 1.22	DW = 1.64	DW = 1.92
Ψ_l	0.339	0.158	0.183	0.275
	17.48**	2.952**	13.91**	6.217**
Ψ_k	0.87E−6	0.87E−10	−0.170	−0.266
	0.206	0.171	−2.095*	−3.481**
Π_m	0.660	0.841	0.312	0.096
	34.01**	15.66**	0.339	2.747**
Ψ_m	0.94E−4	0.10E−3	0.974	0.876
	13.20**	7.027**	118.90**	24.22**

APPENDIX B. (*Continued*)

Parameter	L. America	Africa	Asia	Caribbean
Π_n	0.014	−1.740	−71887	2398.1
	0.063	−2.807**	−0.258	0.331
Ψ_n	0.014	0.12E−8	−1.422	0.129
	0.063	1.262	−4.423**	1.671
LR7	−0.276	0.052	0.008	−0.157
	−1.166	0.205	0.469	−0.158
	$N = 649$	$N = 718$	$N = 346$	$N = 178$
	$R^2 = 1.00$	$R^2 = 1.00$	$R^2 = 0.99$	$R^2 = 0.97$
	DW = 1.43	DW = 1.21	DW = 1.63	DW = 1.92
Ψ_l	0.339	0.161	0.184	0.276
	17.45**	2.994**	14.04**	6.236**
Ψ_k	0.60E−6	0.12E−9	−0.163	−0.266
	0.141	0.228	−1.952*	−3.468**
Π_m	0.660	0.839	0.003	0.095
	33.98**	15.62**	0.357	2.719**
Ψ_m	0.949	0.10E−3	0.974	0.875
	13.17**	7.010**	119.20**	24.18**
Π_n	0.008	−1.688	−99704	2777.6
	0.038	−2.717**	0.363	0.382
Ψ_n	0.008	0.12E−8	−1.337	0.128
	0.038	1.251	−4.177**	1.66
LR8	−0.009	−0.223	−0.002	−0.035
	−0.052	−1.009	−1.517	−0.490
	$N = 649$	$N = 718$	$N = 346$	$N = 178$
	$R^2 = 1.00$	$R^2 = 1.00$	$R^2 = 0.99$	$R^2 = 0.97$
	DW = 1.44	DW = 1.22	DW = 1.64	DW = 1.92

*Significant at 0.05 level.
**Significant at 0.01 level.

APPENDIX C

CROSS-NATIONAL TIME SERIES ANALYSIS RESULTS WITH EXTERNAL AND INTERNAL CONFLICTS AS CONTROL VARIABLES

Parameter	LR4	LR5	LR6	LR7	LR8
ALL STATES					
Ψ_l est. *t*-stat	0.403	0.403	0.402	0.402	0.403
	28.07**	28.16**	28.07**	28.03**	28.06**
Ψ_k	0.08E–10	0.78E–10	0.78E–10	0.842	0.95E–10
	0.230	0.218	0.217	0.233	0.262
Π_m	0.597	0.597	0.598	0.597	0.597
	41.49**	41.56**	41.60**	41.54**	41.57**
Ψ_m	0.94E–4	0.94E–4	0.94E–4	0.94E–4	–0.94E–10
	19.01**	19.12**	19.07**	19.00**	19.04**
Π_n	–0.67E–5	–0.77E–5	–0.75E–5	–0.69E–5	–0.71E–5
	–2.497**	–2.831**	–2.765**	–2.542**	–2.620**
Ψ_n	–0.20E–9	–0.19E–9	–0.19E–9	–0.21E–9	–0.19E–9
	–0.299	–0.284	–0.284	–0.304	–0.287
LR1	–0.33E–6	–0.92E–7	–0.68E–6	–0.487E–6	–0.563E–5
	–0.108	–0.289	–0.219	–0.157	–0.181
LR2	–0.310	–0.313	–0.311	0.319	–0.310
	–2.442**	–2.746**	–2.454**	–2.505**	–2.448**
LR4-8	0.050	0.276	–0.201	–0.064	–0.119
	0.533	2.817**	–1.968*	0.548	–1.254
	$N = 2349$	$N = 2349$	$N = 2349$	$N = 2349$	$N = 2349$
	$R^2 = 1.00$	$R^2 = 1.00$	$R^2 = 1.00$	$R^2 = 1.00$	$R^2 = 1.00$
	DW = 1.24	DW = 1.24	DW = 1.24	DW = 1.24	DW = 1.24
AFRICA					
Ψ_l est. *t*-stat	0.161	0.160	0.160	0.161	0.163
	2.983**	2.981	2.976**	2.977**	3.018**
Ψ_k	0.91E–10	0.95E–10	0.832E–10	0.894	0.12E–9
	0.177	0.186	0.162	0.174	0.237

APPENDIX C. (*Continued*)

Parameter	LR4	LR5	LR6	LR7	LR8
Π_m	0.839	0.839	0.11E−3	0.839	0.837
	15.49**	15.50**	6.950**	15.50**	15.47**
Ψ_m	0.10E−3	0.10E−3	1.656	0.10E−3	0.103
	6.929**	6.944**	−2.631**	6.935**	6.925**
Π_n	−1.759	−1.764	0.12E−8	−1.766	−1.711
	−2.822**	−2.833**	1.256	−2.837**	−2.742**
Ψ_n	0.12E−8	0.119E−8	−0.18E−5	0.12E−8	0.12E−8
	1.254	1.248	−0.415	1.261	1.246
LR1	−0.15E−5	−0.129E−5	0.236	−0.13E−5	−0.12E−5
	−0.379	−0.292	0.709	−0.350	−0.424
LR2	0.220	0.230	0.359	0.228	0.172
	0.660	0.689	0.535	0.262	−0.388
LR4-8	−0.034	0.139	−0.308	0.067	−0.234
	−0.149	0.552	−1.101	0.262	−1.052
	$N = 718$	$N = 718$	$N = 718$	$N = 718$	$N = 718$
	$R^2 = 1.00$	$R^2 = 1.00$	$R^2 = 1.00$	$R^2 = 1.00$	$R^2 = 1.00$
	DW = 1.22	DW = 1.22	DW = 1.22	DW = 1.22	DW = 1.22
ASIA					
Ψ_l est. t-stat	0.183	0.183	0.184	0.183	0.184
	13.98**	13.92**	13.94**	13.89**	14.01**
Ψ_k	−0.153	−0.178	−0.164	−0.179	−0.151
	−1.774*	−2.079*	−1.89*	−2.071**	−1.747*
Π_m	0.036	0.003	0.003	0.003	0.003
	0.391	0.308	0.349	0.335	0.387
Ψ_m	0.975	0.975	0.974	0.975	0.975
	119.3**	118.9**	118.7*	118.7**	119.00**
Π_n	−20629	−19812	−91519	−74542	−91919
	−0.074	−0.070	−0.330	−0.267	−0.3327
Ψ_n	−1.449	−1.568	−1.372	−1.423	−1.325
	−4.553**	−4.644**	−4.268**	−4.418**	−4.121**
LR1	−0.003	0.008	−0.002	0.002	−0.006
	−0.173	0.515	−0.115	0.125	−0.377
LR2	−0.003	0.008	−0.002	0.002	−0.006
	−0.173	0.515	0.535	0.125	−0.377
LR4-8	−0.238	0.008	−0.010	0.008	−0.025
	−1.910*	0.515	−0.687	0.479	−1.601
	$N = 347$	$N = 347$	$N = 347$	$N = 347$	$N = 347$
	$R^2 = 0.99$	$R^2 = 0.99$	$R^2 = 0.99$	$R^2 = 0.99$	$R^2 = 0.99$
	DW = 1.63	DW = 1.63	DW = 1.63	DW = 1.63	DW = 1.63

APPENDIX C. (*Continued*)

Parameter	LR4	LR5	LR6	LR7	LR8
MENA					
Ψ_l est. t-stat	1.422	1.437	1.422	1.424	1.422
	24.61**	24.58**	24.62**	24.57**	24.64**
Ψ_k	−1.924	−0.748	−0.797	−0.748	−0.857
	−1.335	−1.093	−1.168	−1.096	−1.254
Π_m	−0.002	0.003	0.004	0.225	0.004
	−0.050	0.064	0.086	0.047	0.093
Ψ_m	0.14E−3	0.14E−3	0.14E−3	0.13E−3	0.14E−3
	20.38**	20.14**	20.27**	20.19**	20.28**
Π_n	0.394	0.675	1.471	0.655	1.081
	0.097	0.166	0.361	0.162	0.268
Ψ_n	−0.899	−0.757	−0.816	−0.743	−0.785
	−0.927	−0.783	−0.845	−0.776	−0.815
LR1	−0.44E−5	−0.41E−5	−0.433E−5	−0.40E−5	−0.45E−5
	−2.251*	−2.083*	−2.219*	−2.058*	−2.289*
LR2	−0.382	−0.396	−0.373	−0.391	
	−2.625**	−2.341*	−2.206*	−2.293*	−2.111*
LR4-8	−0.163	0.410	−0.319	0.038	−0.383
	−1.474	0.022	−1.440	0.0204	−1.839*
	$N = 451$	$N = 451$	$N = 451$	$N = 451$	$N = 451$
	$R^2 = 0.72$	$R^2 = 0.72$	$R^2 = 0.72$	$R^2 = 0.72$	$R^2 = 0.72$
	DW = 1.16	DW = 1.15	DW = 1.16	DW = 1.14	DW = 1.16
LATIN AMERICA					
Ψ_l est. t-stat	0.341	0.342	0.340	0.341	0.340
	17.50**	17.560**	17.49**	17.52**	17.49**
Ψ_k	0.18E−6	0.16E−5	0.54E−6	0.83E−6	0.67E−6
	0.042	0.383	0.124	0.196	0.157
Π_m	0.659	0.658	0.659	0.659	0.659
	33.87**	33.81**	33.89**	33.92**	33.88**
Ψ_m	0.95E−4	0.96E−4	0.95E−4	0.95E−4	0.95E−4
	13.21**	13.28**	13.20**	13.24**	13.21**
Π_n	0.49E−9	0.045	0.049	0.058	0.055
	0.219	0.202	0.223	0.262	0.246
Ψ_n	0.049	0.045	0.050	0.058	0.055
	0.220	0.202	0.223	0.262	0.246
LR1	−1.105	−1.261	−1.083	−1.054	−1.114
	−0.605	−0.690	−0.592	−0.578	−0.609
LR2	−0.349	−0.338	−0.362	−0.388	−0.360
	−1.284	−1.252	−1.336	−1.433	−1.330

APPENDIX C. (*Continued*)

Parameter	LR4	LR5	LR6	LR7	LR8
LR4-8	0.070	0.223	−0.007	−0.300	−0.046
	0.414	1.339	0.172	−1.263	−0.567
	$N = 694$	$N = 694$	$N = 694$	$N = 694$	$N = 694$
	$R^2 = 1.00$	$R^2 = 1.00$	$R^2 = 1.00$	$R^2 = 1.00$	$R^2 = 1.00$
	DW = 1.45	DW − 1.45	DW = 1.45	DW = 1.44	DW = 1.45
CARIBBEAN					
Ψ_l est. t-stat	0.277	0.277	0.277	0.277	0.278
	6.240**	6.227**	6.225**	6.235**	6.261**
Ψ_k	−0.267	−0.267	−0.265	−0.267	−0.565
	−3.471**	−3.477**	−3.459**	−3.471**	−3.456**
Π_m	0.096	0.098	0.093	0.096	0.095
	2.736**	2.754**	2.656**	2.737**	2.703**
Ψ_m	0.875	0.875	0.874	0.875	0.873
	24.09**	24.11**	24.12**	24.09**	24.04**
Π_n	2293.5	1719.80	3278	2358.1	2841.5
	0.3168	0.2319	0.449	0.325	0.3905
Ψ_n	0.128	0.129	0.127	0.128	0.127
	1.666*	1.670*	1.653*	1.666*	1.652*
LR1	−0.074	−0.068	−0.072	−0.074	−0.085
	−0.627	−0.568	−0.618	−0.631	−0.712
LR2	−0.074	−0.068	−0.072	−0.074	−0.085
	−0.627	−0.568	−0.618	−0.631	−0.712
LR4-8	−0.005	−0.027	−0.063	−0.015	−0.043
	−0.059	−0.314	−0.873	−0.149	−0.587
	$N = 178$	$N = 178$	$N = 178$	$N = 178$	$N = 178$
	$R^2 = 0.97$	$R^2 = 0.97$	$R^2 = 0.97$	$R^2 = 0.97$	$R^2 = 0.97$
	DW = 1.93	DW = 1.93	DW = 1.93	DW = 1.93	DW = 1.93

*Significant at 0.05 level.
**Significant at 0.01 level.

SUBJECT INDEX